CONTEMPORARY SOCIAL RESEARCH SERIES
General Editor: MARTIN BULMER

20

Research Methods and Organization Studies

CONTEMPORARY SOCIAL RESEARCH SERIES

Research Methods and Organization Studies

ALAN BRYMAN

Loughborough University

London and New York

First published 1989
by Unwin Hyman Ltd

Reprinted 1992, 1995 (twice)
by Routledge
11 New Fetter Lane, London EC4P 4EE

Simultaneously published in the USA and Canada
by Routledge
29 West 35th Street, New York, NY 10001

Typeset in Times by Columns of Reading
Printed and bound in Great Britain by
Biddles Ltd, Guildford and King's Lynn

British Library Cataloguing in Publication Data
A catalogue record for this book is available from the British Library

Library of Congress Cataloguing in Publication Data
A catalogue record for this book is available from the Library of Congress

ISBN 0-415-08404-0

For my parents and parents-in-law
(as well as Sue and Sarah, as usual)

Contents

Glossary of abbreviations

CEO   Chief executive officer
GM   General manager
GNS   Growth need strength
ICI   Imperial Chemicals Industries
ICV   Internal corporate venture
JDS   Job Diagnostic Survey
LBDQ   Leader Behavior Description Questionnaire
LOS   Leader Observation System
LPC   Least Preferred Co-worker scale
MPS   Motivating potential score
OCQ   Organizational Commitment Questionnaire
OD   Organizational development
OE   Organizational effectiveness
PIMS   Profit Impact of Market Strategies programme
QWL   Quality of Working Life
R & D   Research and development
ROC   Return on capital
ROE   Return on equity
ROI   Return on investment

Preface

The field that is variously called 'organization studies', 'organizational behaviour' and even 'organizational science' has grown enormously since the late 1950s from a field comprising a small number of scholars, working on topics deriving from their particular disciplinary backgrounds (mostly psychology and sociology), to a major interdisciplinary subject in its own right with its own journals and professional associations. In spite of this massive growth and the strong emphasis among the field's practitioners on empirical knowledge about organizations, with one or two exceptions, textbooks concerned specifically with organizational research have been conspicuous by their absence. The student has been forced, by and large, to rely on textbooks concerned with research methods in the fields of psychology and sociology and to translate these discussions to the organizational context. This tendency is particularly surprising since management and business students, many of whom choose topics deriving from organization studies, invariably have to carry out projects for their degrees. This book has grown out of a belief that a research methods textbook tailored to the particular needs of students of organizations is needed. It has been written with a view to providing a critical approach to the various research strategies discussed in the book. This approach is necessary in order both to provide students with a critical understanding of the research that they read in their courses, so that findings are not treated simply as 'facts', and to instil a critical approach to the research strategies that they might employ in their own investigations, so that informed choices can be made. Also, there has been a burgeoning in recent years of discussions of various methodological issues within the specific context of doing research in organizations, so that an aim of this book is to synthesize some of this work.

I have been particularly concerned to meet the needs of students doing undergraduate and postgraduate degrees in management and business. Accordingly, I have tended to emphasize examples of research deriving from industrial, commercial settings. It has not always been possible to provide this slant, but this is not a handicap, since it should be recognized that organizational research is undertaken in a host of milieux. Moreover, I feel that the book will be relevant for many courses on research methods in psychology and sociology degrees, particularly those which seek to focus tuition on particular contexts. I have found it useful to provide students with such a focus in fifteen years of teaching research methods to sociology students.

This book appears fairly hot on the heels of my previous book in the series – *Quantity and Quality in Social Research* (1988) – and once again Martin Bulmer has provided me with much critical commentary from which this book has benefited greatly. Michael Bresnen has also read the chapters and has greatly enhanced the book at a number of points. My wife, Sue, has offered much useful advice on style. All of these people are, of course, absolved from any responsibility for errors, which are entirely my own. Finally, Sue and my daughter, Sarah, have again provided a highly supportive environment, in spite of the inconvenience that my writing often presents.

Alan Bryman
Loughborough University

1

The nature of
organizational research

Do satisfied workers perform better in their jobs than their less
satisfied peers? And what makes some people more satisfied in
their work than others? These are reasonable questions to ask
and indeed have been asked on numerous occasions by
organizational researchers. But how might one go about answering them? This book is about the ways in which organizational
researchers approach the task of answering such questions and
the myriad other questions with which they are habitually
concerned. But why a book specifically on the task of organizational research? Is the task of doing research in organizations
not fundamentally the same as any social science research? After
all, much organizational research borrows and relies upon
concepts and approaches to the conduct of research deriving from
the social science disciplines (especially psychology and sociology) that have given and continue to give organizational research
much of its impetus and character. Many of the field's
practitioners were trained in the social sciences, and it is
therefore not surprising that much organizational research bears
the imprint of the contributing social sciences and also shares
many of the guidelines and difficulties associated with conducting
research that social scientists have identified.

On the other hand, it might be that doing research in
organizations presents particular problems, or at least such
problems appear in particularly sharp relief. Further, some
approaches to research have been employed more extensively in
the context of studying organizations than elsewhere and have
undergone substantial development within organizational contexts. Certain methodological problems have even been identified
and elaborated through the study of organizations. Finally, there
is a sense in which the inculcation of an awareness of
methodological issues is more likely to be effective when it is
tailored to the reader's specific needs. It is anticipated that
students of organization studies, organizational behaviour and
similar courses and students carrying out projects in and on

organizations will find this book more helpful and of greater interest in addressing methodological issues than a general textbook on social science research methods.

A flavour of the particular considerations that organizational research entails can be provided by returning to the two research questions encountered at the outset of this chapter. One of the most frequently encountered research methods that is likely to be considered in order to answer these two research questions is a questionnaire survey of employees. Perhaps we might consider conducting our research in three industrial firms operating with different technologies, but possibly in the same product sector, in order to ensure a fair degree of variation in the types of job performed by the people who complete the questionnaires. At this point, our imaginary research is likely to encounter the first of a number of problems, which, while not unique to organizational research, is none the less a pervasive and intractable one within the field; we need access not just to the individuals who will complete the questionnaires, but also to the firms themselves. Unlike social science research in the community, organizational research often entails substantial negotiation to obtain access to firms and their members. This is not to say that research in the community is easier, but that the bounded nature of organizations imposes an additional layer between organizational researchers and their subjects. Consequently, problems of access tend to preoccupy organizational researchers a great deal (Brown, De Monthoux and McCullough, 1976; Bryman, 1988c), and researchers who have conducted investigations in both organizational and community contexts have remarked on the special problems which the need to negotiate access entails (Whyte, 1984). Many organizations are resistant to being studied, possibly because they are suspicious about the aims of the researcher. Further, those persons who act as 'gatekeepers' between the researcher and the organization (usually fairly senior managers) are likely to be concerned about the amount of their own and others' time that is likely to be consumed by the investigation. Sutton's (1987) experience of conducting research on the experiences of 'dying' organizations, while possibly somewhat extreme, illustrates this point, in that his attempts to gain access to appropriate firms elicited such responses as 'All of us are working 70-hour weeks' (p. 546). Precisely because of such worries, organizational researchers are often rebuffed. In order to achieve access many researchers offer to produce reports of their findings which may be of assistance to the firm in order to infuse an element of reciprocity (Buchanan, Boddy and McCalman, 1988). However, such incentives do not always succeed, and many firms will refuse access for a variety of reasons: it may be company policy not to co-operate; they may not approve the specific project; the researchers' assurances may not assuage worries about the amount of time that is taken up; the firm may just have been involved with another organizational researcher, and so on. The mere fact that some firms agree to participate and others refuse is often perceived as posing a problem, since the representativeness of findings may be jeopardized, a point that will be returned to at a number of junctures in later chapters. Once in the organization, our imaginary researcher will still need to gain the co-operation of the people to whom the questionnaire is administered, but this particular difficulty is common to all studies using such a technique.

A second issue that is a particular problem in organizational research is the level of analysis at which the research should be conducted. This difficulty reveals itself in a number of ways. First, who should be included in the study? For example, the research questions are not specific to any occupational stratum, so should managerial (including senior managers) as well as non-managerial employees be included? Second, the research questions imply that job satisfaction may vary according to the kinds of work that people do. Such a question could be handled at the individual level of analysis or by grouping respondents according to the kind of work they perform or according to sections within the firm. At an individual level of analysis, people may be asked to describe the nature of the work that they perform in terms of characteristics presented to them in the questionnaire; their responses are then aggregated to see whether there are any patterns, such as whether people who describe their work as routine and repetitive tend to exhibit low levels of job satisfaction. The researcher may even wish to extend such considerations to the level of the organization; are there systematic differences in job satisfaction and the features with which it is deemed to be associated between the three industrial firms examined? Consequently, organizational research tends to involve decisions about appropriate levels of analysis in at least two senses: the level or levels at which the research is conducted within the organization and the most appropriate ways of aggregating data (as well as recognizing that data collected at one level may be employed to make inferences about another level).

Again while not unique to organizational research, our imaginary investigator must be sensitive to the ethical and political dimension of the study. If access has been negotiated through senior management, the researcher may face the possibility of suspicion from many employees and unions regarding the 'true' aims of the research. The research may readily be perceived as a tool of management for rationalizing the workforce, engendering worries about lay-offs. Since entry was via management and if there is the promise of a report as a means of facilitating access, employees' views about the study's aims may harden against the proposed research. If the researcher succeeds in reassuring union representatives about his or her own and the company's aims, the problem of being caught between sides in the firm has to be guarded against. For example, researchers must resist the attempts by adversaries within organizations to use them as sources of information about each other, such as the union seeking to pump the researcher for information about what is going on in the boardroom. In short, the researcher must be cautious about being seen as taking sides within the organization. This is often not easy, since the nature of the issues with which a researcher is concerned often appear to imply a particular stance. For example, the emphasis on job performance in the first research question could easily be taken to imply a pro-management stance and therefore could be a cause of considerable consternation among non-managerial employees, in spite of reassurances by the researcher that he or she is a neutral observer only concerned with the investigation of academic issues. Thus, it is not surprising that many researchers have experienced problems in dealing with the delicate webs of relationships that organizations comprise (Bryman, 1988b, pp. 12–13).

Finally, organizational research is pervasively concerned with the promulgation of practical knowledge. There are other areas in the social sciences which reflect a similar commitment, but a very large proportion of organizational studies are directly or indirectly concerned with practical issues. This preoccupation reveals itself in the widespread concern with organizational effectiveness. As one commentator has put it:

> The theory of effectiveness is the Holy Grail of organizational research . . . It is assumed . . . that there is some stable, reliable relation between effectiveness as an outcome, on one hand, and some precursor or partial precursor, on the other.
> (Mohr, 1982, p. 179)

Similarly, the considerable emphasis in much research on the performance or effectiveness of individuals (as in the first research question in our imaginary research project) or groups is strongly related to the preoccupation with organizational effectiveness and hence to the production of 'relevant' research. In fact, much research on the sources of job satisfaction, absenteeism, stress and the like is related to the focus on organizational effectiveness because of a widespread view that these phenomena have implications for individual effectiveness. Similarly, at an organizational level, interest in topics like the sources of innovation is connected to the fixation with organizational effectiveness.

Another striking feature of this state of affairs, which is well illustrated by the above quotation from Mohr (1982), is not just the fact of the preoccupation with organizational effectiveness, but the *form* that the preoccupation assumes. Organizational effectiveness is perceived as an entity that is dependent upon other things. In other words, it is seen as an entity whose variation is caused by other entities. This approach to asking research questions is common to many of the topics addressed by organizational researchers, and in fact occurs with considerable frequency in other fields of social science as well. Organizational effectiveness is perceived as a dependent variable, variation in which is influenced by other factors (what Mohr calls 'precursors'), which are often referred to as independent variables. A great deal of organizational research comprises this causal imagery, and many of the research designs discussed in this book are specifically concerned with the extraction of causal connections. The experiment constitutes an approach to research which is particularly well equipped to produce findings in which cause and effect relationships are established. Unlike the questionnaire survey approach delineated in the imaginary study, in an experiment the researcher actively manipulates a social setting and observes the effects of that intervention on the dependent variable of interest. Experimental research designs are given a detailed treatment in Chapter 3, while the topic of organizational effectiveness is given more attention in Chapter 9. As some of the discussion in this section implies, much organizational research exhibits many of the trappings of what is often taken to be a scientific approach to research – the emphasis on causes, variables, experiments, measurement and so on. This theme receives a more detailed treatment in the next section. However, not all strands of organizational research reflect this predilection for the paraphernalia of a scientific approach, as the section on qualitative research will reveal.

The nature of quantitative organizational research

A great deal of organizational research can be described as exhibiting many of the characteristics of 'quantitative research' (Bryman, 1988a; Podsakoff and Dalton, 1987). The essentials of this model of the research process resemble closely a 'scientific' approach to the conduct of research. A term like 'scientific' is inevitably vague and controversial but in the minds of many researchers and writers on methodology it entails a commitment to a systematic approach to investigations, in which the collection of data and their detached analysis in relation to a previously formulated research problem are minimal ingredients. One way of construing this research process is presented in Figure 1.1, which contains the chief elements typically delineated by writers on social science research methodology. According to this model, the starting point for a study is a theory about some aspect of organizational functioning. A theory entails an attempt to formulate an explanation about some facet of reality, such as why some people enjoy their work and others do not, or why some organizations are bureaucratic and others are not. From this theory a specific hypothesis (or hypotheses) is formulated which will be tested. This hypothesis not only permits a test (albeit possibly a partial one) of the theory in question, but the results of the test, irrespective of whether the findings sustain it or not, feed back into our stock of knowledge concerning the phenomenon being studied. It is the generation of data to test a hypothesis that in many respects constitutes the crux of the quantitative research process, reflecting a belief in the primacy of systematically collected data in the scientific enterprise. This general orientation to the research process has bred a number of preoccupations which will be briefly discussed. In the following section a detailed example will be provided of a research programme that comprises many of the elements to be discussed below as well as the steps implied by Figure 1.1.

First, hypotheses contain concepts which need to be *measured* in order for the hypothesis to be systematically tested. A theory might lead to a hypothesis that 'An organization's size and its level of bureaucratization will be positively related'. In order to test this hypothesis it will be necessary to provide measures of the two constituent concepts within the hypothesis: organizational size and bureaucratization. The process of translating concepts into measures is often termed *operationalization* by writers on the research process, and many organizational researchers refer to *operational definitions* (the specification of the steps to be used in the measurement of the concepts under consideration) in reports

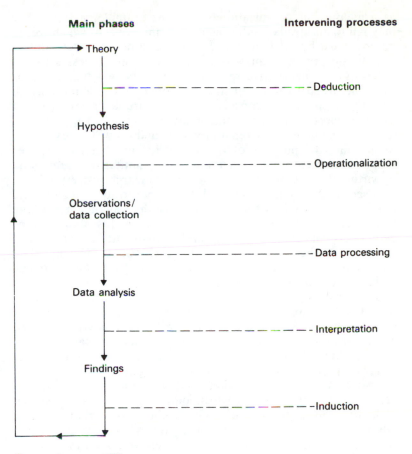

Source: Bryman, 1988a

Figure 1.1 The logical structure of the quantitative research process

of their investigations. These measures are treated as *variables*, that is, attributes on which people, organizations, or whatever exhibit variability. Thus, organizational size is often operational- ized by the number of employees in a sample of organizations (Pugh *et al.*, 1969) and is a variable in the sense that organizations will vary considerably in respect of this concept and its associated measure. There is always a recognition that a measure is likely to be a relatively imperfect representation of the concept with which it is purportedly associated, since any concept may be measured in a number of different ways, each of which will have its own limitations. In using the number of employees as a measure of organizational size, for example, a researcher may fail to encapsulate other aspects of this concept which would be addressed by other measures such as turnover, assets and so on. Because of the centrality of measurement processes to the enterprise of quantitative research, considerable attention tends to be accorded to the refinement of operational definitions. In Chapter 2 some of the considerations that are taken into account by researchers in enhancing the quality of measures (in particular the examination of their reliability and validity) will be explored. Meanwhile, the purpose of this discussion has been to register that measurement is a preoccupation for quantitative researchers, by virtue of its centrality to the overall research process.

A second preoccupation is with the demonstration of *causality*, that is, in showing how things come to be the way they are. Many hypotheses contain implicit or explicit statements about causes and effects, and the ensuing research is frequently undertaken to demonstrate the validity of the hunches about causality. The quotation from Mohr (1982) on page 4 reflects this tendency within research on organizational effectiveness. The concern about causality has a strong impact on the kinds of results that are considered 'findings'. In a study of Japanese organizations, Marsh and Mannari (1981) were concerned with the relative impact of an organization's size and its technology on its internal structure. One of their findings was that 'structural differentiation or complexity [the degree to which an organizational structure comprises many or few sections and/or hierarchical levels] was linked to size more than to technology' (p. 52). This research seeks to establish the factors which account for variation in the internal structure of organizations; in this case, two putative causes – size and technology – have been examined in order to establish which of the two has the greater causal impact upon organization structure. This preoccupation with the demonstration of causal effects is often mirrored in the widespread use of the terms *independent variable* and *dependent variable* in quantitative organizational research. In Marsh and Mannari's investigation, size and technology are considered independent variables, meaning that they are assumed to have a causal impact upon the dependent variable – organization structure. The term 'cause' is often taken to denote that something determines something else. This is clearly an inappropriate connotation, since size, for example, does not determine organization structure. Other variables, such as technology, are known to impinge on structure, so that variation in the latter cannot be wholly attributed to size. As Chapters 3 and 4 will reveal, the ability to establish cause-and-effect relationships is a major preoccupation among researchers using experimental and social survey designs, the two major research approaches within the field. Experimental research more readily permits causal statements to be established, because of the considerable control that researchers exert over the settings being studied and because they are able to manipulate directly the independent variable and observe its effects on the dependent variable. In survey research, this facility is not present, so that causal relationships invariably have to be inferred. None the less, among both groups of practitioners, the pursuit of findings which can be construed in causal terms is a major concern.

A third preoccupation is *generalization*, that is, the pursuit of findings which can be generalized beyond the confines of a specific investigation. Like the preoccupations with measurement and causality, the pursuit of generalizable findings is associated with the scientific ethos that pervades much organizational research. If findings have some generality beyond the particular and possibly idiosyncratic boundaries of a particular investigation, the researcher is moving closer to the law-like findings with which the natural sciences are frequently associated. In social survey research, the issue of generalizability reveals itself in an emphasis, especially in textbooks, on how far the samples upon which research is carried out are representative of a larger population. Although such an issue is relevant to the aims of experimental research, the extent to which the findings of experimental research can be generalized is affected by a number of considerations in addition to the representativeness of the study's participants.

Finally, quantitative research exhibits a concern that investigations should be capable of *replication*. This means that it should be possible for a researcher to employ the same procedures as those used in another study to check on the validity of the initial investigation. Replication can act as a check to establish whether a set of findings can be repeated in another milieu; for example, do findings which derive from a study of civil service organizations apply equally well to industry? In this sense, the issue of replication links closely to the question of generalizability. A second rationale for emphasizing the replicability of research is to ensure that the biases and predilections of researchers can be checked, by allowing their findings to be verified. If the same research design and measurement procedures can be employed by someone else, confidence in the initial findings can be enhanced. Again, the belief in the importance of replication can be traced to the use of the natural sciences as a model of the quantitative research process, since it is generally assumed that it should be possible to verify a scientist's findings by using the same procedures. One of the reasons for the distrust of qualitative research among some proponents of quantitative research is that the former does not readily permit replication. The account of the research process that has been provided exhibits an ordered, somewhat linear sequence of steps (as in Figure 1.1) and a strong commitment to a scientific model of research. Each of the four preoccupations exemplifies the proclivity for a scientific approach to the conduct of research. This account of quantitative organizational research is not without problems which will be addressed below. Meanwhile, a field of research which embodies many of the essential qualities of quantitative research in organizations will be employed as an illustration of a number of the themes encountered so far.

The case of job characteristics
Organizational researchers have long displayed an interest in the ways in which people's experience of work is affected by the content of the jobs they perform. In particular, it has been suggested that by reversing the trend towards simplifying work and by 'enriching' the content of jobs, so that work can be more challenging and enjoyable, productivity and the quality of work will be enhanced. Hackman and Oldham (1976) drew on the work of a number of other researchers (for example, Turner and Lawrence, 1965) within this tradition who had demonstrated that whether people responded positively to enriched work (that is, by exhibiting greater productivity and superior work experience) was affected by their personal characteristics. In spite of the intuitive appeal of the notion that people will work harder and enjoy their jobs more if work is made more interesting and involving, previous research demonstrated that people's responses to more challenging work did not always align with this expectation. This research led Hackman and Oldham to

> propose and report a test of a theory of work redesign that focuses specifically on how the characteristics of jobs and the characteristics of people interact to determine when an 'enriched' job will lead to beneficial outcomes, and when it will not.
> (Hackman and Oldham, 1976, p. 251)

The essence of their approach is to suggest that particular job characteristics ('core job dimensions') affect employees' experience of work ('critical psychological states'), which in turn have a number of outcomes for both the individual and the organization

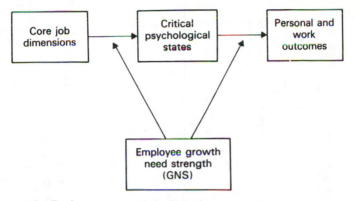

Figure 1.2   Basic structure of the job characteristics model

('personal and work outcomes'). Further, individuals' responses
to positive job characteristics will be affected by their 'growth
need strength' (GNS), that is, their need for personal growth and
development. Figure 1.2 provides the basic structure of the
model that underpins Hackman and Oldham's theory.

Core job dimensions, critical psychological states and personal
and work outcomes were each conceptualized as having a number
of different components. For example, core job dimensions
comprise five aspects: skill variety, task identity, task significance, autonomy and feedback. Hackman and Oldham propose
that these dimensions can be combined to provide a 'motivating
potential score' (MPS). The critical psychological states are
viewed as comprising three dimensions: experienced meaningful-
ness of the work, experienced responsibility for outcomes of the
work and knowledge of actual results of the work activities.
Definitions of all of the different ingredients of the model are
provided in Table 1.1.[1] In order to test the validity of the theory
on which the connections posited in Figure 1.2 are based, a
questionnaire called the Job Diagnostic Survey (JDS) was
devised and administered to 658 individuals working on sixty-two
jobs in seven organizations in the USA (Hackman and Oldham,
1975, 1976). Employees completed the questionnaires at work.
The questionnaire derives measures of job content from employees' descriptions of their work, as well as measures of
psychological states, growth need strength and affective reactions
to work. Data relating to some concepts, such as absenteeism,
were derived from other sources. In Table 1.1 can also be found
specimen questions from the JDS questionnaire for each
component of the model. Information about variables which were
not derived from the JDS is also provided in Table 1.1.

Table 1.1 Job characteristics theory: concepts, dimensions, definitions, indicators and sample results

Definitions of dimensions	Sample Job Diagnostic Survey questions	Sample findings from, Hackman and Oldham (1975, 1976); correlation between job characteristics and psychological states with:	
		Internal motivation[3]	Absenteeism[4]
(I) Job dimensions			
(a) *Skill variety* – the degree to which a job entails a number of different activities which involve the deployment of the incumbent's skills and talents	The job requires me to use a number of complex or high-level skills[1]	.42 (.15)	–.15
(b) *Task identity* – the extent to which the job entails a complete and discernible piece of work	The job provides me with the chance to completely finish the pieces of work I begin[1]	.22 (.08)	–.18
(c) *Task significance* – how far the job has clear implications for others either in the firm or beyond it	This job is one where a lot of other people can be affected by how well the work gets done[1]	.32 (.07)	.16
(d) *Autonomy* – how far the individual is free to decide about the scheduling of work and how it should be carried out	The job gives me considerable opportunity for independence and freedom in how I do the work[1]	.33 (.08)	–.24

Description			
(e) *Feedback* – the extent to which the employee is provided with unambiguous information about the adequacy of his/her performance	The job itself provides very few clues about whether or not I am performing well (NB this question is scored in reverse to indicate presence of feedback)[1]	.36	(.28)	-.12

| In addition, a job's 'motivating potential score' (MPS) is calculated: | Not applicable | .46 | | -.25 |

$$MPS = \frac{Skill\ variety + Task\ identity + Task\ significance}{3} \times Autonomy \times Feedback$$

(II) Critical psychological states

(a) *Experienced meaningfulness of work* – how far the job is meaningful and valuable to the employee	The work I do is very meaningful to me[2]	.63		-.03
(b) *Experienced responsibility for work outcomes* – the extent to which the employee feels responsible for consequences of his/her work	I feel a very high degree of personal responsibility for the work I do on this job[2]	.66		-.16
(c) *Knowledge of results* – how far the employee is aware of the effectiveness of his/her work performance	I usually know whether or not my work is satisfactory on this job[2]	.25		-.11

(III) Growth need strength
The individual's felt need for personal growth and fulfilment at work

Respondents are asked how much they would like a job which involves, e.g., 'stimulating and challenging work'

continued overleaf

Table 1.1 *continued*
Job characteristics theory: concepts, dimensions, definitions, indicators and sample results

Definitions of dimensions	Sample Job Diagnostic Survey questions	Sample findings from, Hackman and Oldham (1975, 1976); correlation between job characteristics and psychological states with: Internal motivation[3] Absenteeism[4]

(IV) Outcome variables

(a) *Internal motivation* – how far the individual feels self-motivated to perform well

I feel a great sense of personal satisfaction when I perform this job well[2]

(b) *General job satisfaction* – an overall assessment of how happy the employee is with his/her job

I am generally satisfied with the kind of work I do in this job[2]

(c) *Growth satisfaction* – satisfaction with opportunities for personal growth and development

Respondents are asked about their degree of satisfaction with, e.g., 'the feeling of worthwhile accomplishment I get from doing my job'

(d) *Work performance*

Managers are asked to rate each employee in terms of effort, work quality and work quantity

(e) *Absenteeism*

Not applicable. Data on number of days absent per employee were taken from company records

Notes:

[1] Respondents are asked to indicate how far the statement is accurate. A seven-point scale from 'very inaccurate' to 'very accurate' is used.

[2] Respondents are asked to indicate how far they agree with the statement. A seven-point scale from 'disagree strongly' to 'agree strongly' is used.

[3] The coefficients are product moment correlation coefficients. Those in brackets are the correlation coefficients relating job characteristics to internal motivation with the effect of critical psychological states removed.

[4] These are median correlation coefficients, i.e. average correlations for the seven organizations in which the research was conducted.

The job characteristics theory leads to several hypotheses that were submitted to an empirical testing by Hackman and Oldham. First, Figure 1.2 implies that both job characteristics and psychological states will be related to the outcomes addressed by their research. This cluster of hypotheses was confirmed, but it was found that relationships with absenteeism and rated work effectiveness were markedly weaker than with the satisfaction and internal motivation variables. Second, Figure 1.2 implies that relationships between job characteristics and outcomes will be dependent upon the psychological states. This means that it is anticipated that job characteristics and outcomes are related because job characteristics enhance the experience of work (the critical psychological states), which in turn is related to the outcomes; that is, the relationships between job characteristics and outcomes are not direct. This hypothesis was addressed in a number of ways, one of which was to compare the correlations between job characteristics and outcomes with the same correlations when the effects of critical psychological states were controlled. It would be anticipated that the former correlations would be larger than the latter if the hypothesis about the effect of critical psychological states were correct. For example, the correlation between skill variety and internal motivation was .42, but when the impact of critical psychological states was taken into account by controlling for their effects, the correlation fell to .15. Third, Figure 1.2 also implies that people will respond differently to job characteristics as a result of variations in their GNS. This hypothesis was dealt with by separating out respondents in the top and the bottom quartiles in terms of GNS. The intermediate groups (half of the sample) did not figure in the analysis. Figure 1.2 suggests that relationships between job characteristics and psychological states and between psychological states and outcomes will be affected by whether employees have high or low growth needs. Correlations between these two pairs of variables were computed for each of the two groups, with the anticipation that correlations would be larger for high GNS than for low GNS respondents. This was confirmed, although the differences in many cases were not substantial. The tendency for these results to confirm the hypotheses which were deduced from the job characteristics theory (and which are embedded in the model in Figure 1.2) was particularly gratifying to the authors since their ideas and research can be used as a basis for redesigning work.

The validity of the job characteristics theory (and some of the practical themes that are supposed to stem from it) has been a focus for a number of investigators. Orpen (1979) reports a study of seventy-two clerks in three divisions of a local government agency in South Africa. The research proceeded through four phases. Initially, data were collected by questionnaire on a host of variables relevant to the theory. Many of the measures derived from the JDS. In the second phase, one half of the employees were allocated to work which Orpen describes as 'enriched' in terms of the job characteristics approach (that is, greater skill variety, autonomy and so on); the other thirty-six employees continued with the same work that they had been performing prior to the administration of the questionnaire. All other conditions of work relating to the two groups, such as job security and pension benefits, remained unchanged. In phase 3, the two groups worked for six months on their new or original jobs (depending on which of the two groups they had been allocated to). Finally, at the end of this phase, employees completed the same questionnaire that had been administered to them in phase 1. Orpen found that members of the enriched group reported larger increases in job satisfaction, job involvement and intrinsic motivation over the course of the study than members of the unenriched group. Further, there was evidence that absenteeism and turnover were reduced by job enrichment. However, the groups did not differ in terms of their levels of performance and productivity at the end of the research (data were not collected on these variables in the first phase). Since Orpen had administered the JDS to the employees, it was possible to examine the relationships between reported job characteristics and various outcome measures in the same way as Hackman and Oldham (1976) had done. Orpen also examined the possible impact of GNS using their general approach. He found a pattern of results which was similar to that discerned by Hackman and Oldham, in that positive job characteristics were associated with higher levels of job satisfaction and, though less closely, with job involvement and internal motivation. However, there was virtually no association between job characteristics and supervisors' performance ratings of the employees. On the other hand, GNS was found to have some impact on the extent to which positive job characteristics engendered greater job satisfaction, job involvement and so on. This study allows some of the major findings adduced by Hackman and Oldham in support of their theory to be confirmed. However, not all of Orpen's findings were consonant with the theory and Hackman and Oldham's findings; the weak relationships between job characteristics and performance ratings are a case in point. Also, Orpen did not test the 'whole' model implied by Figure 1.2, since the role of critical psychological states was not addressed.

Ganster (1980) also conducted an investigation aimed at testing aspects of job characteristics theory. He recruited 190 US undergraduate students, all of whom completed a questionnaire designed to measure a number of different ways in which people differ from one another. Only one of these – GNS – was specified by Hackman and Oldham, but others (need for achievement, arousal-seeking and commitment to the Protestant ethic) were also examined for their potential in connection with the theory. Students were then asked to work on an electronics assembly task in groups of six. Half the students worked in a milieu in which positive job characteristics (task variety, autonomy, feedback and so on) were enhanced; for the other half, these elements were less pronounced. The work lasted approximately seventy-five minutes, at the end of which the students completed a questionnaire to gauge their perceptions of the task (following the JDS format) and their satisfaction with it. Students performing the enhanced task achieved higher task satisfaction scores than their counterparts performing the simpler task. Further, there were very strong associations between their perceptions of the task, as measured by JDS questions, and satisfaction. However, there was virtually no evidence to suggest that individual differences had any impact upon whether students expressed greater task satisfaction when performing enriched work. Need for achievement was the only measure which implied some tendency for individual differences to have an impact on the relationship between job characteristics and task satisfaction. GNS had no such effect at all. Like Orpen's study, Ganster did not address all aspects of job characteristics theory (again critical psychological states did not form part of the analysis) and some of his findings depart from what the theory would lead us to expect (most notably the virtual absence of any impact from the individual difference variables).

Job characteristics theory has generated a large number of studies, many of which have failed to provide unequivocal support for its major themes, which to a certain degree is the case with Orpen's and Ganster's investigations (Roberts and Glick, 1981). Further, much of the subsequent research has been subjected to methodological criticisms (Roberts and Glick, 1981; Salancik and Pfeffer, 1977), many of which will be encountered in later chapters. Salancik and Pfeffer (1978) have proposed a rival theory which they term 'a social information processing approach'. This perspective draws attention to the possibility that perceptions of job characteristics are affected by the social context within which people work (for example, by informational cues emitted by supervisors and peers) and by individuals' prior work experiences which shape both their expectations and also how they apprehend their jobs. A number of investigations have found support for these ideas (for example, Griffin, 1983; O'Reilly and Caldwell, 1979).

Much of the progress of job characteristics theory exemplifies the general points made about the nature of quantitative organizational research. The starting-point is a theory which is formulated in relation to prior findings and earlier theoretical ideas. The new theory prompts a number of hypotheses to be formulated. Two observations are especially noteworthy about these hypotheses. First, they comprise a number of concepts that need to be rendered measurable; indeed, the JDS seems to have been devised with this purpose very much in mind. Thus, the concept of job characteristics and its postulated aspects, such as task variety and autonomy, need to be measured in order for the investigation to proceed. Second, the hypotheses comprise explicit statements of causality. The arrows in Figure 1.2 embody this tendency in that they imply a clear sequence of cause and effect.

The generalizability of the Hackman and Oldham research is somewhat vague. Their respondents were drawn from a wide variety of both manual and non-manual occupations in both the manufacturing and service sectors. In covering a wide range of settings and job types it might be argued that the generalizability of the investigation is enhanced; on the other hand, we are not informed how these respondents were selected from the pool of potential respondents. This lack of attention to the selection of respondents contrasts sharply with the importance attached to such issues in textbooks concerned with social research methods. The investigations by Orpen and Ganster also invite questions about the selection of both the settings in which the research took place and the selection of the subjects themselves. It is also striking that it is relatively easy to replicate any of the three investigations by following the same procedures, albeit in different settings (perhaps to increase confidence in the generalizability of findings). Perfect replications may be difficult to achieve, particularly in research like that of Orpen and Ganster, but even quasi-replications can enhance confidence in a theory and its associated findings.

A further observation that can be drawn from the case of job characteristics theory is that the three studies described reflect the three major approaches to the collection of data in quantitative organizational research: the questionnaire survey (Hackman and Oldham), the field experiment (Orpen) and the laboratory experiment (Ganster). In the social survey study, data relating to all variables are collected at the same time by questionnaire; in the field experiment, the researcher intervenes in the life of an organization by manipulating the presumed independent variable and observing the effects on the dependent variable; and in the laboratory experiment a work setting is created in the laboratory and the independent variable is manipulated for students rather than 'real' employees. The differences between these three approaches to the collection of data and their respective strengths and weaknesses will be central themes in Chapters 3 and 4.

The theory and research associated with the study of job characteristics are strongly influenced by practical concerns. Hackman and Oldham state, for example, that one of the factors which prompted them to examine the field of job redesign was that there was a gap between existing approaches and problems encountered in the introduction of job redesign programmes. They write: 'Especially troublesome is the paucity of conceptual tools that are directly useful in guiding the *implementation and evaluation* of work redesign projects' (Hackman and Oldham, 1976, p. 251, original emphasis). This orientation represents a concern with the practical benefits of research for organizations and those who work within them. While this emphasis is not exclusive to organization studies, there are few fields associated with the social sciences for which such concerns are so pervasive.[2] This applied emphasis has often been a source of criticism by writers both within and outside the field who have seen this tendency as being deleterious to the subject's development (for example, Goldman, 1978).

It is also striking that the development of theory and research associated with job characteristics exhibits the somewhat linear progression that underpins Figure 1.1. A theory is developed in relation to observations about aspects of a particular domain. Hypotheses are drawn from the theory, and embedded within these are concepts (such as job characteristics and its associated dimensions) which need to be rendered measurable. Subsequent researchers have sought to address various other issues, such as: whether different methods may produce different results (Orpen; Ganster); whether the general approach can be extended to include additional variables (Ganster); whether the nature of the relationships proposed by the theory needs revision (Champoux, 1980); or whether the indicators used to measure a concept like job characteristics really do break down into the five dimensions proposed by theory (Dunham, Aldag and Brief, 1977). The results are then fed back into the theory. For example, some of the findings that are inconsistent with the theory, such as Ganster's (1980) failure to find that individual differences had any impact upon the relationship between job characteristics and outcomes, need to be absorbed by the theory, resulting in some reformulation of the original ideas. The emergence of a competing theory like the information processing approach proposed by Salancik and Pfeffer (1978) is consistent with the model of the research process implied by Figure 1.1, in that it arose as an alternative means of understanding some of the findings which emerged within the context of the job character- istics approach, as well as by way of a reaction to some concerns about the ways in which research associated with the job characteristics theory is carried out. In addition, the emergence of findings which are not entirely consistent with the job characteristics theory acts as a further spur to alternative theoretical reflections.

Model and reality

Although job characteristics theory and research exhibit most of the features of the quantitative organizational research model fairly well, there is a widespread awareness among researchers within the field that many investigations depart from certain elements of the model in important ways. Since one of this book's aims is to provide insights into many of the realities of organizational research, and not just to present the broad characterizations that are often furnished in social research methods textbooks (Bryman, 1988b), discussions of such depar- tures from idealized accounts are clearly required. An insight into one important way in which quantitative research departs from the model implied by Figure 1.1 can be discerned from the following comment from Campbell's reflections as outgoing editor of the *Journal of Applied Psychology*, one of the main journals in which organizational research (especially that with a psychological emphasis) is published:

> The idealized deductive process of developing a theory, deriving hypotheses, and testing them to support or not support the theory, is respected by almost everyone, but at the same time almost everyone realizes that the ideal seldom describes reality.
>
> (Campbell, 1985, p. 328)

Campbell's comment implies that theory probably plays a less prominent role than is implied by the previously described model or by the research that followed in the wake of Hackman and Oldham's formulation of job characteristics theory. This view is consistent with the lack of penetration of theory in a great deal of sociological and psychological research, or in any event the loose connection between theory and research (Bryman, 1988a, pp. 19–22).

Where, then, do the foci of quantitative organizational studies come from? Where, in particular, do hypotheses and their associated concepts come from? First, it is a mistake to think of all quantitative research as concerned with the testing of hypotheses. In many instances, the research is much more exploratory. For example, an investigator may be concerned to establish whether two or more variables are related, but may not have specific expectations about the nature of the relationship that those variables are likely to exhibit; or a researcher may have collected data and subsequently realize these data may have implications for a topic that was not anticipated at the outset. Survey investigations like Hackman and Oldham (1976) are more likely to exhibit a relative absence of hypothesis-testing than experimental investigations, like Ganster (1980) or Orpen (1979), because experiments tend to be highly structured and force the investigator to form relatively explicit hunches about findings. Even when hypotheses are formulated, they may be at a greater level of generality (and therefore more exploratory) than is typically associated with a 'scientific' hypothesis. A case in point is the Aston Studies, a highly influential programme of research that initially derived from a survey study of the correlates of organization structure in forty-six West Midlands organizations. As discussions of the broad orientation of the approach suggest (Pugh, 1981 and 1988; Pugh *et al.*, 1963), the hypotheses formulated by the group of researchers, for example that characteristics of an organization's structure would be related to characteristics of its context (such as size, technology, ownership, market, charter and so on), were extremely general. There do not seem to have been explicit hypotheses about which characteristics of structure would be related to which contextual characteristics, nor were many explicit hypotheses developed about the nature of the relationships anticipated (such as whether positive or negative).

However, as the discussion above suggests, it is a mistake to think that when hypotheses are presented they derive from the author's theoretical reflections about an issue and hence from a desire to test a theory. Very often hypotheses and their associated concepts are the product of deliberations in connection with the literature relating to a substantive field. Prior theoretical issues may arise as justifications for the inclusion of particular variables or for the patterns depicted in the hypotheses. Thus, the lack of, or in any event partial, penetration of theory in much organizational research can occur in a host of ways. An investigation by Keller (1986) of the causes of performance in R & D organizations provides an example. Keller reviewed a number of studies relating to this theme in a search for likely 'predictors' of R & D performance. He writes:

> The *literature* on performance, innovativeness, and communication relating to individuals in R & D organizations suggests that certain variables are likely candidates for explaining project groups' performance in R & D settings. . . . A set of hypotheses, based on the model developed by Katz (1982) *and on the prior literature*, was generated. It was hypothesized that physical propinquity among members of a project group, group cohesiveness, and the self-esteem, innovative orientation, job satisfaction, and educational level of group members would be positively related to a project group's performance.
>
> (Keller, 1986, pp. 716, 717, our emphases)

As this passage suggests, the review of the literature played a major role in the specification of variables likely to have an impact on performance. Further, the discussion of the ensuing findings makes little reference to the study's findings for theoretical issues. Its primary implications are deemed to be practical: 'The results . . . suggest that the managers of R & D organizations that use project groups should encourage the development of cohesive groups' (p. 724). Another way in which the lack of theoretical issues may occur is through a review of the literature on a particular issue and the nomination of a hitherto unexplored aspect which is accorded scant justification in theoretical terms. Lieberson and O'Connor (1972) suggest that the tendency to study the effects of changes in leadership in large corporations on subsequent performance ignores the constraints on new incumbents. Using archival data (a source of information examined in Chapter 7), the authors explored the industry in which each firm was located and the company itself as potential restrictions on leaders of large corporations. The chief rationale for the inclusion of these variables seems to have been that they had not previously been addressed and relevant data were readily available.

Of course, it might be suggested that the tendency for much quantitative organizational research not to be theory-driven is by no means a bad thing, since such research should emphasize practical concerns so that advice for managers and executives can be provided. Keller (1986) seems to have interpreted the significance of his research in this light. Certainly, executives may appear dumbfounded by the relevance of some organizational research to their concerns, as reflected in the comments at a conference by a senior manager at Hewlett-Packard with a doctorate in organizational behaviour (Price, 1985). On the other hand, many theories can have considerable significance for practical managerial preoccupations, the job characteristics theory being a case in point. However, the chief point of the discussion in this section has been to draw attention to the possibility that the neat, linear model implied by Figure 1.1 may not always provide a valid indication of the quantitative research process. While it may provide a useful heuristic, it should not be seen as a definitive representation as is sometimes implied in textbooks. Nor is it the case that the ambiguous position of theory in relation to research constitutes the only source of departure from the model; for example, in Chapter 2 it will be shown that the link between concepts and their associated measures does not always proceed in the manner implied by the model.

The emergence of qualitative research

Since the early 1970s there has been a considerable growth of interest in an approach to research that is variously referred to as 'qualitative' and 'interpretive', the former being the preferred term in this book. Many advocates of qualitative research inveigh against the scientific pretensions of much quantitative research which they see as based on a misunderstanding about how people should be studied.

It is tempting to conceive of the distinction between quantitative and qualitative research in terms of the presence or absence of quantification. This would be extremely misleading on at least two accounts. First, qualitative researchers are not averse to quantification as such, and often include some counting procedures in their investigations. Similarly, quantitative researchers sometimes collect qualitative material for their investigations. Second, there is considerably more to the contrast than the relative importance of quantitative data and associated data collection procedures. The most central characteristic of qualitative, in contrast to quantitative, research is its emphasis on the perspective of the individual being studied. Whereas quantitative research is propelled by a prior set of concerns, whether deriving from theoretical issues or from a reading of the literature in a particular domain, qualitative research tends to eschew the notion that the investigator should be the source of what is relevant and important in relation to that domain. Rather, the qualitative researcher seeks to elicit what is important to individuals as well as their interpretations of the environments in which they work through in-depth investigations of individuals and their milieux. The two most prominent methods of data collection associated with the qualitative approach to organizational research are participant observation and unstructured or semi-structured interviewing (and in organizational research these techniques are usually accompanied by the collection of documents). The nature of these two techniques will be explored in greater detail in Chapter 5. Each entails fairly prolonged contact with the people being investigated and each is somewhat unstructured in that the researcher seeks to constrain people as little as possible. Whereas survey and experimental research, like that conducted within the context of job characteristics theory, comprises specific objectives that derive from the investigators' preoccupations, qualitative research tends to be unstructured in order to capture people's perspectives and interpretations. Consequently, theoretical reflection tends to occur during or towards the end of the data collection process rather than at the outset.

A study by Burgelman (1985) of internal corporate venturing projects (ICV) in the new venture division (NVD) of a large manufacturer of commodity-type products (referred to anonymously as GAMMA) provides an example of such research. These commercial activities are oriented to the identification of new niches into which the corporation might profitably move and to the subsequent development of products. Among other things, Burgelman was interested in the relationships between the NVD and other divisions in the firm, and in the initiation and management of strategy within the NVD. He collected data over fifteen months, during which information relating both to the past and to the present was amassed. Burgelman describes his data collection thus:

> The bulk of the data were collected around the study of six major ICV projects in progress at GAMMA at the time of the research . . . In addition to the participants in the ICV projects, people from the operating divisions and from the corporate level were interviewed. The interviews were largely unstructured and ranged in duration from 1.5 to 4.5 hours . . . After completion of an interview, a typewritten copy of the conversation was made . . . The research also involved the study of documents . . . One key set of documents . . . involved the written, corporate long-range plans concerning the NVD

and each of the ICV projects . . . The purpose [of the research] is primarily to generate new insights that are useful for building theory.

(Burgelman, 1985, pp. 41, 42)

The approach entails starting out with a set of loose concepts and ideas – strategy and relationships between the NVD and the rest of GAMMA – the content of which is gradually 'filled in' during the data collection. The theoretical element of the research is apparent at the end of the research rather than at the beginning. It is also striking that in contrast to the collection of data on numerous organizations, as exemplified by the forty-six organizations in the original Aston research (see page 22), Burgelman has collected data on just one firm. In the eyes of many researchers, including Burgelman (1985, p. 42), the focus on a single case signals a problem of the degree to which the ensuing findings can be generalized, which, as noted earlier in this chapter, is a preoccupation among researchers within the quantitative tradition.

The data from the unstructured interviews allowed Burgelman to draw a number of inferences about managers' perspectives in their own terms. In contrast to the statistical presentation of results that is a feature of the job characteristics and Aston investigations cited above, Burgelman's article is littered with verbatim quotations from the managers and other participants. For example, when discussing frictions between the NVD and GAMMA's corporate level, he notes that reward systems and recognition constituted one source of dissensus. As evidence, he quotes one venture manager:

> Even in the face of the extraordinary growth rate of the venture, the questions corporate management raised when they came here concerned our impact on the overall position of GAMMA, rather than the performance of the venture *per se*.
> (Quoted in Burgelman, 1985, p. 49)

The faithful recording of what people say in interviews and conversations is a feature of the presentation of qualitative data which enhances the impression of the researcher's grasp of subjects' points of view.

Qualitative research is by no means a new innovation within organization studies. Some classic studies within the field made substantial use of the approach (for example, Dalton, 1959; Lupton, 1963; Roy, 1954, 1960). However, qualitative research has attracted increasing attention which was given explicit recognition with the publication of a special issue of the *Administrative Science Quarterly* (vol. 24, no.4 1979), a journal which is traditionally associated with the quantitative tradition. In the eyes of many of its proponents, qualitative research is not simply a matter of a different approach to data collection from quantitative research; it is a different way of 'knowing', that is, it constitutes a different form of knowledge. Quantitative research is claimed to be infused with *positivism*, an approach to the study of people which commends the application of the scientific method. In contrast, qualitative research is often claimed to reflect a different form of knowledge in which people's under-standings of the nature of their social environment form the focus of attention, a focus which contrasts sharply with the tendency in much quantitative research to treat facets of this environment (such as organization structure or job characteristics) as pre-existing 'objects' akin to the physical or biological matter on which natural scientists work. On the other hand, qualitative research may be seen more simply as a different approach to data collection, which allows issues that are less amenable to quantitative research to be examined. This view is explicitly contested by writers who see in quantitative and qualitative research different approaches to what constitutes knowledge about organizations and their participants, as well as other aspects of the social world (for example, Morgan and Smircich, 1980) and not simply different ways of conducting research. These issues will be examined further in Chapter 9.

Regardless of whether qualitative research is conceptualized as a distinctive epistemological stance or as a cluster of research methods, there can be little doubt that it has attracted a good deal more attention in the late 1970s and the 1980s than in earlier periods. It would be a mistake to believe, however, that qualitative studies have become significantly more pervasive in journals and elsewhere. Podsakoff and Dalton (1987) conducted an analysis of the research methods used by articles reporting empirical research in five journals in 1985. The journals selected were known to publish articles relating to organizational research.[3] In spite of the considerable support for the injection of qualitative research into organization studies, Podsakoff and Dalton found that extremely few of the 193 studies analysed derived from qualitative investigations. Indeed, not one article based on participant observation was discerned. In part, this finding can be explained in terms of the tendency for some qualitative studies to be published outside the conventional channels. Further, quite a lot of qualitative studies are published in collections devoted to specific topics, such as organizational culture (for example, Frost *et al.*, 1985; Pondy *et al.*, 1983), an issue which has attracted a considerable amount of attention from qualitative researchers. Also, there may be some resistance to publishing such research in the conventional journals. If the criteria for accepting articles based on quantitative research are applied to qualitative studies, the latter may appear unreliable and idiosyncratic; at worst, they may be accused of being journalism (Schneider, 1985). It is important to realize, therefore, that qualitative research is not as pervasive in organization studies as some of the claims about its potential influence imply.

The purpose of this section has been twofold: to introduce qualitative research in a fairly preliminary way and to draw attention to the presence of disputes about the nature of knowledge in the study of organizations. In drawing attention to the relative prevalence of particular research methods, the intention has been to emphasize that, even though a large number of sources of data will be examined in later chapters, research methods are unequally distributed in terms of the frequency of their use in organizational research.

Research designs and methods of data collection

Although it is not always easy to sustain the distinction, in this book it is proposed to distinguish between research *designs* and research *methods* (or techniques of data collection). The former should be thought of as the overall structure and orientation of an investigation. This structure provides a framework within which data are collected and analysed. While particular designs tend to be associated with particular methods of data collection, a distinction is useful because one does not necessarily imply the other.

The following research designs are distinguished in this book (see also Table 1.2).

Experimental research (D1)   Orpen's (1979) study illustrates the basic framework of an experiment. There are at least two groups – in his case one which is given enriched work and one which is not. The group which does not receive the enriched work acts as a point of comparison, which allows Orpen to say whether, for example, the increase in job satisfaction observed among those who experienced enriched jobs might have occurred in any case. In addition to the distinction between experiments that take place in the field – that is, in real organizations as in Orpen's research, or in the laboratory as in the study by Ganster – a further separation is often drawn between experiments and 'quasi-

Table 1.2 Chief research designs and methods in organizational research

Designs		Methods	
D1	Experiment (major distinctions: laboratory and field experiments; experiments and quasi-experiments)	M1	Self-administered questionnaire
		M2	Structured interview
		M3	Participant observation
D2	Survey (including longitudinal survey design)	M4	Unstructured interviewing
		M5	Structured observation
D3	Qualitative research	M6	Simulation
D4	Case study	M7	Archival sources of data
D5	Action research		

experiments'. The latter constitute a diffuse category of research designs that exhibit most of the characteristics of a real experiment. The nature of experimental research and the various distinctions mentioned in this paragraph receive greater attention in Chapter 3.

Survey Research (D2) Hackman and Oldham's (1976) study illustrates the basic features of the survey design fairly well. Data are collected, usually either by interview or by questionnaire, on a constellation of variables. The objective then is to examine patterns of relationship between the variables. For example, Hackman and Oldham were concerned to establish how far there was a relationship between particular job characteristics and various other variables like internal motivation. Unlike experimental research, the researcher does not intervene in the organization and observe the effects of the intervention. Information is collected on a number of variables, and the degree to which they are causally related has to be inferred. Most survey research entails the collection of data at a single juncture, as in Hackman and Oldham's research. Survey research can be extended to include further questioning of respondents, at which point the research becomes elaborated into a longitudinal survey design. These points receive attention in Chapter 4.

Qualitative research (D3) As in Burgelman (1985), the emphasis in qualitative research tends to be on individuals' interpretations of their environments and of their own and others' behaviour. The presentation of data tends to be sensitive to the nuances of what people say and to the contexts in which their actions take place. The emphasis tends to be on understanding what is going on in organizations in participants' own terms rather than those of the researcher.

Case study research (D4)   Case studies entail the detailed examination of one or a small number of 'cases'. The unit of analysis is often the organization, but can equally be either departments and sections in organizations or inter-organizational networks. It is often difficult to distinguish qualitative from case study research, because the former often takes place in a single organization (as in Burgelman's research on corporate venturing) or in a small number of organizations (for example, Dalton, 1959; Lupton, 1963). Therefore, as a research design, the case study throws up definitional problems, which along with a variety of other issues will be addressed in Chapter 6.

Action research (D5)   In action research, the researcher is involved, in conjunction with members of an organization, in dealing with a problem that is recognized as such by both parties. The researcher feeds information about advisable lines of action back to the organization and observes the impact of the implementation of the advised lines of action on the organizational problem. In a sense, the researcher becomes part of the field of investigation. It is the nature of the relationship between the researcher and his or her subjects that constitutes the prime reason for conceptualizing action research as a distinct design.

   Within these designs a large number of methods of data collection and sources of data can be and are used. The main categories covered in this book are as follows.

Self-administered questionnaires (M1)   These are collections of questions that the respondent completes on his or her own.

Structured interviews (M2)   These are collections of specific and precisely formulated questions which are asked of a respondent by an interviewer.

Participant observation (M3)   A technique which involves the researcher spending a period of time making observations in a particular organizational context. The degree of participation varies from study to study.

Unstructured interviewing (M4)   Unlike M2, the researcher interviews in a very informal way, allowing respondents considerable latitude in what they say. There may not even be a pre-formulated series of questions.

Structured observation (M5)   The researcher records observations in terms of a predetermined schedule, rather than the somewhat unstructured recording of behaviour associated with M3, and does not participate a great deal in the day-to-day life of the organization.

Simulation (M6)   Individuals are asked to imitate real-life behaviour in order to observe how they react in different settings. People's behaviour can then be recorded with the aid of instruments like M5.

Archival information (M7)   This is not so much a method of data collection, but a source of data, in that the researcher uses pre-existing materials on which an analysis is carried out. This category includes historical documents, contemporary records and existing statistics. The data can be handled qualitatively or quantitatively. Archival research is examined in Chapter 7 along with a related method, the secondary analysis of social survey data.

M1 and M2 will be examined in Chapter 2, in conjunction with a general discussion of measurement issues. Although some of the general issues about measurement raised in this chapter apply to other methods of collecting quantitative (or quantifiable) data, the considerable prominence of questionnaires and interviews means that many of these issues have been specifically developed in relation to these two methods. M3 and M4 will be examined in Chapter 5, as the chief methods of qualitative research. M5 and M6 will be examined in Chapter 7, along with language studies – a little-used approach which is becoming more prominent. Chapter 8 also comprises brief discussions of a number of methods of data collection which are rarely used but are none the less worthy of mention.

Although a distinction has been drawn between designs and methods, there is frequently a correspondence between the two: D2 is typically associated with M1 and M2; D3 usually entails M3 and/or M4. However, D1, D4 and D5 can each be associated with a variety of different sources of data, and most of the methods can be employed in relation to different designs. Thus, although there may be a tendency for an association between design and method to be noticeable, the correspondence is a good deal less than perfect.

Overview

This chapter has sought to introduce the nature of organizational research. The prevailing ethos of research is one which gives priority to what might loosely be termed a 'scientific' approach. This predilection cannot be easily explained, but undoubtedly the cachet that an association with a scientific approach confers cannot be discounted. This cachet is all the more significant in the light of the strong emphasis on practical and applied issues, since in the eyes of some commentators it is just such an approach that is most likely to produce 'relevant' knowledge and to gain support among practitioners. A model of the quantitative organizational research approach was also presented along with the example of job characteristics theory and research which seem to mirror its qualities fairly well. However, it has also been observed that investigations frequently depart from this model in significant ways. The model is best thought of as a representation, even a characterization, rather than as a description. The idea of qualitative research was introduced to draw attention to the presence of another perspective on the research process in organizations, as well as to point to a controversy about the nature of knowledge in the field.

As Figure 1.1 implies, the measurement process occupies a central role in quantitative research. In the next chapter the nature and problems of measurement in the context of quantitative research are examined. The emphasis will be upon measurement through questionnaires and interviews, since they are the most intensively used sources of quantitative data (Podsakoff and Dalton, 1987). Other major sources of quantitative data – such as structured observation and archives – will be addressed in later chapters.

Notes

1 It should be noted that the presentation of the job characteristics model has been simplified slightly. In particular, the model specifies that particular job characteristics will enhance particular critical psychological states. For example, autonomy is supposed to enhance 'experienced responsibility for outcomes of the work'. However, the model's chief ingredients are represented in the text.

2 The edited collections of Kilmann *et al.*, 1983 and Lawler, 1985b, are recent indications of this concern with practical, applied topics in organizational research.

3 The journals examined by Podsakoff and Dalton, 1987, were:

Academy of Management Journal, Administrative Science Quarterly, Journal of Applied Psychology, Journal of Management and *Organizational Behavior and Human Decision Processes.* This last journal was formerly known as *Organizational Behavior and Human Performance.*

2

Measurement in organizational research: questionnaires and structured interviews

---

Measurement is a key step in the quantitative research process. It is the procedure that links theoretical categories (concepts) with empirical research and is therefore the means by which such categories are rendered researchable. Concepts constitute the linchpin of the whole process in that much organizational research entails attempting to establish connections between measures which are taken to be indicative of underlying concepts.

But where do concepts come from? To a very large extent, they are the result of our general reflections about the social world. We can return to the two research questions with which Chapter 1 began, both of which have to do with the notion of job satisfaction. The concept of job satisfaction derives from our reflections about the different ways that people experience their jobs. It is clear that some people enjoy their work, while others dislike their jobs intensely. Some people seem to be indifferent, having no clear views at all. Between these positions are shades of variation in people's experience of their work. Moreover, these variations are not random, but seem to exhibit patterns: doctors and solicitors seem to enjoy their work a great deal, but people whose job entails the routine operation of a machine which repeatedly does the same thing or who check that an apparently endless pile of forms are properly completed seem to enjoy their work much less and even express considerable dislike of what they do. The concept of job satisfaction allows us to achieve two ends. First, it summarizes the variety of views that people have about their work, as well as the different ways that they experience their jobs. Thus, concepts have a synthesizing function in that they summarize and afford a sense of coherence to an otherwise amorphous mass of relatively unsystematic observations. Second, once formulated, the concept of job satisfaction provides a focus for subsequent reflection on the experience of work; future deliberation and research are about job satisfaction as such. Further, the very fact that part of the reflection that acted as a spur to the formation of the concept of job satisfaction may have entailed a recognition that chief executive officers (CEOs) seem to like their work much more than unskilled manual workers in the same firm points to the sorts of lines of enquiry that research into job satisfaction can fruitfully pursue in exploring its causes.

Once formulated, a concept presents a paradox to the intending investigator. If it is intended to conduct systematic research into the causes of job satisfaction, precise ways of distinguishing people in terms of their levels of job satisfaction will be required. How can differences between people in terms of job satisfaction be recognized? The contrast between the CEO and the unskilled manual worker may allow a fairly ready contrast in levels of job satisfaction. However, within the CEO's company there may be a host of different manual tasks which vary in skill level. If the focus for an investigation is the relationship between the amount of variety in a job and satisfaction with that job, how could possibly minute variations in job satisfaction be gauged? In much the same way, we can distinguish between hot, warm and cold, or between tall, medium height and short, but more discreet differences cannot be encapsulated so readily in words and therefore require some form of measurement to allow fine distinctions to be made. Such considerations prompt the question: how do we measure job satisfaction? This issue – how we provide measures of concepts and the difficulties entailed in such an exercise – constitutes the basic theme of this chapter. There is a considerable paradox here; observations about the experience of work led to the concept of job satisfaction, but once the concept is formulated, the problem of how to make systematic observations (measurement) presents itself. None the less, it is with this connection between concepts and quantitative observations (often referred to as 'indicators', see below) that this chapter is concerned.

Sometimes concepts are embedded in hypotheses which either are formulated on the basis of theoretical reflection or derive from reviews of the literature in a particular domain. For example, consider the following hypothesis which was one of a number formulated in advance of a study of employee reactions to job characteristics: 'Hypothesis 2: Levels of employee satisfaction and motivation are expected to vary across technology. These differences are expected to be due to variations in job characteristics across technology' (Rousseau, 1977, p. 25). This hypothesis was formulated following a review of two areas of study: job design research and socio-technical systems theory. The former is essentially the job characteristics approach discussed in Chapter 1; socio-technical systems theory proposes that it is necessary to harmonize the technical infrastructure and the social organization of work in order to enhance both organizational performance and employee satisfaction. The hypothesis contains a number of concepts which will need to be rendered observable in order for it to be confirmed or rejected. In line with the predilections of quantitative researchers, this means that the concepts must be made capable of measurement in order for systematic research to be undertaken. The hypothesis implies that firms' technologies affect the characteristics of production jobs; these job characteristics in turn affect employee satisfaction and motivation. We have four concepts in need of measurement – technology, job characteristics, employee satisfaction and motivation – in order for the hypothesis to be tested. Technology is the independent variable, while employee satisfaction and motivation are dependent variables in the context of the hypothesis; job characteristics are visualized as constituting an 'intervening variable', a term that will be examined in Chapter 4. The case of technology is interesting in the context of the present discussion, in that the 'measurement' of this concept entailed classifying the nineteen firms studied by Rousseau into one of three different types, according to a scheme devised by Thompson (1967). Measurement frequently entails the subsumption of firms, individuals, or whatever into categories, and not just the more obvious sense of assigning numbers to a characteristic. The term *operationalization*, which derives from physics (Bridgman, 1927), is often used to denote the procedure whereby concepts are given measures.

Operationalizing a concept

The following discussion provides an exposition of the procedures associated with the operationalization of concepts in organizational research. It emphasizes the use of questionnaires and structured interviews as potential data collection instruments. The rationale for this approach is that quantitative organizational research makes intensive use of these methods of data collection (Podsakoff and Dalton, 1987). Both methods allow the researcher to question people about their own behaviour (and possibly that of others) and their attitudes to and perceptions of various aspects of their work environment. Questionnaires and structured interviews are conventionally associated with survey research, so that their use in this context may seem surprising, particularly since organizational researchers make heavy use of experimental research. However, it is important to realize that questionnaires and structured interviews are very often used by researchers employing an experimental design, as will be apparent from the discussion in the next chapter.

The idea of operationalization entails the provision of *indicators* which can stand for the concept in question. It is possible to imagine, and indeed this frequently occurs, the use of one indicator of a concept. For example, the following question was used as a single indicator of job satisfaction in a structured interview survey in the USA: 'On the whole, how satisfied are you with the work you do – would you say that you are very satisfied, moderately satisfied, a little dissatisfied, or very dissatisfied?' (Ebeling, King and Rogers, 1979, p. 390). While this appears to be a quite reasonable question, it suffers from the limitation of being very general and hence not providing a very specific frame of reference for respondents.

A great deal of the organizational research which uses questionnaires and structured interviews entails the provision of more than one (and often many more than one) indicator. The idea is to add up these indicators (often called 'items') to form an overall score for each respondent. In this way, it is possible to provide an index or scale for the underlying concept. As an example can be cited an index of job satisfaction devised by Brayfield and Rothe (1951). The index comprises eighteen statements, and each respondent is asked to indicate how well each statement describes his or her job. Respondents are asked to indicate whether they strongly agree, agree, are undecided, disagree, or strongly disagree with each statement. Examples of statements are:

- My job is like a hobby to me.
- My job is usually interesting enough to keep me from getting bored
- I find real enjoyment in my work

This approach to measuring job satisfaction is one of the most intensively used methods in organizational research. It is known as a Likert scale (after the person who devised it) and comprises a series of statements to which respondents indicate the intensity of their agreement; the responses are then aggregated for each respondent. Someone affirming 'strongly agree' to 'My job is like a hobby to me' would be given a score of 5, with the other responses being scored 4, 3, 2 and 1 respectively. Since there are eighteen items, the minimum possible score is 18 and the maximum is 90. In fact, respondents typically differ substantially from these two extremes. The Likert procedure can readily be adapted to include a larger range of possible responses to each statement (for example, seven or nine points) in order to allow finer distinctions to be used by respondents. Other approaches to devising indices or scales are found in organizational research. One is to ask respondents how often particular statements pertain. In the Leader Behavior Description Questionnaire (LBDQ) developed at Ohio State University (Halpin and Winer, 1957) respondents are asked to indicate whether statements with which they are presented always, often, occasionally, seldom or never apply to their superiors. The questionnaire is designed to measure patterns of leader behaviour. Examples of statements are:

- Lets group members know what is expected of them.
- Is friendly and approachable.
- Assigns group members to particular tasks.
- Looks out for the personal welfare of group members.

In the JDS, in addition to indicating degrees of agreement to some statements, respondents have to answer other questions in terms of whether the statement is accurate. Yet another style is to ask respondents the degree of importance they attach to different issues or phenomena, and so on. Collectively, these styles of questioning are referred to as 'rating scales' and are frequently used because of their simplicity and ease of interpretation. When more than one indicator is used, it is best referred to as a 'multiple-indicator (or -item) rating scale'.

The discussion so far has not addressed the question of why more than one item might be required for each concept. One reason for the widespread use of multiple indicators is that many of the concepts with which researchers deal are broad and it is unlikely in many cases that a single indicator will adequately reflect the full range of every concept. Second, a respondent may make a mistake in answering questions; if a researcher has only asked one question then the respondent will be incorrectly classified in terms of that particular question. The presence of additional items can offset an incorrectly or inappropriately answered question. Third, if only one question is asked, it must be very competently designed because if it is faulty it will produce inappropriate data for that particular concept. Again, the presence of more than one indicator allows the impact of a poor question to be offset. Finally, the presence of more than one indicator allows much finer distinctions to be drawn between people. Compare the item used to measure job satisfaction in the Ebeling, King and Rogers (1979) study, which only allows people to be classified in terms of a fourfold division, with the Brayfield and Rothe (1951) index which allows people to be located on a scale from 18 to 90.

One embellishment of the multiple-indicator approach is the examination and elucidation of underlying dimensions to a concept and its associated indicators. This can be established in advance by deriving a priori dimensions of a concept. Lazarsfeld (1958) proposed that the establishment of different facets of a concept is an important step in the development of an operational definition. The JDS, for example, seeks to examine five dimensions of job characteristics (see Table 1.1), each of which is measured by a number of questions. This approach contrasts with the Brayfield and Rothe index which does not reflect underlying dimensions of the concept. When a dimensional approach is employed, the indicators of each dimension can be aggregated to reveal profiles for each individual, job, organization, or whatever. A job may comprise skill variety and autonomy, a moderate level of feedback and task significance, and little task identity.

Another approach to the elucidation of dimensions is through factor analysis, a technique which aims to discover 'bunching' among variables. It can be used in relation to a multiple-indicator measure which does not specify a priori dimensions of a concept. The LBDQ is a case in point. The questionnaire comprised 130 questions and was administered to 300 respondents. The factor analysis revealed that certain questions tended to cling together and to form clear patterns. These bunches of indicators are referred to as 'factors'. Two factors were especially prominent. One comprised questions that the researchers took to be indicative of a leader who is 'considerate'. Of the four indicators from the LBDQ listed on page 38, the second and fourth statements are examples of descriptions of a considerate leader. The second factor was called 'initiating structure', because it refers to a description of a leader who tightly structures work and provides clear guidelines of responsibility for subordinates. The first and third questions cited on page 38 are examples of this aspect of leader behaviour. Factor analysis can also be used to confirm whether there is a close correspondence between a priori dimensions and the question items to which they have been assigned. For example, some doubt has been cast on whether there is a neat correspondence between the five dimensions of job characteristics measured by the JDS and the associated questions (Dunham, Aldag and Brief, 1977).

A type of questioning that is increasingly encountered is the use of vignettes, whereby the researcher produces a 'story' and asks the respondent to answer questions in relation to it. Leblebici and Salancik (1981) were interested in the effects of environmental characteristics on the amount of uncertainty that is perceived in decision-making. The focus for their inquiry was the degree of uncertainty perceived by loan officers in US banks. Seven hypothetical loan applications were constructed to reflect a range of degrees of potential risk. Each vignette comprises information about the applicant's appearance, age, gender, residence, job, income, dependants, amount and purpose of loan and so on. Each loan officer was asked to indicate the likelihood that the loan would be repaid and also how the decision would be handled within the bank. Another example is a study by Fredrickson and Mitchell (1984) which was concerned with the extent to which firms attempt 'to be exhaustive and inclusive in making and integrating strategic decisions' (p. 402). Following preparatory interviews with CEOs in firms in the sawmills and planing industry, 123 executives were presented with a five-page 'decision scenario' which depicted a hypothetical forestry firm faced with a major problem, along with the background to the problem. The vignette also dealt with the firm's approach to handling the problem. Each executive was then asked a battery of Likert-type questions which aimed to indicate how their own firm would have dealt with the problem. Two advantages of the vignette approach are very clear. First, the focus for respondents is considerably more concrete than the general questions that normally pervade survey instruments; and second, the technique more accurately reflects the complexity of people's thinking in relation to complicated topics (Finch, 1987). Both of the cited studies deal with decision-making, an area in which complex thought processes are likely to be in evidence.

Organizational research utilizes a variety of approaches to the establishment of operational definitions. Single item measures coexist with multiple-item ones. Since the late 1960s quantitative research appears to be making increasingly greater use of multiple-item measures. Many researchers use multiple-item measures that have been employed in earlier studies. In other words, some measures seem to establish a reputation and are used again and again by other researchers. The bulk of the research findings deriving from Rousseau's (1977) afore-mentioned study of the link between technology, job character-istics and worker responses employed four multiple-item measures previously devised by other researchers (for example, the JDS and the Brayfield–Rothe index).

Structured interviews and self-administered questionnaires

Up to now, structured interviews and self-administered question-naires have been referred to as though there is little or no difference between them. The chief similarity is that they are both highly structured approaches to gathering data on fairly to very large numbers of respondents. In many respects, the structured interview is simply a questionnaire that is administered in a face-to-face setting. Both approaches to data collection are highly structured in order to make people's responses as comparable as possible. Each respondent is given the same instrument and answers each question in the same order as other respondents. These practices allow the questioning to be standardized, so that variation in people's responses can be attributed to genuine variations and not to divergences in the manner or order of asking questions. The structured interview can be contrasted with the unstructured interview in which the interviewer has a very loose assemblage of topics that are to be asked in any order and in a variety of ways. Between the two extremes of structured and unstructured interviewing is a host of possible variations. By and large, quantitative research tends to use interviews at the structured end of the continuum; unstruc-tured interviews tend to be used in the context of qualitative research and will be returned to in Chapter 5, where such research is discussed in greater detail.

When considering questionnaires, the contrast is often drawn between interview and postal questionnaire approaches. The term 'self-administered questionnaire' has been preferred to 'postal questionnaire' in the preceding discussion, because in organizational research respondents frequently fill in on their own questionnaires which have not been sent to them through the mail. It is often the case that questionnaires are handed out to respondents who return them at a collection point or through the mail. As an example of the latter, the following procedure was followed by Rousseau (1977):

> Questionnaires were distributed to employees on the job by both the researcher and a member of management. A letter accompanied the questionnaire explaining the purpose of the project. Subjects were not asked to identify themselves and mailed the completed questionnaires directly to the resear-cher . . . subjects completed it in their own time.
> (Rousseau, 1977, p. 28)

Research based on multiple-item rating scales, like the JDS and the LBDQ, tend to use this or a similar approach to the distribution of questionnaires. It would seem inappropriate to refer to this procedure as denoting the use of a postal questionnaire, so the more inclusive term 'self-administered' is preferred.

Structured interviews and self-administered questionnaires each possess advantages and disadvantages. There are few if any guidelines to assist in knowing when to use one rather than the other. The amount of detail may be one factor, in that it is likely to be difficult to induce a high level of co-operation when self-administered questionnaires are being used to collect a large body of information. Self-administered, and particularly postal, questionnaires often engender poor response rates (the proportion of designated individuals who agree to paticipate), a tendency which may be exacerbated by excessive length. However, if a questionnaire comprises many clusters of questions with identical response formats, like the LBDQ and the JDS, its administration by interview could be extremely tedious, so that self-administration could be much less time-consuming and irritating for respondents. A consideration of the advantages and disadvantages of self-administered questionnaires may be of assistance in deciding which to choose.

Advantages of self-administered questionnaires
(1) Self-administered questionnaires are invariably cheaper than interviews, especially when there is a large number of respondents and if respondents are geographically dispersed. Interviews are much more costly; it would have cost Rousseau (1977) much more money to hire interviewers for 201 respondents, or more time if she had conducted interviews herself. Handing out or posting questionnaires is much less expensive, even when postage has to be provided for their return. If respondents are far apart from each other the costs of interviewing would be even greater, because of the cost of travel between interviewees.

(2) Self-administered questionnaires are usually quicker than interviews. The former can be distributed *en masse*, but interviews cannot be conducted in the same way unless many interviewers are employed.

(3) There are several problems associated with the presence of interviewers. Characteristics of interviewers, such as their age, appearance, race, gender and social class, have been shown by researchers to have an effect on the preparedness of respondents to answer questions in the interview situation and on the nature of the answers they provide (Sudman and Bradburn, 1974). Further, there is evidence that characteristics of interviewers and

of respondents may combine to produce special effects, though such effects are heavily influenced by the nature of the questions being asked. For example, social class differences between interviewers are most likely to have an effect on respondents' answers when respondents are trade union members and the questions are concerned with labour issues. Further, there is evidence that interviewers have expectations which can be communicated to respondents and affect their answers. Finally, there is a good deal of evidence to suggest that people's responses to questions can be affected by their perceptions of the social desirability of certain kinds of answer (for example, Thomas and Kilmann, 1975), a topic which will receive further attention below. It has been suggested that this source of error in people's replies is more pronounced when an interviewer is present (Sudman and Bradburn, 1982). Obviously, if there is no interviewer present, as in the case of self-administered question-naires, such sources of error may be eliminated.

Disadvantages of self-administered questionnaires
(1) While it is always essential to make questions clear and unambiguous (see the discussion below on asking questions), this requirement is even greater with self-administered question-naires, since there is no interviewer to help the respondent if a question is not understood. Similarly, the format of the questionnaire has to be especially easy to follow.

(2) Respondents can read the whole questionnaire before starting to answer the first question, so that answers to early questions may be influenced by their knowledge of the later ones, perhaps making answers more consistent than they would otherwise be.

(3) The researcher can never be certain who has answered a self-administered questionnaire. When questionnaires are sent to chief executives of firms, for example, it is impossible to know whether the person to whom it was sent has answered it. Indeed, in view of the propensity of managers to delegate, there is a fair chance that a questionnaire will be passed on. As a result, there may be a good deal of variety in the roles and statuses of respondents, a factor that may have implications for the comparability of the data.

(4) If an interviewer visits firms to carry out a large number of interviews, he or she can collect additional data through making observations or requesting documents. This possibility is removed if questionnaires are posted, though when they are distributed (as in Rousseau's study) the collection of such additional material may be feasible.

(5) In the eyes of many commentators, the most fundamental drawback of self-administered questionnaires is that they can generate lower, and in many instances much lower, response rates than interview-based research. The bulk of the discussion about this issue in the methodological literature relates to postal questionnaires, which appear to be particularly prone to low response rates. The problem with refusals is that they may introduce an element of bias as respondents and non-respondents may differ from each other in terms of characteristics relevant to the research. Consequently, there is a voluminous literature drawing attention to the ways in which refusals can be minimized (for example, Lockhart, 1984). While the provision of a covering letter with a clear explanation of the aims and importance of a piece of research, a reply-paid envelope, assurances of confidentiality and anonymity, and following up non-respondents constitute essential basic manoeuvres in minimizing refusals, it is evident that response rates may still be poor. The field of organizational research reveals examples of both very low and reasonably high response rates. Instances of very low response rates are particularly evident when postal questionnaires are sent to firms: Carter (1984) and Hitt, Ireland and Stadter (1982) achieved low response rates of 21 and 25 per cent respectively in such circumstances. In addition, there is evidence that people's preparedness to respond to questionnaires and surveys is declining (Goyder, 1988), a problem that is bound to compound the poor response rates associated with postal questionnaires.

Personal and telephone interviewing
The comparison of interviews and questionnaires has not distinguished between face-to-face and telephone interviewing. With the former, interviewer and respondent are in direct contact, but in the case of telephone interviews they can be hundreds or thousands of miles apart. Telephone interviews are relatively rarely undertaken in the field of organizational research, but two good examples can illustrate the sorts of use to which they may be put. Yin (1979) reports the results of an investigation into the responses of nineteen public organizations (such as police, educational and welfare organizations) to six different types of innovation. This research mainly entailed personal interviews with various personnel. In order to broaden the span of the research, telephone interviews, each comprising seventy-eight questions, were carried out with senior representatives of ninety other organizations affected by one of the six innovations, covering such topics as the nature of the innovation, its staffing, opposition from municipal representatives and

employee training for the innovation. The ensuing data are obviously much less detailed than those deriving from the nineteen case studies, but they allowed Yin to establish the prevalence of some of the patterns gleaned from the case study material.

Pennings (1987) used telephone interviews for some portions of the data he required for a test of some hypotheses deriving from the contingency approach to organizational effectiveness, in the context of a study of 108 branches of a large commercial US bank. In addition to personal interviews with managers and other employees and the use of some archival data, telephone interviews were conducted with 2,354 clients. The telephone interviews yielded data on characteristics of each branch's environment (in particular indicators of customer variability) and on organizational effectiveness through questions on customer satisfaction (such as satisfaction with employees' knowledge, responsiveness and courteousness, and waiting time). One important function of the telephone interviews was to mitigate the problem of 'common method variance', which occurs as a consequence of data relating to pairs of variables deriving from a single source. This topic is discussed later in this chapter.

In view of the considerable use which both Yin and Pennings have made of the telephone interview, it is slightly surprising that it is not used more widely. Telephone interviews afford a number of advantages over personal interviews. They are cheaper, though still more expensive than postal questionnaires; they are generally quicker to administer; interviewers can be much more readily supervised; and the effects of the personal and social characteristics of interviewers on respondents' replies are probably less pronounced. Considerable coverage is possible with telephone interview studies. For example, in a study within the population ecology tradition, which was concerned to examine the relative likelihood of demise among specialist and generalist organizations, Freeman and Hannan (1983) conducted telephone interviews in 1977 with the owners or mangers of restaurants in eighteen Californian cities. Interviews were repeated in 1978 and 1979, with establishments being added to the sample to replace failed restaurants. In total, data were obtained for 958 restaurants. Further, telephone interview response rates are at least as good as those with personal interviews (Groves and Kahn, 1979). Therefore, telephone interviewing seems largely to enjoy the advantages associated with personal interviewing. It was once advocated that telephone interviews needed to be brief, because of a belief that interviewees would have a limited attention span, but this view is not supported by research evidence (Dillman,

1978; Groves and Kahn, 1979), though it is clearly easier for telephone respondents to terminate the interview than when in a face-to-face environment. On the other hand, telephone interviewers, as against personal interviewers, cannot collect additional observational material which may be of interest; they cannot respond to the look of puzzlement that affects interviewees when they fail to understand a question; and they cannot employ interview aids, such as cards printed with answers from which respondents must choose. One potential use of telephone interviewing is in the context of the selection of samples or cases with particular features. For example, it could be used to find organizations which have particular strategies, or which have a certain structure, or which have introduced an innovation (or are about to do so). Indeed, the telephone interview would seem well suited to the predilection in some areas of organizational research for key informant interviewing (see next section). In any event, the telephone interview warrants serious consideration for a number of research topics as an alternative or adjunct to personal interviews and questionnaires.

Key informant research
Although not unique to organizational research, the use of key informants to provide data is a characteristic feature of many quantitative studies. Data are collected either by interview (personal or telephone) or by questionnaire (usually postal). Key informants are often used in the context of providing quantifiable data on characteristics of their organizations. The informant is usually someone of seniority who can speak for the organization. A number of studies of organization structure have employed this approach (for example, Blau *et al.*, 1976; Pugh *et al.*, 1969). In the context of their study of New Jersey manufacturers, Blau *et al.* write:

> Information was collected at each of the 110 plants with a structured questionnaire administered to senior managers; these included the chief executive officer, the head of production, and the personnel manager. Data were collected at the site on day-to-day operations. All the data obtained refer to attributes of a plant's social structure and objective conditions, such as size, personnel distributions, production technology, and automation.
>
> (Blau *et al.*, 1976, p. 22)

Studies of strategic management also make considerable use of key informants. Grinyer, Yasai-Ardekani and Al-Bazzaz (1980) conducted structured interviews with the director or senior manager responsible for corporate planning in forty-eight UK companies, while Hitt, Ireland and Stadter (1982) sent question-naires to CEOs of 1,000 US firms. Similarly, in their research on decision-making, Hickson *et al.* (1986) interviewed one or more individuals as informants about decisions in which they had been involved. As this brief list of procedures suggests, key informant studies are undertaken either by interview or by postal question-naire and can involve one representative or more in each organization. The problem with using a postal questionnaire is that one cannot be sure whether the person to whom it was sent (for example, the CEO) actually answered it, so that some variability in the status of informant may occur across organiz-ations and may have implications for the comparability of data. The emphasis tends to be upon eliciting 'factual' rather than attitudinal information. Thus, in the Aston Studies (Pugh *et al.*, 1969) an attribute of organization structure like functional specialization is measured by asking informants whether the organization has people who spend all of their time working in each of sixteen functional areas (such as employment, accounts and market research).

An obvious consideration regarding such investigations is whether it is possible for individuals to provide accurate information on the organization as a whole. A study by Phillips (1981) of wholesale distribution companies, in which questions about organizational characteristics were asked of more than one informant in each firm and then informants' answers compared, indicates that the potential for error, as a result of bias or ignorance, is considerable. If a number of informants is used it is possible to cross-check and then reconcile the conflicting accounts. Simply aggregating accounts may not eliminate error, since extremely incorrect versions may have an adverse net effect on accuracy. Obviously, when only one informant is employed, as in the studies by Grinyer, Yasai-Ardekani and Al-Bazzaz and Hitt, Ireland and Stadter, there is even more chance of error.

In the 1970s key informant research was implicated in a controversy about the validity of different measures of organiz-ation structure. An alternative approach, often using dimensions of organization structure similar to those of writers within the Aston tradition, was separately developed by a number of researchers (such as Hall, 1968) by administering questionnaires to samples of members of a number of organizations. Measures of dimensions of organization structure are created by aggregat-ing respondents' answers to questions. For example, in order to measure the dimension 'division of labour' – a putative equivalent to the Aston researchers' notion of functional specialization – Hall asked respondents how true statements such as 'Everyone has a specific job to do' were. An organization-level measure of division of labour is then derived from individuals' replies. When both types of measure – key informant and individual – were combined in the same study, a number of researchers found that there was a poor correspondence between these apparently equivalent measures of seemingly identical dimensions of organization structure (for example, Ford, 1979; Pennings, 1973; Sathe, 1978). For instance, Sathe found correlations between the two types of measure for centralization, formalization and specialization to be .08, .17 and –.14 respectively. The finding of a negative relationship is especially worrying since it implies that more specialization in terms of the key informant approach is accompanied by less specialization in terms of the individual-based measures. There has been considerable speculation about the meaning and implications of such disconcerting findings. Sathe, for example, has suggested that the two approaches to the measurement of organization structure address different facets: key informant measures tap the formal or designed structure, while individual-based measures reflect day-to-day experiences and so an organization's emergent structure. It would seem that the divergences revealed by investigators are in large part produced by the different aspects of structure each type of measure addresses. However, the distortion that may arise when only one or two informants are used is rarely considered by researchers; in particular, the question of whether the correspondence between the two types of measure can be improved by using a larger number of informants is largely unanswered.

Ostensibly, the use of key informants to derive measures of strategy is less problematic, since it is usually a company's overt strategy, as formulated by senior executives (often precisely the same persons who would be used in a key informant study), that is the object of attention. On the other hand, there may be important nuances which are poorly captured by a reliance on only one informant, although documents and statements of company philosophy can be important additional sources of data for checking informants' answers.

All of the illustrations mentioned above involve informants imparting information about their own organizations, departments, or whatever. A variation on this theme is suggested by a study of Dutch firms by Geeraerts (1984), who believed that it was virtually impossible to acquire from firms themselves the information on strategy and performance that he needed for his research. Accordingly, he sought the requisite information from senior consultants in leading Dutch consulting firms. Eighty-four consultants completed questionnaires relating to 142 firms. However, such research could raise a number of difficult ethical issues if such information, which is not in the public domain, is divulged without firms' consent.

The time and cost involved in administering large numbers of questionnaires in each of a number of organizations to glean equivalent measures to those that can be derived from key informant studies are often considerable. One of the main arguments in favour of key informant studies is that they provide an economical approach to gaining 'global' data on an organization and its operations. The discussion in this section points to the advisability of using more than one informant and preferably three or more. The significance of the failure of key informant and individual-based measures to be related should not be exaggerated. At least part of the problem may be to do with the fact that the dimensions of structure addressed by researchers operating with the two approaches to measurement were not designed to be equivalent; their equivalence (for example, that the Aston functional specialization measure is much the same as Hall's notion of the division of labour) is something that has been suggested by later writers employing both types of measure within the same study.

Asking Questions

Assuming that a researcher does not intend to rely exclusively upon pre-existing measures of the concepts that the investigation is to examine, the need to devise new measures will mean that a number of prerequisites of questionnaire construction will need attention. One of the most basic decisions is whether to employ open-ended or forced-choice (often called closed-ended) questions. With an open-ended question the respondent has considerable latitude over what kind and length of response may be given. For example, in their structured interviews with top executives Lawrence and Lorsch (1967) used the following question in conjunction with others to determine the nature of demands emanating from the external environments in which firms operated: 'Would you list for me the major kinds of problems an organization encounters competing in this industry?' (Lawrence and Lorsch, 1967, p. 247). Once all of the answers to a question like this have been collected, they will need to be *coded*. By 'coding' is meant the assignment of numbers to each answer category so that common answers can be aggregated.

Coding is necessary for answers to be processed by computer. The advantage of such a question is that it permits respondents to answer in their own terms. The problem for the researcher is that it is likely to engender a wide variety of responses which may be highly resistant to coding and hence quantification. It is also necessary to ensure that interviewers record exactly what is said and do not embellish responses in any way, since they may introduce error and bias as a result.

Forced-choice questions remove these two problems by forcing respondents to choose between a limited range of possible answers. Such questions are often called 'pre-coded' questions, because the assignment of numbers to answer categories is usually undertaken prior to their administration to respondents. Coding then becomes a relatively simple task whereby each respondent's answer can easily be ascribed the appropriate code (for example, respondents who answer 'agree' to a Likert-style statement will receive a code of 4 for that question). With open-ended questions, the task is much less easy since each answer has to be scrutinized and its meaning interpreted in order to determine the most appropriate code. In a sense, the questions which make up multiple-item rating scales like the JDS, Brayfield–Rothe, or LBDQ scales are forms of forced-choice question, but it seems to be sensible to make a distinction between such rating scale questions and a question like the following, in which the respondent is asked to choose between a number of statements:

> This next question is on the subject of work. People look for different things in a job. Which one of the following five things would you *most* prefer in a job?
> 1 Work that pays well.
> 2 Work that gives a feeling of accomplishment.
> 3 Work where there is not too much supervision and you make most decisions yourself.
> 4 Work that is pleasant and where the other people are nice to work with.
> 5 Work that is steady with little chance of being laid off.
> (Schuman and Presser, 1981, pp. 95–6, original emphasis)

The obvious disadvantage with such a question is that the prescribed answers may impose what is to the respondent an inappropriate frame of reference or set of answers. Further, great care has to be taken to ensure that the answers do not overlap, that they cover an adequate range of possibilities and that they are equally attractive to respondents. These problems do not apply to the same degree to rating scale questions as in the LBDQ, but all forced-choice formats share the problem of whether respondents interpret answers in the same way. When a person indicates that his or her supervisor is 'often' friendly and approachable, is that respondent using the same frame of reference as other respondents? None the less, forced-choice questions are widely employed in organizational research because of the ease with which responses can be classified and quantified and because they are less likely to be prone to interviewer embellishments. Further, forced-choice questions can have the important advantage of clarifying questions for respondents by providing further information about the kind of information required. Superficially, it appears that one must choose between the apparently greater accuracy and sensitivity of open questions and the ease of analysis permitted by forced-choice questions. However, two points must be borne in mind. First, Schuman and Presser (1981) have conducted a number of experiments which compare the two types of question and have concluded that when the answer choices which make up a forced-choice question derive from pilot studies, in which open-ended questions have been used to generate forced-choice responses, there is virtually no difference between the two types of question. In this connection, it is worth noting that pilot studies are often recommended in order to reduce errors in subsequent research. However, many forced-choice questions are probably designed with little of the pre-testing that Schuman and Presser advocate. Second, if a self-administered questionnaire is being used, a large number of open-ended questions will almost certainly deter prospective respondents, who will not relish the prospect of writing large amounts of text. Consequently, the choice between the two types of question applies primarily (though not exclusively) to the structured interview context.

The literature on questionnaire design reveals a large body of prescriptions about how to ask questions. These can be mentioned briefly.

(1) Questions should be clear and unambiguous. If they are capable of more than one interpretation, quantifying people's responses will be highly suspect. A question like 'How satisfied are you with your job?' is likely to be interpreted in a variety of ways by people, some of whom may be thinking in terms of intrinsic aspects (the work itself), others in terms of extrinsic factors (pay, conditions). If the researcher was interested in satisfaction with the work itself, it is clear that the question has not provided an adequate frame of reference, because some

people might clearly be thinking in terms of pay and conditions. Therefore, a question should be specific as well as unambiguous. As suggested above, terms like 'often', 'usually' and 'sometimes', though frequently employed, constitute additional sources of ambiguity when used in questions or for forced-choice responses since they are capable of a variety of interpretations. An extreme example of a question which is both ambiguous and lacking in specificity is the final question employed in Marx and Engels's *Enquête Ouvrière*, a questionnaire sent to 20,000 French socialists: 'What is the general, intellectual and moral condition of men and women workers employed in your trade?' (Bottomore and Rubel, 1963, p. 218). Not only is the term 'condition' vague, the question as a whole spans far too widely and so fails to provide a specific frame of reference.

(2) Wherever possible simple language should be used, so that respondents can readily comprehend questions. Consequently, it is common for questionnaire designers to recommend that jargon or words which do not have an everyday usage be avoided.

(3) It used to be the case that questions were recommended to be short. Payne (1951) is often cited for his advice that questions should not exceed twenty-five words. In recent years, some commentators have modified this view. Sudman and Bradburn (1982) suggest that the recommendation to keep questions short when attitudes are being asked about is probably correct, but that when questions relate to behaviour, longer questions seem to assist respondents to recall events. This effect seems to be more pronounced in connection with self-administered questionnaires than with structured interviews. An important role of longer questions is that they can allow investigators to clarify the terms that they are using. The following question is taken from the JDS:

> To what extent does your job involve doing a *'whole' and identifiable piece of work?* That is, is the job a complete piece of work that has an obvious beginning and end? Or is it only a small *part* of the overall piece of work, which is finished by other people or by automatic machines?

This question contains fifty-five words, thereby transgressing Payne's rule considerably, but it makes clear to the respondent precisely what a ' "whole" and identifiable piece of work' means to the researcher, so that ambiguity is kept to a minimum.

(4) There is agreement that the 'double-barrelled' question – in which the respondent is asked about two things in one question – should be avoided, since it can be confusing to both respondent

and researcher. The latter cannot be sure about which of the two topics an answer refers to. Yet this rule is often broken. One of the JDS questions asks respondents to indicate how far their 'job is simple and repetitive'. Is it not possible for a job to be one but not the other?

(5) It is often advocated that questions should not contain negatives, since they can be readily misinterpreted. This recommendation is possibly broadly true, but there are likely to be occasions when they cannot be avoided, especially when groups of multiple-item scales and indexes are being used. One of the problems with such groups of questions is that of 'response sets', whereby the respondent answers in the same way (such as 'strongly agree') to every question. Indeed, one of the reasons why formats of the 'strongly agree' to 'strongly disagree' or 'very often' to 'very rarely' kind are not recommended by writers on questionnaire design (who often prefer forced-format questions in which a number of possible different answers are provided) is that people often fail to give a great deal of consideration to their answers (Converse and Presser, 1986). Yet multiple-item rating scales are widely used in organizational research for the reasons stated above. One way of dealing with the response-set problem is to include negative items which point in the opposite direction to the rest. If a person, for example, indicates that he or she strongly agrees with all the items, including the negative ones, that person's answers have to be discarded since the inconsistent replies are likely to be indicative of a response set. Thus, the JDS includes the following item: 'The job itself is not very significant or important in the broader scheme of things.' The sample JDS question in Table 1.1 to measure feedback is another example. There is a strong possibility that these negative questions were included to check on response sets in respect of the other questions asked. When such negative items are provided, they are scored in the opposite direction to the others. For example, if the positive indicators are scored from 5 to 1 for 'strongly agree' through to 'strongly disagree', negative items will be scored 1 to 5 for the same answers in order to ensure that each individual's answers to the questions making up the index or scale can be aggregated to form a score for that person.

(6) Leading questions and presuming questions should be avoided. A question like 'How many years have you been a member of the – trade union' should be avoided since it assumes membership. It would be better to have a filter question that asks whether the respondent is a member of the union and only asks those who are members about the number of years that they have been members. Non-members will simply bypass the question on

number of years. Similarly, questions which appear to force answers in a particular direction should be avoided at all costs.

The problem of how to phrase questions is by no means the only area in which care is needed in questionnaire design. The format of the questionnaire requires attention so that it does not confuse interviewers or people filling in self-administered questionnaires. For example, it is important to check that instructions are clear so that particular questions are not habitually missed out. In this regard, pilot studies can be invaluable. There is also the issue of question order. Beyond the injunction that respondents should be eased into an interview or self-administered questionnaire through simple, non-threatening questions (so that they are not put off from continuing) and that researchers should be sensitive to the implications of early questions for answers to questions included later in the questionnaire (since respondents may be sensitized to the themes raised in earlier questions), there are few recommendations that can be made since experiments with question order usually fail to produce clear-cut effects (Schuman and Presser, 1981).

Reliability and validity of measures

When a measure is devised, it should not be presumed to be appropriate and adequate; rather, it is necessary to establish that it meets the researcher's aims and that it has adequate measurement properties. Discussions of such issues usually involve a consideration of whether the measure is reliable and valid. The following treatment of these issues will employ a number of illustrations. In particular, the Organizational Commitment Questionnaire (OCQ) will be used as an example at a number of junctures, since a fairly complete account of the assessment of its validity and reliability is available (Mowday, Steers and Porter, 1979). The OCQ was devised 'to measure the relative strength of an individual's identification with and involvement in a particular organization' (p. 226). The questionnaire comprises fifteen statements with which respondents have to indicate their degree of agreement or disagreement on a seven point Likert-format scale. Examples of the statements are:

- I am willing to put in a great deal of effort beyond that normally expected to help this organization be successful.
- I feel very little loyalty to this organization. (This statement is scored in reverse, so that it is disagreement that is indicative of commitment.)

- I really care about the fate of this organization.
- For me this is the best of all possible organizations for which to work.

Mowday, Steers and Porter report evidence relating to the validity and reliability of the OCQ from a variety of investigations. In all, it was administered to 2,563 respondents in a wide variety of work settings and representing nine different organizations.

Reliability
Reliability refers to the consistency of a measure. This notion can be taken to comprise two elements: external and internal reliability. External reliability refers to the degree to which a measure is consistent over time. If I weigh a bag of flour on my kitchen scales and find that there is variation in the recorded weight on each occasion, then my scales are failing to provide a consistent and hence reliable measure of weight. Similarly, if I devise a new measure of job satisfaction, I would hope that my measure will not fluctuate; I would hope that people's propensity to answer in a particular way will not change markedly over time. The most obvious way of establishing reliability in this sense is to administer a measure on two different occasions and to examine the degree to which respondents' scores are consistent between the two time periods. This approach to gauging reliability is known as *test/retest reliability*. In two of the studies carried out by Mowday, Steers and Porter, test/retest reliability was estimated: for a sample of psychiatric technicians, the correlation coefficients relating test and retest scores over two-, three- and four-month periods were .53, .63 and .75 respectively; for a sample of retail management trainees the reliability estimates over two and three months were .72 and .62. The different patterns for these two studies – that is, increasing over time for the technicians and decreasing for the trainees – is somewhat disconcerting, but the results are basically indicative of a questionnaire with fairly good external reliability.

Sometimes the results of a number of examinations of test/retest reliability can be very inconsistent. Fiedler (1967) has devised a well-known measure known as the Least Preferred Co-worker (LPC) scale. The measure asks respondents to describe the person with whom they have least enjoyed working, currently or in the past, in terms of between sixteen and twenty-five pairs of adjectives (the number varies). Each pair is on an eight-point scale. Examples of the items used are:

Pleasant 8 7 6 5 4 3 2 1 Unpleasant
Friendly 8 7 6 5 4 3 2 1 Unfriendly
Rejecting 1 2 3 4 5 6 7 8 Accepting
Distant   1 2 3 4 5 6 7 8 Close

This kind of questioning is known as a 'semantic differential' scale. The LPC scale is meant to be indicative of the orientation of leaders to their leadership role. Leaders who derive high scores from the scale and who therefore describe their LPC in predominantly favourable terms (pleasant, friendly, accepting and so on) are deemed to have a primary orientation to relationships with people; low scorers are deemed to be primarily oriented to tasks. Rice (1978b and 1979) found a considerable range in test/retest reliability across twenty-three studies using the measure. Correlations between tests and retests ranged between a low of .01 and a high of .92, with a median of .67. The median test/retest interval was eight weeks. Some of the coefficients seem unacceptably small (eight are below .50). However, as Rice (1979) observes, one reason for the variation in the magnitude of the coefficients, and in particular for some of the low ones, is that intervening experiences between the initial test and the retest affected people's subsequent scores. For example, seven of the eleven coefficients below the median of .67 derive from respondents who had important experiences between the two tests. 'These experiences included basic training in the military, management development workshops, or business games lasting several weeks' (Rice, 1979, p. 292). Herein lies an important problem with test/retest reliability estimates: indications of low levels of stability over time may at least in part be attributable to intervening events and changes to the respondent. If the span of time between the tests is reduced to minimize such effects, it is not inconceivable that the proximity of the test and retest will engender a spurious consistency, since people may recollect their initial responses. In order to deal with such effects an experimental design (see Chapter 3) would be required so that a control group which had not received the original test could be compared with the group of subjects who do receive an initial test. It is fairly unusual to find this type of testing, however.

Internal reliability refers to the degree of internal consistency of a measure. This issue is of particular importance in the context of multiple-item measures in which the question may arise as to whether the constituent indicators cohere to form a single dimension. One method of establishing reliability in this sense is through *split-half* methods. If we wanted to establish the internal reliability of an eighteen-indicator index using this method, the index would be administered to a group and then the eighteen items would be divided into two groups of nine (on a random or odd/even basis), and the level of correlation between the two groups of items would be computed. Alternatively, the *average inter-item correlation* between all eighteen items might be established by computing all of the possible correlation coefficients between all eighteen indicators and then computing the mean coefficient. In more recent years, researchers tend to use *Cronbach's alpha* as a measure of internal consistency. In essence this method computes the average of all possible split-half correlation coefficients. It is widely employed because it uses a great deal of information about the items in question and their correlations. Most researchers accept .80 as the minimum acceptable level of internal reliability for a multiple-indicator scale. The OCQ achieved high levels of coefficient alpha, ranging from .82 to .93 across the studies reported by Mowday, Steers and Porter, with a median of .90.

It is interesting to note that external and internal validity may not be consistent. Whereas Fiedler's LPC scale can be interpreted as having questionable test/retest reliability, its internal consistency as measured by Cronbach's alpha tends to be high (Rice, 1979). For example, a study of construction project managers in the UK used the LPC scale and found an alpha coefficient of .89 (Bryman *et al.*, 1987a). Similarly, the OCQ achieves higher levels of internal than external reliability. The tendency of multiple-indicator measures to exhibit greater internal than external reliability is probably a common one, at least in part reflecting a tendency for coherence to be a more exacting requirement than stability over time. However, the practical problems in inferring stability from studies which administer questionnaires to samples at two different times should not be underestimated.

Validity
The question of the *validity* of a measure raises the issue of whether it really relates to the concept that it is claimed to measure. If we devise a new index of job satisfaction, how can we be sure that it is really to do with job satisfaction and not some other entity? When people doubt that IQ tests really measure differences in and levels of intelligence, they are raising the question of the validity of the IQ test as a measure or operational definition of intelligence. But how can we know that a measure really does relate to the concept for which it is supposed to be standing?

The most basic way of establishing validity is to gauge whether a measure has *face validity*. Quite simply, this means that it is necessary to examine whether there appears to be a correspondence between the measure, be it a single indicator or a multiple-indicator index, and the concept in question. Clearly, this approach to establishing validity is highly judgemental and easily prone to error. The problems associated with this rudimentary way of examining validity will be even greater when the meaning of the concept itself is controversial and complex (as in the case of organizational effectiveness, about which more will be said in Chapter 9). Kidder and Judd (1986) suggest that panels of judges can be used to check that the content of measures appears to match the concept. However, the suggestion that questions of validity may be decided on the basis of a show of hands is not very sensible, since minority views may be indicative of real problems with the measure and may even point to the possibility of collective error on the part of judges. None the less, the use of judges is clearly superior to individual decisions.

A more stringent test is examining *criterion validity*. Here the researcher aims to connect the measure with a relevant criterion. Criterion validity can take either of two forms: *concurrent validity* or *predictive validity*. In the case of the former, the measure is correlated with a coterminous criterion measure. If a new scale of job satisfaction is devised, to test for its validity a criterion of interest might be absenteeism. Data on absenteeism may be taken either from a question to respondents or from company records relating to the recent past. It seems reasonable to assume that more satisfied employees will be less likely to be frequently absent than those who are dissatisfied. If this were not the case, one might be tempted to doubt that the scale is really tapping job satisfaction. Mowday, Steers and Porter submitted the OCQ to a number of tests. They examined the correspondence between individuals' OCQ scores with their reported intention to leave the organization in four studies. The reporting of intention to leave derived from a question which respondents were asked in addition to the OCQ and other questions. Fairly high negative correlations were achieved, indicating that people who are committed to their organizations are less likely to intend to leave than those who are uncommitted. However, if there is a lack of correspondence between a measure and the criterion used to test its validity, the interpretation of the finding is not without difficulties. In the case of the job satisfaction measure, it might reasonably be objected that it is the criterion that is faulty and not the measure of job satisfaction. This kind of dispute cannot readily be resolved, but the use of multiple criteria may heighten one's confidence in (or mistrust of) a measure.

Predictive validity entails a future criterion measure. We may use subsequent levels of absenteeism from the firm as the criterion against which the job satisfaction measure can be tested. The predictive validity of the OCQ was examined by Mowday, Steers and Porter for five samples by relating respondents' scores to subsequent voluntary turnover. One would anticipate that those who expressed high levels of organizational commitment through the OCQ would be less likely to have left their organizations by a later date. Although the relationship between OCQ and turnover was negative, as anticipated, the magnitude of the correlations was not large, with a median of −.41. The chief problem with testing for predictive validity is that the strength of the relationship between the measure and the criterion is likely to be affected by the amount of time that is allowed to elapse before the analysis is undertaken. On the other hand, its main advantage over concurrent validity is that the ability to predict a future state of affairs may be much more convincing and perceived to have greater practical benefit.

An even more exacting test of validity is assessing the *construct validity* of a measure (Cronbach and Meehl, 1955). Construct validation entails drawing hypotheses about the likely connection between the concept of interest and another concept. This procedure links validation with a theoretical arena, since hypotheses will be established on the basis of theoretical deductions about the likely ramifications of the concept in question. For example, from the meaning of the concept of job satisfaction it might be deduced that individuals who are satisfied with their jobs will exhibit lower levels of stress than their less satisfied counterparts. Such a view may derive from views about the importance of the job for individuals' well-being. Consequently, a sizeable negative correlation between people's scores on a scale measuring job satisfaction and a scale measuring stress would be anticipated. However, the problem with seeking to establish construct validity is that the results deriving from the exercise are capable of a number of interpretations. If it is found that there is a low correlation between the two measures, does this necessarily mean that the job satisfaction measure is faulty? At least two alternative arguments can be proffered. First, the theoretical deduction that prompted the suggestion that the two variables should be connected may be incorrect, either because the theory is poor or because the specific deduction was inappropriate. Second, the measure of stress may be invalid in relation to its underlying concept, so that what has been established is the absence of a connection between job satisfaction and the measure of stress, rather than stress *per se*. None the less, Mowday, Steers and Porter addressed the construct validity of the OCQ as follows:

> according to theory, commitment should be related to motivational force to perform and intrinsic motivation. That is, highly committed employees are thought to be motivated to exert high levels of energy on behalf of the organization.
> (Mowday, Steers and Porter, 1979, p. 236)

Moderately high (.35 to .45) correlations were achieved in the four studies in which questions were asked of respondents in respect of these two aspects of motivation, thereby providing acceptable construct validity for the OCQ.

All of the methods of establishing validity encountered thus far are means of demonstrating what Campbell and Fiske (1959) refer to as *convergent validity*; that is, they seek to demonstrate that a particular way of measuring a concept converges with other measures. Campbell and Fiske propose that convergent validation should really involve the employment of more than one method of data collection in seeking to validate a measure. Thus, in order to validate a measure of job characteristics through a self-administered questionnaire like the JDS, an observation schedule might be compiled to check on characteristics of jobs and to see how far the two methods correspond (see Chapter 8 for a discussion of structured observation). It is extremely rare to find this approach to validation in organizational research. An approach to multiple-method convergent validation that is encountered is the simultaneous use of different self-administered questionnaire measures that are deemed to tap the same underlying concept. Gillet and Schwab (1975) administered two different measures of job satisfaction – the Job Description Index and the Minnesota Satisfaction Questionnaire – to production employees and were able to establish that the two measures exhibited a high degree of convergent validity for the four aspects of job satisfaction that were covered by both questionnaires (satisfaction with pay, promotion, supervision and co-workers). Similar exercises in respect of other concepts can be found in Yunker and Hunt (1975) in the context of measures of leader behaviour and in Withey, Daft and Cooper (1983) with regard to measures of technology.

Likewise, Mowday, Steers and Porter tested the convergent validity of the OCQ by relating individuals' scores to another questionnaire measure of organizational commitment – the Sources of Organizational Attachment Questionnaire. Tests of convergent validity were conducted for six sets of data and were found to exhibit high levels of correlation, varying between .63 and .74. However, two problems with procedures such as those used by Gillet and Schwab and Mowday, Steers and Porter may be mentioned. If there had been an absence of a correspondence between the two measures of job satisfaction a similar difficulty to that alluded to in the discussion of construct validity would have presented itself; which of the two measures would be the valid one? Second, in using different measures which are not the product of different methods of data collection (that is, contrary to Campbell and Fiske's recommendation), the problem of 'common method variance' is likely to be present. This means that evidence of convergent validity may at least in part be attributable to the fact that common methods of data collection – the self-administered questionnaire in the research by Gillet and Schwab and Mowday, Steers and Porter – were employed. The use of common methods may induce a degree of consistency, and therefore provides a much less stringent test than is required by Campbell and Fiske's recommendation.

Campbell and Fiske went further in recommending that a measure should exhibit not only exhibit convergent validity with other methods but also *discriminant validity*. The idea of discriminant validity means that a measure should reveal *low* levels of correlation with measures of different concepts; if there is a close correspondence between the measures of two different concepts, it is not possible to distinguish them. Ideally, once again, the contrasting measures should derive from different methods of data collection but this is very rarely found. In the Gillet and Schwab study, a stringent test for discriminant validity was taken to entail low levels of correlation (or at least levels lower than the correlations denoting the convergent validity of the four aspects of job satisfaction noted above) between the various dimensions of job satisfaction when measured by either of the two questionnaires. This means that, for example, the different aspects of job satisfaction when measured by the Job Description Index should be weakly intercorrelated and should not exceed the convergent validity correlations; similarly, the measures of the twenty facets of job satisfaction denoted by the Minnesota questionnaire should achieve weaker intercorrelations than the convergent validity correlations. It is necessary to note that this procedure is only an approximation to the approach recommended by Campbell and Fiske since it examines not the discriminant validity of measures of different concepts but only that of divergent measures of different facets or dimensions of the same concept (that is job satisfaction). Mowday, Steers and Porter sought evidence of discriminant validity by comparing

OCQ scores with scores on three other work-related attitude measures: job involvement, career satisfaction and facets of job satisfaction. The authors found that discriminant validity was weakest when organizational commitment was correlated with satisfaction with work (that is, high correlations), but concluded that overall the correlations 'are sufficiently low as to provide some indication of an acceptable level of discriminant validity' while simultaneously recognizing that they were 'higher than might be desired to demonstrate conclusively discriminant validity' (Mowday, Steers and Porter, 1979, p. 237). This procedure is again only an approximation to Campbell and Fiske's recommendation, since it relies on the same method – the self-administered questionnaire – for all of the measures. Since this implies the possibility of common method variance, the discriminant validity estimates may be inflated as a result. Consequently, the discriminant validity of the OCQ may be better than that implied by the results provided by Mowday, Steers and Porter.

In the end, the OCQ can be regarded as a reliable research instrument with an acceptable level of validity. Indeed, its demonstrated validity is probably greater than that of comparable measures in the field of organizational research. Like many similar measures it exhibits strong internal reliability, reasonable test/retest reliability and acceptable levels of validity. As regards the latter, the evidence for predictive and discriminant validity is the least convincing.

Problems in establishing reliability and validity
A number of difficulties associated with testing reliability and validity have already been mentioned. These difficulties appear to point to a common theme, namely, the presence of alternative ways of interpreting some of the ensuing findings. The fruits of examining test/retest reliability, construct validity and criterion validity in particular are often not definitive because they are capable of more than one interpretation.

In addition, there can be conceptual difficulties in the procedures that have been elucidated. For example, it is often not easy to distinguish between the aims of convergent and discriminant validity. Mowday, Steers and Porter (1979) employ job satisfaction as a concept whose measures ought to exhibit discriminant validity in relation to the OCQ. One might reasonably ask what the ensuing correlations between the measures of facets of job satisfaction and the OCQ mean. A number of writers (such as Bateman and Strasser, 1984) see organizational commitment and job satisfaction as correlates.

Here, then, is a paradox; when the two concepts are being investigated to discern how far they are correlated within a framework of researching substantive issues, a high correlation is anticipated; in the context of discriminant validity, a low correlation is anticipated. Indeed, many of the correlations relating to discriminant validity in Mowday, Steers and Porter (1979) are quite high (especially between commitment and satisfaction with work) and within another context could be taken as indicative of 'findings' which demonstrate that one variable influences the other. As such, if a theory were proposed which postulated a link between organizational commitment and job satisfaction, the findings of Mowday, Steers and Porter could be taken to point to a reasonable level of construct (and hence convergent) validity.

In part, such a confusion derives from the absence of clear criteria allowing the researcher to choose measures of concepts which provide strong tests of discriminant validity. Tests of convergent validity are probably easier to envisage. However, a further confusion relates to knowing when a test for construct validity is being carried out. Much research entails seeking to draw hypotheses from a pre-existing body of theory and research relating to a domain of organizational research, and then submitting the hypotheses to an empirical test. As such, a huge amount of research could be interpreted as construct validation since much the same logical procedure is exhibited. How are we to know when a piece of research is meant to be generating a set of findings or whether it is an exercise in construct validation? Indeed, does the distinction matter? To a certain extent, the decision about which is happening may be retrospective. For example, Schriesheim and Kerr (1977) reviewed research relating to Fiedler's LPC scale. Fiedler's research is predicated on the argument that leaders who have high LPC scores evince better performance from their subordinates when the situation is favourable to the leader; low-scoring leaders will extract better performance when the situation is unfavourable. Schriesheim and Kerr take the view that many of the findings associated with this framework are inconsistent and conclude that the LPC scale therefore has a low level of construct validity. However, many of the studies reviewed by these authors will have been concerned to test the wider contingency model of leadership in which the LPC scale is embedded; in other words, the research will have been concerned with substantive issues. None the less, the question of when research is being conducted for substantive purposes (to add to a body of knowledge in a field) or as a construct validation exercise can be confusing.

The foregoing discussion of reliability and validity has followed the pattern that can be discerned in textbooks dealing with social research methods in describing the various means by which measures of concepts can be verified. It is also necessary to recognize that the validity of many measures used in organizational research is unknown, because validity testing is relatively rarely reported and presumably, therefore, rarely conducted (Bryman, 1988a; Payne, 1976). Podsakoff and Dalton's (1987) analysis of 193 organizational research articles published in 1985 found that reliability tests and factor analyses were reported in 67 per cent and 20 per cent of articles examined respectively. However, reports of reliability relied almost exclusively on Cronbach's alpha, implying that tests of internal consistency are much more likely to be provided than examinations of test/retest reliability, a finding confirmed by Mitchell (1985). This tendency has implications for validity, since an externally unreliable measure cannot be valid; if my kitchen scales provide a different indication of weight every time I weigh the same item, they cannot be giving me a valid measure of weight since it fluctuates. Particularly disconcerting is the finding that only 3 per cent of articles reported attempts to gauge convergent or discriminant validity. Assuming that the absence of any report of a validity test means that one was not carried out (a reasonable assumption since when internal consistency tests are carried out they do seem to be reported), and assuming that test/retest stability is rarely examined, Podsakoff and Dalton's (1987) findings seem to suggest that many measures developed in the field are of unknown external reliability and validity. Much of the discussion of validity and reliability presented in the previous section can be viewed as referring to procedures associated with good practice but which are rarely adhered to in reality. The good practice procedures seem most likely to manifest themselves in relation to measures that acquire a prominence in the field (such as the OCQ, the LPC scale, the JDS and so on), but many other measures that are devised do not share the apparent rigour to which these more prominent measures are subject. Further, the tendency among many researchers to tinker with prominent measures of known reliability and validity – most notably by dropping items from scales in order to reduce the number of questions being asked of respondents – may alter the properties of those scales and consequently may mean that the revised measures are no longer valid and reliable.

The reasons for the relative lack of evidence for validity and external reliability are almost certainly to do with the time and cost involved in providing the relevant tests. External reliability requires two waves of measurement, and if done properly would probably require an experimental design. Internal reliability can easily be gauged once a scale has been administered by computing Cronbach's alpha. Validity testing that goes beyond mere face validity is also likely to involve investments of time and resources which many researchers may see as diverting their attention from the essence of the research enterprise – of adding to the stock of knowledge in a substantive domain. It should not be assumed that the relative absence of reliability and validity testing is specific to organizational research in that it is common to much social research; indeed, the tendencies referred to in this and the previous paragraphs are indicative of the linkages that exist between organizational research and the social sciences generally in connection with research methodology.

The departure from good practice can occur in a number of other ways. Fiedler's LPC scale provides an example of a measure which is not the operationalization of a prior concept, in that the measure arrived first and its meaning(s) have been subsequently elucidated. The interpretation of the LPC scale provided on page 56 is one of a number that Fiedler and others have put forward. It posits a 'motivational hierarchy' in which high-scoring leaders are conceptualized as oriented primarily to people and secondarily to tasks; low scorers are concerned primarily with tasks and secondarily with people. However, in earlier writings Fiedler interpreted high scoring, as against low scoring, as indicative of: an emphasis on people rather than tasks (that is without the recognition of secondary goals that the motivational hierarchy approach entails); cognitive complexity rather than cognitive simplicity; and emotional and psychological closeness to others rather than aloofness. Rice (1978a) has proposed yet another interpretation which emphasizes attitudinal differences between high- and low-scoring leaders. In view of the variety of interpretations of the LPC scale that have been proffered, it is scarcely surprising that it has been referred to as 'a measure in search of a meaning' (Schriesheim and Kerr, 1977, p. 23). In spite of its departure from the normal practice of entailing the operationalization of a pre-existing concept, the LPC measure and the associated contingency model of leadership have been highly influential (Bryman, 1986).

The problem of reactivity
The validity of measures based on interviews and questionnaires is also jeopardized by the obtrusiveness of the methods from which they are derived. People are conscious of the fact that they are being studied; they may have limited recall, they may

perceive certain issues incorrectly, and so on. These issues are often referred to collectively as the problem of 'reactivity' (Webb *et al.*, 1966). For example, the intrusion of 'response sets' in questionnaire and interview answers has long been recognized by social researchers. This term refers to 'the presence of several irrelevant but lawful sources of variance' (Webb *et al.*, 1966, p. 19), that is, systematic but extraneous sources of variance in people's responses to questionnaires and similar instruments. 'Acquiescence' is a problem that is often addressed in multiple-question scales. Some individuals show a tendency routinely to endorse statements (and some, though fewer, tend to respond persistently negatively). In order to weed out this contaminating effect, as noted earlier in this chapter, multiple-item indices use negative items.

Less easy to deal with is the problem of 'social desirability bias', which refers to the propensity to reply in socially desirable ways when responding to questionnaires. This tendency suggests that many people seek to present themselves in a positive light when answering questions. Crowne and Marlowe (1964) and Edwards (1961) have devised scales which facilitate the detection of respondents who are likely to exhibit such distortions in their responses. The Crowne and Marlowe scale asks people to respond to a number of statements, each of which is either socially desirable but probably untrue of most people or socially undesirable but probably true of most people. Edwards's (1961) approach entails soliciting people's estimates of the desirability of particular traits or characteristics. There is considerable evidence of the operation of social desirability bias in social research and a number of investigators have detected its operation in relation to topics associated with organization studies. Thomas and Kilmann (1975) administered three different measures of conflict-handling approaches (including that used by Lawrence and Lorsch, 1967) to graduate students along with the Crowne and Marlowe and Edwards scales. It was found that a substantial proportion of the relative propensity of the different conflict resolution modes to be endorsed could be attributed to the social desirability of their associated questionnaire items. A similar exercise was conducted by Arnold and Feldman (1981), who found that individuals who score high on the Crowne and Marlowe scale tend to over-report the importance of both having the opportunity to use special skills and abilities at work and autonomy and independence. Since self-report questionnaires are widely used to provide measures of people's perceptions of their job characteristics and of their affective responses to jobs (for example, the JDS), the potential for the intrusion of the biases deriving from social desirability effects in some areas of organizational research is considerable.

The problem with the social desirability effect, as against the acquiescence syndrome, is that it is much less easy to check in a routine fashion since it necessitates the administration of an extra scale, such as the Crowne and Marlowe scale. Not only is this likely to be viewed by many researchers as a distraction, the social desirability questions could be seen as potential contaminants of people's other responses, possibly by raising their sensitivity to such topics. Further, since it relies on asking extra questions, there is the additional worry that the social desirability scales may be subject to the same sort of error that they are designed to detect.

A further kind of response set that has attracted the attention of many investigators concerned with organizational research is the operation of lay theories of social processes which can contaminate measurement procedures. People often carry around with them their own notions of the phenomena that researchers seek to address. There is evidence that these lay theories can contaminate their responses to questionnaire items designed to address the same issues as the lay theories. The operation of 'implicit leadership theories' provides an example of this process. Bryman (1987) and Rush, Thomas and Lord (1977) have administered the LBDQ to British and US students respectively, asking them to describe the behaviour of an imaginary leader in terms of the LBDQ items, but on the basis of very little information about that person. In each case, it was found that the description provided by respondents was more or less identical to the description typically discerned when people answer the questions in relation to real leaders. These findings suggest that when describing real leaders (people's own superiors when the LBDQ is employed) people's responses may be substantially affected by their beliefs about how leaders in general behave. The idea of implicit leadership theories also has implications for the nature of the inferences that can be drawn about the relationship between leader behaviour and various correlates (see Chapter 4). However, research on lay theories has obvious relevance for considerations of validity, since the implication of these findings would be that a measure like the LBDQ may not be providing a measure of leader behaviour as such. Further, unlike the problems of acquiescence and social desirability, solutions are not very evident; it is not a case of detecting those respondents who exhibit the source of bias and eliminating them, since lay theories presumably apply to the sample as a whole. On the other hand, Gioia and Sims (1985) have presented evidence to suggest that when questionnaire measures of leader behaviour comprise statements which reflect specific behaviour patterns on the part of leaders (rather than general statements about what leaders do) the distorting effect of lay theories of leader behaviour is minimized.

These considerations imply that there is likely to be a gap between what people say they and others do and their own and others' behaviour, or between what they say they feel and how they actually feel about their work, firm, or supervisor, and so on. In this light, the fairly low correlations for predictive validity obtained by Mowday, Steers and Porter in connection with their organizational commitment scale are scarcely surprising. Equally, these considerations reinforce the desirability of gleaning measures of organizational phenomena from sources other than the ubiquitous self-report questionnaire, as advocated by Campbell and Fiske (1959). One approach to closing the gap between, for example, what people say they do and what they actually do would be to test questionnaire data against observational information. When such an exercise is carried out the results can be salutary. Jenkins *et al.* (1975) report the results associated with the development of a structured observation scale to measure the nature of jobs. Observers were trained to examine job characteristics according to a pre-formulated schedule. Each person whose job was observed was also interviewed by a structured interview schedule about the nature of their job. Respondents were drawn from three organizations and worked in a variety of manual and non-manual jobs. The data collection strategy permitted a comparison of the interview and observational data relating to a number of job characteristics (not all characteristics were amenable to such comparison). Data relating to six job characteristics were collected by both interview and observation: variety, skills, certainty, autonomy, worker pace control and co-operation. The correlations between the two data collection methods were not high, varying between .14 (certainty) and .48 (skills). These results are not particularly encouraging in that one might have hoped for somewhat higher levels of concordance between the two methods. However, it is not possible to be certain which of the two methods of data collection is responsible for the disappointing levels of correlation (or whether both are). Further, structured observation schedules share with interview and self-administered questionnaires the characteristic of obtrusiveness, which possibly adversely affects the utility of exercises such as that undertaken by Jenkins *et al.*, though it is almost certainly superior to a slavish reliance on one method.

Research by O'Reilly, Partlette and Bloom (1980) suggests that questionnaire approaches to the measurement of job characteristics may be flawed. They conducted research on seventy-six public health nurses who were all performing the same task. That these nurses were doing the same work was verified by interviews with senior management and by a job analysis conducted by 'expert judges'. Thus there was no prima-facie reason to suggest that these respondents would exhibit variety in their descriptions of their work. Task characteristics were measured by the JDS. O'Reilly, Partlette and Bloom found that there *was* variety in nurses' descriptions of their jobs, and that these variations were systematically associated with their general frames of reference and job attitudes. Age, tenure in their public health unit, total income and higher education were found to be associated with a number of dimensions of job characteristics, as was the degree to which respondents conceived of nursing as a profession. Particularly strong correlations were found between the job characteristics and nurses' orientation to their job, as indicated by overall job satisfaction and temporal commitment to the job. For example, nurses who were satisfied with their job were more likely than those who were less satisfied to perceive greater variety, task identity, autonomy, feedback and task significance in exactly the same work. These findings imply that as a description of 'objective' job characteristics, a widely used self-administered set of questions such as that used in the JDS may be flawed, since respondents' answers are likely to be affected by their frames of reference. It is conceivable that similar flaws arise in relation to other measurement devices based on questionnaires.

Overview

This chapter has focused upon the approach to measurement associated with questionnaires and structured interviews. It will become apparent from later chapters that these two data collection methods are by no means the only sources of measurement in organizational research. However, they are widely used in survey and experimental research, albeit in greater degree in the former. The self-administered questionnaire is particularly intensively used and typically comprises a very large number of rating scales. One of the chief foci of this chapter has been the validity and reliability of measurement in the field. While there are clear guidelines about the proper procedures to be employed in this context, they are widely disregarded or adopted in a piecemeal fashion, though there are exceptions. Indeed, much quantitative research derives from investigations in which measures of largely unknown reliability and validity were employed. In addition, a number of measurement problems – such as social desirability bias and lay theories – have been addressed as potential assaults on validity in particular. The recognition in this chapter of the relative paucity of measures which have been thoroughly validated and tested for reliability should not be taken to imply that 'anything goes' in organizational research and that readers may simply follow the lead of others and attach little significance to, or invest little effort in, the area of concept operationalization. This book aims to provide an account of organizational research which both pinpoints areas of good practice and also shows how the reality of research often entails departures from textbook procedures. Nor should this recognition be taken to mean that many organizational researchers are dilatory and unconcerned about the value of their investigations. The point has been made a number of times in this chapter that exercises in validity and reliability testing can be time-consuming and costly, and beyond the reach of many researchers seeking simply to carry out an investigation. The increasing use of measures with relatively well-known validity and reliability is a step in the right direction, though as the field spreads into new areas the utility of such measures is bound to decline, thereby engendering the need for new ones. Equally, it has been recognized in this chapter that some measurement problems are highly intractable and may limit the utility of even the better-researched measures. Many of these issues will rear their heads once again in later chapters concerned with other measurement devices.

3

Experimental research

Experimental designs are of considerable importance in organizational research on at least two counts. First, their particular strength as a research strategy is that they allow the investigator to make strong claims about causality – that one thing has an effect on something else. Within a field that has a strong orientation to a natural science approach to the study of social phenomena (and which perceives the detection of cause-and-effect relationships to be an important ingredient of that approach), the ability to make robust claims about causality cannot be understated. Indeed, the predilection for the scientific approach is underlined by the increasing use of terms like 'organizational science' or 'sciences' to describe the field (for example, Cummings and Frost, 1985).

However, the ability to establish causality is important to many organizational researchers, not simply by virtue of its association with a scientific approach, but because it is perceived as leading to practical, relevant knowledge. Thus, if it is possible to demonstrate that a participative approach to organizing work engenders greater job satisfaction and individual performance than non-participative approaches, the resulting evidence may be deemed to have considerable practical importance, since the evidence contains an implicit prescription about the appropriate distribution of influence within work organizations. Similarly, the investigations reported in Chapter 1 by Ganster (1980) and Orpen (1979) allow claims about the effectiveness of job enrichment to be directly evaluated; does enriched work cause greater job satisfaction and individual performance than non-enriched work? The experimental design that was employed by each of these researchers allows the causal hypothesis that underpins this question to be examined. In this chapter, the factors that facilitate the detection of causality from experimental designs will be elucidated.

Second, because of the facility with which researchers employing experimental designs are able to establish cause and effect, the experiment is frequently perceived as a model research design. This point will be especially apparent when survey research, from which causal findings are less easy to establish, is examined.

In everyday speech, we frequently employ the term 'experiment' very loosely to denote trying something out and observing the consequences of our action. Social scientists and others who write about experiments see them as involving something more than merely trying something out; in particular, the idea of 'control' is essential. The idea of control implies the elimination of alternative explanations of the apparent connection between a putative cause and a particular effect. We may say that we are going to 'experiment' with a different route when we drive to work one day; if we find that the time taken is a few minutes more, we should be very careful about saying that the alternative route was the cause of the greater time taken; the volume of traffic may not have been typical, and we may have driven more tentatively because of our unfamiliarity with the route. In other words, we have not controlled, and hence eliminated, these alternative possibilities. This notion is akin to the need to control the potentially contaminating effects of heat, light and humidity in the natural scientist's laboratory. What we want to be able to demonstrate is that our supposed independent variable, and that variable alone, is the cause of variation in the dependent variable.

On the other hand, to anticipate slightly some of the issues that will be examined below, conducting research on themes deriving from organization studies runs into some specific problems when the natural scientist's laboratory is used as a yardstick. Most obviously, experimental organizational research is conducted on people rather than on relatively inert matter. The very fact that people will know that they are objects of study may have an impact on their behaviour. Natural scientists acknowledge that experimentation can have an independent impact on the matter that they study (for example, the Heisenberg principle), but this matter is not capable of the self-knowledge and awareness to which human beings are susceptible. Of course, this problem is not specific to organizational research, but pervades all experimental research in the social sciences. What is particularly conspicuous in organizational research is the special cluster of problems that doing research in organizations as such entails. Much organizational research based on experiments can be construed as either laboratory or field experimentation. The research studies by Ganster (1980) and Orpen (1979) respectively are examples of each of these two types of study. When research is conducted in real organizations – field experiments – special difficulties may be anticipated. Researchers are unlikely to have the relatively free hand in setting up experimental arrangements that they can confer upon themselves in the laboratory; those on whom the research is conducted may be suspicious of the true aims of the study (for example, perceiving it to be an instrument of senior management); subjects may have a vested interest in certain outcomes; and so on. The first of these three difficulties – field experimentation rarely permitting a *carte blanche* to the researcher – means that many field experiments are not 'true' experiments in terms of the principles that will be stipulated in the next section. In recognition of this fact, a distinction is often drawn between experiments and 'quasi-experiments', the latter term referring to experiments in which the researcher is unable to fulfil all of the requirements of a genuine experimental study. The researcher's control over the allocation of subjects to different groups within the experimental design is the key to the distinction, as the discussion later in the chapter will reveal.

The next section deals with the nature of experimental designs, emphasizing in particular what it is about true experiments that allows the researcher to make definitive statements about cause and effect. These principles are independent of the specific focus with which this book is concerned, that is, they have been developed in the context of a consideration of experimental research in general. The specific problems of conducting experimental research in organizations to which the previous paragraph has alluded will be dealt with in later sections.

Internal validity

In saying that we are concerned with being able to generate definitive findings in which competing explanations of an apparent causal connection are eliminated, we are saying that a piece of research must be designed so as to have 'internal validity', a term which denotes being able to conclude that the independent variable really does affect the dependent variable (Campbell, 1957). In the following exposition of the nature of internal validity, an imaginary example will run through the various designs – experimental and non-experimental – that will be examined. The example is concerned with the question of whether greater participation in decision-making at work causes the productivity of those involved in such schemes to improve. Thus participation can be visualized as an independent variable which is deemed to have an impact on people's productivity at work. It is proposed to examine this contention in a firm which has a work group in which people carry out visual quality checks on chocolate biscuits. The group members are allowed greater opportunity to decide how to do their work. By following this example through from non-experimental to the various types of experimental design, the problems of inferring causality from the former can be discerned, while the facility with which internal validity can be established in experimental designs can also be discerned. The study of participation at work has been the focus of numerous experimental studies (Bryman, 1986), so that while the example is imaginary, the specific focus is not. In addition, examples of studies of job enrichment will be employed at a number of points in order further to illustrate the nature of true experiments.

A non-experimental design, which will be referred to as the 'one-group non-experimental design with pre- and post-testing' (Design 1), provides a useful starting-point in allowing the problems of inferring internal validity from a non-experimental study to be demonstrated. In the presentation of this design, a notation will be employed that will be followed through in the remainder of this chapter: Exp denotes an experimental treatment (that is, the independent variable: participation); Obs refers to an observation made in relation to the dependent variable (that is, productivity); and T refers to the timing of the observations that are made in relation to the dependent variable. Subscripts are employed to refer to different instances of the these three items of notation; thus, if subjects are measured in terms of their levels of productivity on two occasions, Obs_1 and Obs_2 would refer to the two measures and T_1 and T_2 would refer to the timing of the two measures.

In order to investigate the effects of participation on productivity with Design 1, a measure of the group's productivity (the pre-test) is taken at the outset. Thus, productivity is gauged (Obs_1) at T_1 before participation is introduced. The experimental treatment (Exp) is introduced. Then, after about three months (at T_2) group productivity is measured again (Obs_2, the post-test). Thus, measures of group productivity (Obs_1 and Obs_2) are taken at two junctures (T_1 and T_2), that is, before and after the period of enhanced participation (Exp). The structure of this design is provided in Figure 3.1.

Let us imagine that group productivity has increased by some 20 per cent over the period in question; an encouraging finding, but can we be certain that it can be attributed to participation alone? The problem is that there are a number of competing explanations for the suggestion that greater participation 'caused' the surge in productivity:

(1) Over the three month period, other things may have been

Time ────────────────▶

T_1 T_2

Obs$_1$ Exp Obs$_2$

Figure 3.1 Design 1. One group non-experimental design with pre- and post-testing

happening in the firm or to do with their jobs. These further changes could have had an impact on the difference between Obs$_1$ and Obs$_2$.

(2) It is possible that changes occurred to the subjects and which may account at least in part for the increase in productivity. It is also conceivable that their productivity would have been enhanced anyway without the introduction of greater participation.

(3) The fact of having their productivity measured at T_1 (that is, Obs$_1$) may have sensitized the group members to their productivity so that they became more aware of the speed of their work and hence started to work faster.

(4) It may be that the procedures for estimating Obs$_2$ were different from those for Obs$_1$, because a different system was used or a different person conducted the calculations.

It is important to realize that none of these rival explanations of the Obs$_2$ – Obs$_1$ difference may be true. It is quite possible that enhanced participation really did account for the productivity increase. The problem is that we do not (and indeed cannot) know whether any of the rival explanations are true. The issue of internal validity relates to the availability of competing explanations which thereby render the posited causal connection questionable. It is the fact that the competing explanations cannot be discounted that is the source of the problem.

One solution to the problem of rival explanations would be to include a second group. This second group is usually known as the 'control group'. We can envisage a second group doing exactly the same work as the group that receives the experimental treatment (Exp), but which does not actually experience greater participation (that is, No Exp). The term 'control group' derives from a natural science context and does not travel particularly well when applied to the study of people. The control group in this study is not devoid of any experimental stimulus; the biscuit workers are still working, so that in a sense the control group is a second experimental group which acts as a point of comparison. None the less, the convention of referring to the

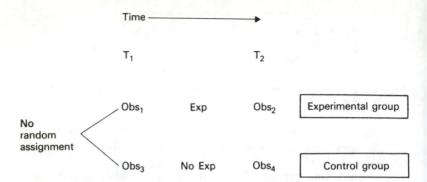

Figure 3.2   Design 2. Non-equivalent control group design with pre- and post-testing

comparison group as a control group will be followed. We now have two groups: an experimental group that enjoys greater participation, and a control group without participation (see Design 2 in Figure 3.2). We might suggest that if any of the rival explanations have any veracity they will become evident when we compare the results of the two groups. Remember that the experimental group's productivity (that is, $Obs_2 - Obs_1$) has increased by 20 per cent. Thus, if we find that Obs_4 is 18 per cent greater than Obs_3, we might well be tempted to conclude that the experimental group's increase in productivity cannot be attributed to the experience of participation. The increase in productivity would be marginally greater in the experimental group than in the control group but is not of a sufficient magnitude to lead one to believe that participation at work induces greater productivity. On the other hand, if the difference between Obs_4 and Obs_3 had been considerably smaller, such as an increase of 3 per cent, we would have been much more tempted to view participation as an important source of the increase in productivity.

We would be jumping to an unjustifiable conclusion if we drew this latter inference, however. The design in Figure 3.2 jeopardizes internal validity by permitting an alternative explanation of the apparent causal link between participation and productivity:

(5) The subjects in the two groups may differ from each other in a number of ways, so that any differences between the results deriving from the experimental and control groups cannot be attributed to the experimental treatment (Exp). It may be

that the members of one group have more work experience than those of the other group, or there may be differences in personal characteristics (such as gender).

The subjects in the two groups need to be *randomly assigned* so that they are 'equivalent'. If there is no random assignment, the possibility exists that any observed differences between the experimental and control groups can be attributed to the divergent characteristics of the two groups. If they are randomly assigned there should be no prima-facie reasons for believing that there is a lack of equivalence, so that any observed differences between the two groups can be regarded as reflecting real differences in experiences. However, it sometimes occurs that random assignment is either not feasible or even undesirable. This may occur when the experiment takes place in a field setting rather than in the laboratory. The reasons for, and implications of, this problem will be addressed below. As a substitute for random assignment researchers often seek to 'match' subjects in terms of known characteristics. Thus, subjects may be matched in terms of work experience, gender, type of work undertaken and so on. Matching is undoubtedly an inferior method of establishing equivalence, since you can only match in terms of factors that occur to you or which are evident. Other factors on which the two groups differ may contaminate the results of the experiment and so render the conclusions invalid. Indeed, some writers on experimental design seem to be unprepared to treat a study as an experiment if matching rather than random assignment has taken place (for example, Kidder and Judd, 1986). However, matching is often used in field experiments in organizational research, so it is proposed to suspend some of these reservations and treat it as a surrogate for random assignment.

These reflections on the selection of subjects lead to the first true experiment that has been encountered so far: the 'equivalent control group experiment with pre- and post-testing', which is often referred to as the 'classical experimental design' (see Design 3 in Figure 3.3). This design is exactly the same as Design 2, except that there is random assignment to the experimental and control groups. The presence of a control group allows the researcher to eliminate the first four assaults on internal validity previously encountered, since any of these effects would be present in both groups, while the establishment of equivalence through random assignment (or possibly matching) ensures that observed differences between the two groups cannot be attributed to differences in the subjects. Data from Orpen's (1979) research on the effects of job enrichment, which was described in

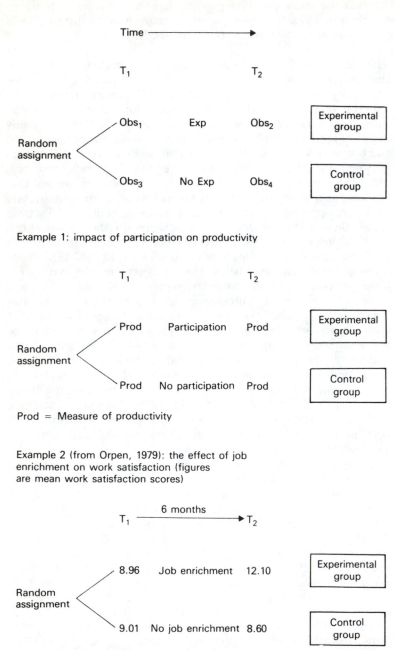

Time ─────────►

T₁   T₂

Obs₁   Exp   Obs₂   Experimental group

Random assignment

Obs₃   No Exp   Obs₄   Control group

Example 1: impact of participation on productivity

T₁   T₂

Prod   Participation   Prod   Experimental group

Random assignment

Prod   No participation   Prod   Control group

Prod = Measure of productivity

Example 2 (from Orpen, 1979): the effect of job enrichment on work satisfaction (figures are mean work satisfaction scores)

T₁ ──── 6 months ────► T₂

8.96   Job enrichment   12.10   Experimental group

Random assignment

9.01   No job enrichment   8.60   Control group

Figure 3.3 Design 3. Equivalent control group experiment with pre- and post-testing

Chapter 1, are also presented in Figure 3.3. The data in Figure 3.3 relate to Orpen's findings in connection with the impact of job enrichment on job satisfaction, the latter being one of the dependent variables he investigated. The measure of job satisfaction was a multiple-indicator rating scale in which the respondent indicated his or her agreement with each of eighteen adjectives which could be taken to describe the job (such as 'fascinating', 'routine' and 'challenging'). The figures are mean pre- and post-test work satisfaction scores for each of the groups. The following procedure was employed in assigning subjects to the unenriched and enriched conditions respectively: 'each subject was randomly assigned to one of the two conditions, with their jobs either remaining unaltered or being substantially enriched' (Orpen, 1979, p. 194). Work satisfaction in the experimental (that is, enriched) group increased by 3.14, whereas in the control group it declined. By controlling for the various rival explanations of the finding that job enrichment causes job satisfaction, including the possibility that the two groups were not equivalent, the robustness of Orpen's results are greater. It should be noted that there are other potential sources of internal invalidity. For example, if members of the two groups declined to participate in the experiment any further, the experiment could be jeopardized if the loss of subjects was differential between the groups. The groups would no longer be equivalent if this were to occur. However, the chief and most basic sources of internal invalidity are those five mentioned above.

Of course, following the discussion in Chapter 2, the examination of internal validity presupposes that the concepts with which the researcher is concerned have been operationalized so that they provide valid measures. If the operational definitions are inadequate, the meaning of the ensuing internally valid findings will be unclear and misleading. Many experimental researchers carry out 'manipulation checks' to verify that their manipulation of the independent variable is consistent with what they believe it to be reflecting. In Orpen's (1979) research, subjects were assigned to either enriched or unenriched conditions. This manipulation was checked by recording subjects' answers to JDS questions on job characteristics. Subjects in the enriched condition were found to exhibit higher levels on each of the five dimensions measured by the JDS than those doing unenriched jobs, though in the case of two dimensions (task significance and feedback) the differences were not pronounced. The author concluded that the manipulation was fairly successful, since those subjects whose jobs had been enriched 'perceived their jobs as higher in most of the characteristics associated with enrichment, whereas those whose job content was unaltered did not' (Orpen, 1979, p. 203).

Variations of the 'equivalent control group experiment with pre- and post-testing' are frequently encountered. First, there is the 'multiple equivalent groups experiment with pre- and post-testing' (see Design 4 in Figure 3.4). In this design, the independent variable is viewed as assuming either a number of different forms or a number of different degrees. Thus, a study of the effects of participation on productivity may take the view that participation is not something that is either present or absent, but an entity which is a matter of degree. Therefore, the four different treatments might reflect different amounts of participation. This design can readily be changed in order to incorporate more or fewer than four levels (or types) of the independent variable. In this context, the 'no participation' condition is best thought of as providing an experimental group, since it is one among four levels of the experimental variable.

Another frequently used design is the 'factorial experiment with pre- and post-testing'. It is often the case that we are interested in not just one experimental variable but two. This can occur for a number of reasons, one of which may be a conviction that an additional variable is capable of moderating the relationship between the independent variable and the dependent variable. For example, we may take the view that the benefits of participation at work are more likely to manifest themselves when the work in which people are engaged is non-routine. When the work is routine, the opportunity for participation to have an effect on productivity is minimal, since the work has to be carried out in a particular way. In order to investigate the veracity of this contention a factorial design (see Design 5, Figure 3.5) can be envisaged. If we take Exp_1 and Exp_2 to denote the presence and absence of participation respectively, and Exp_A and Exp_B the presence and absence of routine work, the possible combinations yield four groups. For example, the first group receives the combination $Exp_1 + Exp_A$ denoting participation in relation to routine work. If the view that routine work moderates the participation–productivity relationship is true, we would anticipate experimental group$_2$ to exhibit a much larger increase in productivity than the other groups including Group$_1$. The factorial experiment is often used in organizational research because of the widespread interest in relationships that are moderated by other variables. This interest has been engendered by an awareness that, if causal relationships are moderated, it can be very misleading if the sources of moderation are not specified. The study by Day and Hamblin (1964) which is discussed later in

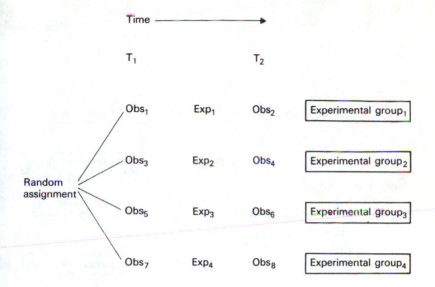

Example: impact of participation on productivity

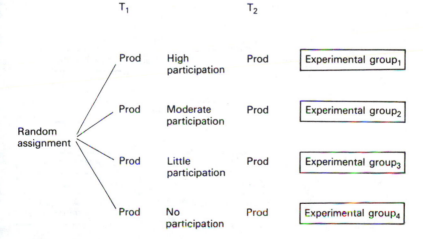

Prod = measure of productivity

Figure 3.4 Design 4. Multiple equivalent groups experiment with pre-
and post-testing

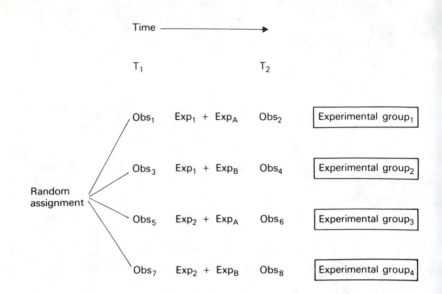

Example: impact of participation and work routineness
on productivity

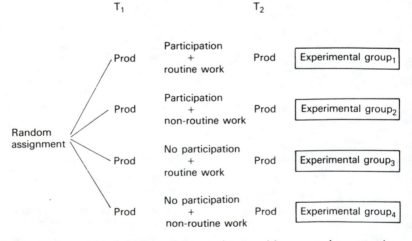

Figure 3.5 Design 5. Factorial experiment with pre- and post-testing

this chapter is a good example of a factorial experiment.

Finally, there is the 'post-test-only equivalent control group experiment', Design 6 (see Figure 3.6). This design is exactly the same as the 'equivalent control group experiment with pre- and post-testing', except that there is no pre-testing of either of the groups. It is widely used in field experiments in organizational research, because it is often not feasible to conduct pre-tests. The 'post-test-only equivalent control group experiment' allows the researcher to discern whether there are differences between the two groups in terms of the dependent variable. Thus, it is possible to envisage a comparison between two randomly

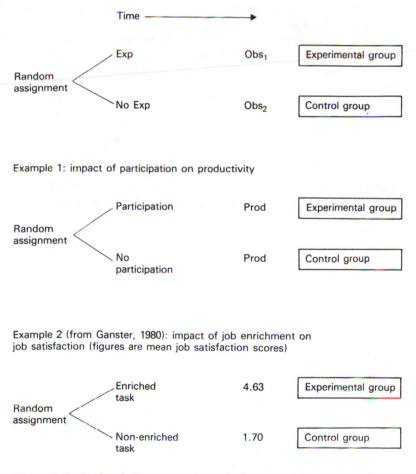

Example 1: impact of participation on productivity

Example 2 (from Ganster, 1980): impact of job enrichment on job satisfaction (figures are mean job satisfaction scores)

Figure 3.6 Design 6. Post-test-only equivalent control group experiment

assigned groups, one of which receives a participation treatment, while the other does not. The two groups are compared at a later date in terms of the dependent variable, productivity. The presence of both a control group and random assignment allows the researcher to control for the chief sources of internal invalidity. However, the design can only allow the researcher to establish whether participation makes a difference to productivity; it cannot establish how far productivity increases as a consequence of participation. When the latter kind of question is likely to be important, the 'post-test-only equivalent control group experiment' will not suffice. None the less, this experimental design has much to recommend it by virtue of its simplicity and adaptability to a variety of circumstances. Designs 4 and 5 are also frequently employed without pre-testing, so that the 'post-test only' design can be found in several guises.

Experimental designs are frequently extolled in the field of organizational research because of the widespread concern to establish findings which provide clear-cut demonstrations of causality. However, experimental designs tend to be regarded as less helpful in regard to establishing the generalizability of findings. This is the focus of the next section.

External validity

External validity is concerned with the extent to which the fruits of a piece of research can be generalized beyond the specific confines of the setting in which the study was undertaken. Thus, if it is found, following a study utilizing one of the experimental designs cited above, that there is a causal connection between participation and productivity we are left with the question of whether we can generalize this finding to other settings. Could it be that the finding is specific to the particular firm in which the study took place? This possibility implies that a rigorously conducted experiment which exhibits a high level of internal validity could be of limited use and interest by virtue of the results being idiosyncratic.

There are several potential sources of external invalidity:

(1) When an experiment involves pre-testing subjects – as in all of the experimental designs which entail pre-testing subjects – it is possible that the pre-test may sensitize subjects and make them more receptive to the experimental treatment than they would otherwise be. The mere fact of having their productivity measured at the outset of the experiment may make subjects in the imaginary participation experiment more

sensitive to participation than they would have been if they had not been pre-tested. This would limit the generalizability of the findings, since we could not say with any certainty that they could apply to populations that had not been pre-tested.

A control group cannot control for this problem because it too is pre-tested. In order to deal with the problem of the effects of pre-testing the 'Solomon four-group experiment' is frequently suggested. This design (see Figure 3.7) comprises two experimental and two control groups. The first two groups are as in Design 3. The third group is not pre-tested, receives the experimental treatment and is post-tested. The fourth group is only post-tested at T_2. The idea is that, assuming random assignment, notional pre-test scores can be computed for the third and fourth groups, by summing Obs_1 and Obs_3 and dividing by 2. This gives the average score for the two pre-tested groups, and this score can then be treated as a surrogate pre-test score for the third and fourth groups. However, these latter two groups have not in fact been pre-tested, so that we can compare their post-test scores with the two pre-tested groups to see if there is any evidence to suggest that pre-testing has sensitized subjects. In this way it is possible to discern how far an increase in productivity is due to participation and how far it is due to the effects of pre-testing.

In fact, the Solomon design is not used a great deal. The requirement of two additional groups simply in order to test for the effects of pre-testing necessitates the diversion of time and money which many investigators seem to be unprepared to countenance. Many investigators would probably prefer to use extra groups within a multiple-group or factorial design, rather than to test for a possible methodological flaw. None the less, the effects of pre-testing cannot be ignored. From an analysis of a number of studies that have specifically examined the effects of pre-testing, Willson and Putnam (1982, p. 256) concluded that 'there is a general pretest effect which cannot be safely ignored'. This effect was found to impinge on experimental and control groups in roughly equal degree. The most obvious solution to the problem is not to pre-test. Studies using Design 6 (and its various adaptations) do not pre-test either experimental or control groups and so do not suffer from the effects of pre-testing. Herein probably lies one of the reasons for the widespread use in organizational research and the social sciences generally of experiments in which subjects are only post-tested.

However, the problem of the effects of pre-testing does not

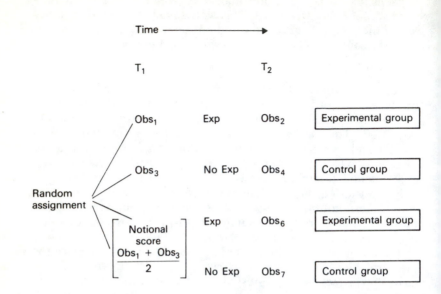

Example: impact of participation on productivity

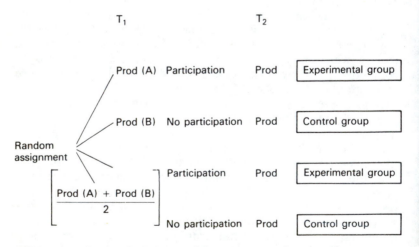

Figure 3.7 Design 7. Solomon four-group experiment

exhaust the range of factors that may adversely affect external validity:

(2) Bias in the selection of subjects may mean that subjects' responses to the experimental treatment are unrepresentative.

There are several interrelated aspects to this problem. Researchers who conduct experiments often do not employ random sampling procedures (Dipboye and Flanagan, 1979), so that the representativeness of subjects is unknown (see Chapter 4 for a discussion of random sampling). They sometimes rely on volunteers, but this is a flawed means of selecting subjects since there is evidence that people who volunteer for experiments differ from those who do not in a number of ways. Rosenthal and Rosnow (1969) have reviewed a large body of data on this topic and concluded that volunteers tend to be better educated, to have greater need for approval, to score higher on IQ tests, to be less authoritarian and to be better adjusted than non-volunteers. The reliance on volunteers can readily be seen as having an adverse effect on external validity.

An alternative non-random means by which experimental subjects are obtained is through inducements. Money and course credits (for example Ganster, 1980, offered credit) are frequently employed to acquire subjects (Dipboye and Flanagan, 1979). It is not known how far persons who are responsive to such inducements differ from others, but the possibility of such bias is disconcerting. In a large number of laboratory experiments, researchers rely on college and university students to act as subjects. Students tend to have a highly specific cluster of personal, attitudinal and socioeconomic characteristics which differ from those of the wider population. At the very least, their age range is very narrow and this alone is bound to make them different from people in general. When researchers conduct laboratory experiments in which they rely on student volunteers or use inducements such as money and course credits, they are clearly compounding the problems associated with using a group of people like students with such a limited range of characteristics. In fact, it is often not clear how student subjects were acquired. Consider the following statement regarding the selection of subjects for an experimental simulation of decision-making:

The subjects of this experiment were 120 students enrolled in an introductory course in psychology. These students were asked to participate in a role-play exercise in which decisions would be made among several alternative sources of funds. To facilitate student interest, an exercise was designed in which each subject played the role of an allocation officer in the World Bank.

(Staw and Ross, 1978, p. 50)

We do not know whether all students who were asked to participate did so, whether psychology students are representative of all students, and so on.

In the case of field experiments in firms, public sector organizations and elsewhere, there is often a reliance on volunteers, but there are also numerous instances in which subjects are selected by their superiors. Alternatively, pre-existing departments are nominated to act as experimental or control groups. An example of this procedure is the study by Morse and Reimer (1956) of clerical workers in a department of an insurance company. The department comprised four parallel divisions, two of which constituted one experimental group, the other two forming another group. The implications of subjects being directed to participate in an experiment for the external validity of findings have not been addressed a great deal in the literature.

Finally, we come to a source of external invalidity that has attracted a particularly large amount of attention over the years.

(3) The experimental setting may set in train a number of 'reactive effects' which limit the researcher's ability to generalize beyond the experimental setting, because such effects are likely to be unique to the experimental context. Reactivity is likely to occur because of subjects' awareness that they are participants in an experiment. This very awareness is likely to induce responses that are specific to the experimental milieu.

One of the best known instances of this kind of response is that known as the 'Hawthorne effect'. This term derives from the Hawthorne Studies, a series of interlinked investigations carried out at the Hawthorne works of the Western Electric Company in the USA in the late 1920s and early 1930s (Roethlisberger and Dickson, 1939). One phase of these investigations entailed a group of women carrying out manual tasks being taken away from their department and working in a separate room. The aim of the study was to discover how changes in the number and duration of rest pauses, in length of the working day, in heating and lighting and so on affected productivity. It was found that productivity increased over the duration of the study irrespective of the changes introduced. It was eventually recognized that the women were responding to the positive and special treatment that they were receiving. The researchers recognized that the women were influenced by the favourable circumstances that the experimental arrangements had introduced. While this finding did much to stimulate the idea of a 'human relations' approach to the study of work, by pointing to the potential advantages of providing people with a benign atmosphere at the workplace, it neatly demonstrates that experimental arrangements may induce an effect over and above the intentions of the investigator.

Orne (1962) has pointed to the phenomenon of the 'demand characteristics' of the experimental situation as a potential source of reactive effects. He argues that experimental subjects are not passive; they frequently try to divine the aim of an experiment and to adjust their behaviour in line with what they take (possibly erroneously) to be its goals. This effect implies that subjects frequently modify their behaviour in order to support the hypothesis around which the experiment is organized. Riecken (1962) has also suggested that experimental subjects seek to discern the aims of an experiment and argues that they seek to present themselves in a favourable light in terms of the experiment. For their part, researchers who conduct experiments are aware of the possibility of such effects. They often employ a variety of tactics to deflect subjects from ascertaining the aims of experiments. The use of deception, of stooges (confederates of the experimenter who participate in the experiment), post-experimental debriefing and the selective use of information about the research are part of the repertoire of strategies for concealing the true aims of an experiment. However, the tendencies pinpointed by Orne and Riecken are still likely to occur, even when the researcher engages in diversionary tactics. On the other hand, some writers have sought to dismiss the degree to which phenomena like demand characteristics have a contaminating influence (for example, Kruglanski, 1975).

This discussion should not be taken to imply that experimental subjects constitute the only source of reactive effects. In a large number of studies, Rosenthal has demonstrated that experimenters are themselves a source of bias since they often unwittingly seek to provide support for the experimental hypotheses that they formulate (Rosenthal and Rubin, 1978). One of the main formats of Rosenthal's research is to take groups of subjects, some of whom are allocated the role of 'experimenter' and others the role of 'subject'. The 'experimenters' are led to believe that certain outcomes are likely to obtain when they conduct studies with their 'subjects'. In one study, 'subjects' were asked to rate photographs in terms of whether the people in the photographs were successes or failures. The photographs had in fact been chosen because of the apparently neutral appearance of the people they depicted. Each photograph was to be rated on a scale going from −10 (extreme failure) to +10 (extreme success). One group of 'experimenters' was led to believe that their subjects would rate their photographs on an average of +5, the other group of experimenters being told that their subjects would average −5. Naturally, the same photographs were shown to each group of subjects. Rosenthal found that the expectations of the 'experimenters' clearly affected the scores of their subjects. The problem with such research is that it is difficult not to feel slightly uneasy about experiments which are designed to undermine claims in favour of the external validity of experiments!

It is possible to discern in much of the foregoing discussion an implicit suggestion that experimental studies seem to be capable of producing findings with strong claims to internal validity but weak external validity. The presence of a control group coupled with random assignment of subjects provides a setting in which the researcher can have considerable confidence in findings indicative of the presence or absence of a causal relationship. However, the provision of a control group can do little to help the researcher to gauge the degree to which sources of external invalidity have arisen in an experiment, because both experimental and control groups are conceivably likely to be affected by problems associated with pre-testing, selection of subjects and reactive effects. In the view of many commentators, external validity is an even greater problem when experimental research is conducted in the laboratory rather than in the field, a topic which is the focus of the next section.

Laboratory or field experiments?

It is often argued that laboratory experiments are of little use because the settings in which they take place are artificial and so the results of the ensuing findings have little validity beyond the confines of the laboratory. An example of a laboratory experiment is Day and Hamblin's (1964) study of the effects of different styles of supervision. Twenty-four groups, each comprising four women, were recruited from the student population at Washington University. On arrival at the laboratory, each group was administered a pre-experimental questionnaire and then received instructions about the task that they were to perform. The task comprised the assembly of models of molecules and in the view of the authors simulated quite well an industrial task, in that it was both complex and had affinities with assembly-line work. Each session took forty minutes and was followed by the administration of a post-experimental questionnaire. The sessions comprised ten-minute periods with the supervisor in the room, with intervening five-minute periods during which she was absent in order to allow aggressive feelings towards the supervisor or the experiment to be expressed. The supervisor was a trained member of the experimental staff. The researchers used an adaptation of the factorial design outlined in Figure 3.5, in that they were concerned to establish the effects of both close (Exp_1) or general supervision (Exp_2) and a style exhibiting high (Exp_A) or low (Exp_B) levels of punitiveness. This design yields four possibilities, such as close and high punitive ($Exp_1 + Exp_A$). Each group was randomly assigned to each of the four possible experimental conditions, that is, six groups per condition. The design differs from that in Figure 3.5 in that, in spite of the presence of a pre-experimental questionnaire, no pre-test scores were reported by Day and Hamblin. The supervisor's style was operationalized by varying her behaviour in relation to her subordinates. When exhibiting close supervision, for example, she administered forty instructions and watched her workers a great deal; with general supervision, only the eight most important instructions were administered. The dependent variables were derived from both questionnaires and observation. Data on self-esteem and feelings of aggression towards the supervisor or co-workers were collected by questionnaire. In addition, observers recorded details of overt aggression and the number of molecule kits constructed (which was used as a measure of productivity). The authors were able to examine the effects of different combinations of supervisory style on these dependent variables.

In this example, the researchers are able to conform to a number of important principles of experimental design which allow them to establish a high degree of internal validity. But in the eyes of many commentators, the artificiality of the setting renders the study of limited value because it is not 'real'. What is lacking here is 'mundane realism' by virtue of the setting and circumstances not being likely to be found in the real world. By way of defence of laboratory experimentation, it is sometimes suggested that the lack of mundane realism does not matter too much if the experimental task achieves 'experimental realism'. This means that the experimental situation must be real to the subjects in the sense of their being involved and caught up in what is happening. Further, mundane realism can be enhanced by a careful selection and construction of experimental settings in the laboratory (Ilgen, 1986). Day and Hamblin (1964) sought to do this by introducing the supervisor to subjects as though she were a real supervisor, by using words and phrases likely to be encountered in an industrial setting and by using a task which contained certain characteristics of industrial settings. On the other hand, it must be remembered that there are still some important differences between this laboratory situation and that likely to be found in the world of work: the subjects are strangers, they meet for only forty minutes, whereas real workers know each other and anticipate many further years together in their jobs; and the subjects are not part of a wider organization. On the other hand, the overt aggression expressed during the course of the sessions is indicative of a fair degree of experimental realism having been created. While the suggestion that it is important not to neglect the significance of experimental realism points to the limitations of a curt dismissal of laboratory experiments, the lack of mundane realism of laboratory experiments in the field of organizational research has a special significance, because many of its practitioners are concerned to develop findings which can be applied to organizations in everyday life. It can readily be imagined that researchers with a strong orientation to generating applied (or at least applicable) knowledge would feel uneasy about research deriving from a context so far removed from the kind of environment to which it is supposed to apply. Further, there is also the possibility that many researchers feel that investigations with a strong artificial flavour are unlikely to persuade decision-makers in organizations to adopt the implications of their findings.

In view of such considerations there is a strong pull in the direction of field experiments in real organizations. One of the main ways in which such research is likely to arise is when the researcher is in a quasi-consultancy role and is given the opportunity to evaluate the effects of an organizational change. However, one of the chief limitations of field experiments is that they frequently transgress a number of principles of experimentation. The failure to apply basic experimental precepts is largely due to the fact that the researcher is rarely able to exert the same degree of control over experimental arrangements that is possible in the laboratory.

In some instances the study is conducted on one group only, that is, with no control group or comparison group. Jenkins and Lawler (1981) describe a study of a small manufacturer in Ohio whose president wanted to redesign the firm's compensation scheme. The researchers agreed to assist the company in the use of a participative approach to the development of the scheme. Initially, a questionnaire covering a variety of topics, such as satisfaction with the job and pay, intention to leave the firm, job involvement and the like, was administered to provide a battery of pre-test measures. The researchers, along with a committee of hourly-paid employees, devised a pay scheme which was accepted by the company president. The scheme that was introduced was not the first proposal that the group had devised, in that their first offering had been rejected by employees. After the installation of the new pay plan we are told that a pay increase was introduced whereby average pay for hourly workers increased by 12.9 per cent. Four months after the pay scheme had been in operation, a second attitude questionnaire was introduced to provide post-test measures so that changes in levels of job and pay satisfaction and so on could be estimated. Thus, the design used was

$$Obs_1 \ Exp_1 \ Exp_2 \ Obs_2$$

where Obs_1 and Obs_2 are the pre- and post-test measures respectively, Exp_1 is the introduction of the new pay plan, and Exp_2 is the pay increase. Two points are striking about this study. First, there is no control group. This absence is by no means unusual in research on organizational changes and their effects; in 23 out of 58 work experiments analysed by Cummings, Molloy and Glen (1977) no control or comparison groups were in evidence. Jenkins and Lawler are clearly aware that the absence of a control group constitutes a limitation of their research, and that it is therefore not an experimental study. In fact, they indicate that they had originally proposed to have a comparison group which presumably would not have been affected by the pay plan. We are not told why this more rounded design was not introduced, but one possible reason is that the comparison group would have experienced a great deal of resentment at the prospect of not being included in the new pay scheme. Indeed, this possibility points to a recurring problem for the external validity of field experiments when experimental and control or comparison groups are used; the mutual awareness of the groups may occasion feelings of envy or pride depending on whether subjects feel that they are losing out or gaining from the experimental arrangements. In the case of the Hawthorne effect mentioned above, the envy of the members of the department from which the women had been taken was a factor in their sense of being special and different. A second point about the Jenkins and Lawler study is that there are two experimental treatments: the participatively designed pay plan and a pay increase. This means that it is not really feasible to disentangle whether it is the pay plan or the pay increase that is the source of the differences between Obs_2 and Obs_1. One of the difficulties with many field experiments is that they involve the introduction of more than one organizational change, so that it is difficult to establish how far increases or decreases in the dependent variable are due to one change rather than another.

A second area in which field experiments frequently fail to exhibit internal validity is in regard to establishing that experimental and control groups are equivalent. Random assignment is usually not feasible since it would invariably be highly disruptive for the organization concerned; Orpen's study of the effects of job enrichment is an exception to this general tendency. Consequently, matching is often resorted to as an alternative to random assignment. In the Morse and Reimer (1956) experiment, matching was established as follows.

> The two pairs of divisions were comparable on relevant variables such as initial allocation of the decision-making processes, satisfaction and productivity, as well as on such background factors as type of work, type of personnel and types of supervisory structure.
> (Morse and Reimer, 1956, p. 121).

There are also numerous examples of studies in which even matching is not evident. Bragg and Andrews (1973) report a study of the introduction of participative decision-making in a hospital laundry comprising thirty-two workers. We are told that two other hospital laundries in the same city were employed as comparison groups in order to allow the change in productivity in the focal laundry to be evaluated. While the use of two other hospital laundries as points of comparison seems a reasonable strategy, we do not know how comparable the work of the laundries is, nor whether the personnel in the three groups are equivalent in terms of personal characteristics or work experience, nor what levels of participation in decision-making the comparison groups exhibited at the outset of the study and whether those levels were equivalent to that of the experimental group.

One advantage of the Bragg and Andrews study is that experimental and control groups were not aware of each other's existence as co-participants in a study. Such mutual awareness can be an important contaminating factor, as suggested above. An extreme example of this is an attempted quasi-experimental study of a coal mine in Pennsylvania in which the authors were seeking to introduce Quality of Working Life (QWL) principles 'to improve employee skills, safety, and job satisfaction while simultaneously raising the level of performance and earnings' (Blumberg and Pringle, 1983, p. 410). Volunteers were solicited to participate as the experimental group, which would function as an autonomous work group. In order to encourage a degree of job switching and sharing that was consonant with the aims of QWL initiatives, all miners were to earn the same rate as that of the highest-skilled job on that section of the mine. This meant a substantial pay rise for fifteen of the twenty-seven men who made up the experimental group. Miners in other sections of the mine constituted the control group(s). Initially, miners in the experimental group were a source of humour among their co-workers, but this posture gradually gave way to hostility. Miners in the control group became increasingly jealous of the lack of attention they received from the researchers, the favourable working conditions, training and equipment enjoyed by the experimental group and the occasional days off work to attend conferences with top management and union officials. Ten months after the start of the experiment, a new section of the mine was to be opened up and to operate on QWL principles in order to enhance the study. Miners were invited to participate from all sections of the mine. Older miners, many of whom were peeved about the apparently cushy conditions enjoyed by the experimental group, refused to come forward, so that the group tended to be made up of inexperienced miners, with less than one year's training behind them. Because of the incentive scheme, many of these inexperienced miners were earning the same as or even more than highly experienced miners. These developments exacerbated the hostility towards the research in certain quarters, and roughly seven months after the opening of the new section the experiment had to be terminated. Although this case is possibly an extreme instance, it points to the problem of mutual awareness as an extraneous variable in many field experiments and the contaminating effects it may induce. Parenthetically, it is striking that even if the study had continued, it would have been very difficult to disentangle the effects of autonomous group working from the pay incentive received by the experimental group. This point underscores the suggestion above that, in field experiments, experimental changes can be difficult to separate from other changes that are introduced at or around the same time.

It would seem that the greater generalizability of field experiments is more apparent than real, since they are vulnerable to a host of potential assaults on external validity. The point can be underlined by pointing out that by no means all organizations are prepared to allow outside observers on their premises for experimentation, even when there exists an interesting innovation in work organization or a problem to be solved. Consequently, the typicality of some research findings may be questionable because of the potential differences between firms that admit researchers and those that do not. An extreme instance of this is an often-cited experimental study in a pyjama manufacturing firm by Coch and French (1948) on ways of overcoming resistance to changes in work. The research is frequently cited because it was one of the first studies to demonstrate the advantages of a participative approach to the introduction of changes. However, the firm was one in which there was an atmosphere of participation because of the frequent use of referendums by senior management to decide on issues, while the company's chief executive was highly conversant with and appreciative of the social sciences, as well as committed to the idea of participation (Zimmerman, 1978). It is also the case that field experiments frequently fail to exhibit an adequate level of internal validity (for example because random assignment may not be feasible or acceptable to the host firm). Thus the lure of field experiments as exhibiting greater external validity, because they are located in real work settings, has to be weighed against the loss of internal validity that is often incurred and the suggestion that their greater external validity is exaggerated.

Even if the advantages of field experiments were more clear-cut than the foregoing discussion implies, there might still be an important role for laboratory experiments. There are likely to be issues which cannot be investigated in field settings because of practical problems of establishing the right conditions. Also, organizational researchers are likely to be interested in classes of empirical problem that are of little or no interest to organizations, because of the absence of a clear practical benefit. Yet field experiments require a substantial commitment of time and resources to the research which is less likely to be acceptable to firms when the study is perceived to be 'pure' research. In such a context, a laboratory experiment may be necessary in order to investigate the issue at hand. Further, laboratory experimentation can be of considerable use when all the researcher wishes to establish is whether something can be made to happen, which can then be the focus of further research (Ilgen, 1986; Mook, 1983). As an example can be cited a number of laboratory experiments in the late 1960s which established that leaders' styles of leadership can be affected by the performance of their subordinates, whereas the bulk of previous research had depicted the causal connection as operating in the other direction (Farris and

Lim, 1969; Lowin and Craig, 1968). Although sited in the laboratory and using students as subjects, these studies made an important contribution to leadership research and forged a number of areas of further inquiry.

It may be that the question of whether laboratory or field experiments provide greater internal or external validity is an empirical question. Two approaches to such a question can be envisaged. First, experiments in both settings might be combined within a single programme of research. Griffin (1983) reports the results of investigations into the effects of informational cues disseminated by supervisors about their subordinates' work on the latter's perceptions of the nature of that work and their experience of it. In an initial laboratory experiment, the 'supervisor' made eight comments regarding different facets of the work of their 'subordinates' (for example, 'There are a lot of different aspects to this job', which was meant to impart information about task variety). A field experiment was then carried out in two manufacturing plants. While the laboratory conditions were not (and could not have been) recreated in the plants, the general tenor of the research was followed up in the field context. Broadly congruent results were obtained in that Griffin was able to show that information about tasks given out by supervisors in the plants had an effect on the same variables as in the laboratory study. 'Objective' job characteristics were also found to have an impact upon subordinates' perceptions of their work, but supervisors' informational cues were shown also to have an independent effect.

A second way forward is to review areas of research and to seek to discern how far laboratory and field experiments produce congruent findings. In many areas of organizational research, especially those concerned with micro-level research on organizational behaviour, the two types of experiment are pursued in conjunction. A volume edited by Locke (1986b) is an example of such an exercise. Focusing exclusively upon topics pertaining to organizational behaviour (such as goal setting, participation and job design) he collected contributions from various writers on the congruence between findings deriving from the laboratory and those from field settings, although it is important to recognize that the latter included many studies which were of the survey kind discussed in Chapter 4. In his overview, Locke remarked:

> In case after case and topic after topic, basically the same results were obtained in the field as in the laboratory. Variation within laboratory and field settings was, where assessed, typically as great as that across the two settings.
>
> (Locke, 1986a, p. 6)

This comment indicates that studies in laboratory and field settings do not duplicate each other, but that differences between the two are no greater than the variations in findings that are encountered when research employing one method is analysed. However, the presence of broadly congruent findings should not be taken to mean that external validity has been established, since research undertaken in both settings can be questionable in this regard.

A further approach is to examine research that allows the behaviour of student subjects to be compared with that of people employed in real organizations. A study by Staw and Ross points to the possible contaminating effects of an undue reliance on student subjects. Staw and Ross (1980) were interested in people's reactions to different forms of administrative behaviour. A total of 222 subjects was asked to assess eight case descriptions of administrative behaviour. These descriptions differed slightly from each other in terms of a number of characteristics. Since the subjects were made up of both undergraduates and practising managers enrolled on an evening MBA programme, it was possible to compare the different responses of the two groups to the varied characteristics depicted in the accounts. Managers were much less likely than undergraduates to rate the administrator as having performed well when his efforts were apparently successful, but they were more likely to rate his performance highly when his behaviour was consistent. Gordon, Slade and Schmitt (1986) examined thirty-two studies relevant to the field of organization studies in which students and non-students participated in research under the same conditions and in which it was possible to draw comparisons between the two groups of subjects. One of the studies was Staw and Ross (1980). Seventy-three per cent of the studies in which quantitative comparisons were used revealed at least one considerable difference between students and non-students. Since the appearance of the review by Gordon, Slade and Schmitt, Isenberg (1986) has reported the results of an investigation in which general managers and students were asked to think aloud while solving a short business case and found pronounced differences in reasoning processes between the two groups (for example, managers started action planning earlier in the task). While a number of explanations can be proffered for such findings, the differences in the reactions of students and managers may point to a cluster of divergences that may have implications for the generalizability of findings based upon the ubiquitous student subject.

Quasi-experiments

Much of the discussion has drawn a somewhat hard-and-fast distinction between experiments and non-experiments, but increasingly many writers prefer to identify either a class of designs that exhibit almost all of the characteristics of true experiments or those which depart significantly from true experiments but which enable the researcher to discount some major assaults on internal validity. In each instance, these quasi-experimental designs permit the researcher to eliminate some competing explanations of supposed causal relationships, but not all. The presence of this intermediate category is particularly helpful since a large proportion of field experiments could not be considered experiments at all, as the discussion in the previous section suggests. According to Cook and Campbell (1976, p. 224), the fundamental difference between 'true' experiments and quasi-experiments depends 'on whether the various treatment groups were formed by assigning respondents to treatments in random or nonrandom fashion'. The term 'quasi-experiment' is also employed to denote the study of a single group which receives the experimental treatment, but for which additional observations are collected over time, so that there is considerably more information than with Design 1. The case for quasi-experiments is most likely to occur in field settings, in which the opportunity for full control is unlikely to be present. Many quasi-experiments in the field are described as 'naturally occurring quasi-experiments', that is, studies in which change to the normal functioning of an organization is known to be in prospect, thereby offering the opportunity of ascertaining the effects of the change(s).

It is possible to distinguish a vast number of designs that could be deemed quasi-experimental (Cook and Campbell, 1976). Rather than focus upon the formal characteristics of these many forms, it is proposed to take a small number of examples to illustrate the kinds of design that may occur. One of the commonest quasi-experiments has already been encountered: Design 2. The chief source of difficulty with this design is the absence of random assignment. However, in addition to the possibility of matching, it is frequently possible to establish whether subjects in groups are equivalent (for example, by comparing their pre-test scores Obs_1 and Obs_3 on the dependent variables). Two examples can be cited. Hackman, Pearce and Wolfe (1978) report a naturally occurring quasi-experiment which was made possible by the redesign of clerical jobs as a result of the introduction of technological change in a US bank. The changes were introduced without any reference to the implications of the job design changes for the motivation of the clerks. These changes afforded an opportunity to examine the veracity of job characteristics theory (see Chapter 1). Hackman, Pearce and Wolfe found that some jobs were enriched by the change, others were adversely affected (referred to as 'de-enriched'), and still others were unaffected. In this way, three 'groups' were created, but without random assignment. The ensuing design bears similarities to both Design 3 and Design 4, except for the absence of random assignment. In Figure 3.8 the formal characteristics of the study and some sample findings are presented. It is a moot point whether the third group should be described as an experimental or a control group. While its job characteristics remained roughly the same, it was none the less affected by the technological changes, so that it is referred to as an experimental group. Findings like those presented in Figure 3.8 led the authors to conclude that changes in job characteristics had an impact upon various outcome measures.

Oldham and Brass (1979) report the results of another naturally occurring quasi-experiment. The study was concerned with employee reactions to the introduction of an open-plan office in a US newspaper firm. The chief focus of the research was upon an experimental group of seventy-six employees. As Figure 3.9 suggests, in addition to a pre-test, there were two post-tests which took place nine and eighteen weeks after the change. A control group of five employees not affected by the change was also pre- and post-tested. Finally, there was a third group of persons who moved to the open-plan office but were not pre-tested to discern whether pre-test sensitization occurred. The article does not provide sufficient information for sample data to be presented, but the basic structure should be apparent from Figure 3.9. The inclusion of the unpretested group (referred to as a 'quasi-control' group even though it was exposed to the experimental variable) brings it close to Design 7, though there is no control for the sensitization effects of the T_2 post-tests on the T_3 ones.

The quasi-experimental designs that underpin both Hackman, Pearce and Wolfe and Oldham and Brass are essentially experimental designs without random assignment. A second type of quasi-experiment is where time-series data are collected for one or more groups, which permit before and after comparisons of the effects of an intervention. When one group is used the design appears thus:

Obs_1 Obs_2 Obs_3 Obs_4 Obs_5 Obs_6 Obs_7 Obs_8 Obs_9 Obs_{10}

Structure of the research

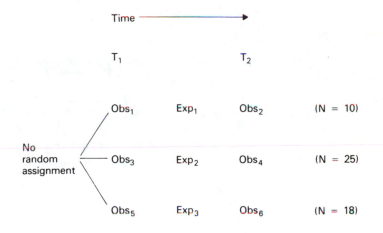

Sample finding: the effect of changes in job characteristics on internal work motivation

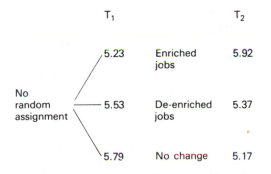

Source: Hackman, Pearce and Wolfe, 1978.

Figure 3.8 Example of a quasi-experiment – effect of changes in job characteristics of work attitudes and behaviour (Hackman, Pearce and Wolfe, 1978)

Structure of the research

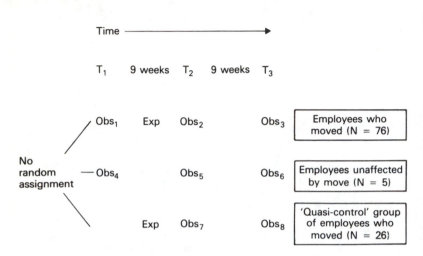

Source: Oldham and Brass, 1979.

Figure 3.9   Example of a quasi-experiment – employee reactions to moving to an open plan office (Oldham and Brass, 1979)

This design allows change in a trend to be recognized and also whether the change coincides with an intervention in the organization. Lawler and Hackman (1969) describe a study in which groups of janitors were allowed greater participation in decision-making. Weekly data on absenteeism were collected over twelve weeks preceding and sixteen weeks after the change. Interestingly, the time-series data were able to show that the level of absenteeism immediately preceding the change was exceptionally high; had single before and after measures been employed, the effects of the change would have been exaggerated. One of the other chief advantages of this time-series design over Design 1 is that the presence of data over time allows the effects of changes occurring to the study participants to be largely controlled. The presence of a control group, even though there may be an absence of random assignment, may considerably enhance the study. Lawler and Hackman were able to collect such data on a group of janitors who did not experience greater participation and were able to strengthen their findings about the effects on absenteeism.

As this discussion suggests, there are many different types of quasi-experiment, and numerous variations on these types can be discerned when studies are examined in detail. If a purist view is taken, they are invariably deficient in terms of the researcher's ability to establish definitive causal findings. On the other hand, they do permit the researcher to study the implications of potentially interesting interventions in organizations (very often ones instigated by organizations themselves) while simultaneously allowing some rival explanations to be discounted.

Overview

There can be little doubt that the experiment is an important and popular approach to the study of organizations. Its appeal derives from the facility with which claims about causality can be established through experimental designs. Since much quantitative research on organizations is couched in the language and orientations of the natural sciences, the ability to impute cause-and-effect relationships is viewed as very important, since the establishment of causal relationships is taken to be an important ingredient of a scientific approach. The distinction between internal and external validity was an important focus for the chapter and led to the suggestion that, whereas internal validity tends to be a strength of experimental research, external validity is often less well established. The distinction between laboratory and field experiments was also examined, and it was suggested that the greater external validity of the latter is not as great as is sometimes supposed. Further, field experiments often suffer from problems of internal validity that can largely be eliminated in the laboratory. The notion of the quasi-experiment provides a framework within which the effects of organizational interventions can be examined.

4

Survey research

The social survey is conventionally associated with questionnaires and interviewing. As such it may appear peculiar that we now come to a discussion of the nature of the survey having addressed questionnaires and interviews in Chapter 2. However, in much the same way that the experiment is not a source of data, but rather a particular framework within which data are collected, the survey too is best conceptualized as a research design. Questionnaires and interviews are methods of data collection which are in considerable use in the context of experimental research as well as in survey investigations. The survey, then, provides a particular kind of structure within which these methods of data collection are employed. The distinctiveness of the survey, in contrast to the experiment, will be a prominent focus of this chapter. Further, just as the experimental approach can be viewed as subsuming different designs, albeit with a number of common characteristics, the survey also reveals itself in contrasting forms. In other words, when referring to experimental and survey designs we are in fact employing fairly broad terms which refer to different orientations to the structure of an investigation, but which comprise a number of variations.

The survey less readily lends itself to a brief definition or delineation of its uniqueness. Some writers deliberately eschew a definition (for example, Moser and Kalton, 1971), while others are more adventurous (for example, de Vaus, 1986). At the very least, we can assert that survey research entails the collection of data (invariably in the field of organizational research by self-administered questionnaire or by structured or possibly semi-structured interview) on a number of units and usually at a single juncture in time, with a view to collecting systematically a body of quantifiable data in respect of a number of variables which are then examined to discern patterns of association. As a number of writers have suggested (such as Marsh, 1982), the tendency to associate survey research solely with interviewing and question-naires is inappropriate, because a design such as this can incorporate investigations using other methods of data collection, such as structured observation or research based on pre-existing statistics.

The phrase 'on a number of units' is significant on at least two accounts. 'Units' is preferred to 'people' because the objects to which the data refer may not be people as such but firms, departments in organizations, or even industries. While a large proportion of the data collected within a survey design refers to people, it is important not to lose sight of these distinctions. Also, the phrase 'a number of' is evidently vague, since it provides no clues as to what number can be taken to constitute a survey. This vagueness is scarcely surprising, since organizational research reveals enormous variation in the numbers of units that have been taken to provide evidence within a survey design. At the lower end of the spectrum can be found a study of seven occupational interest associations (Donaldson and Warner, 1976).

Further, when the objective is to collect data from individuals about themselves, two levels of access are required: to the firm and to the individuals. In Hackman and Oldham's (1976) research on the effects of job characteristics, the nature of the research had to be explained to fairly senior managers before access to respondents could be granted:

The nature of the research was explained to second- or third-level management [in the seven organizations], and permission to administer the instrument was secured. Managers were informed that the project had to do with the refinement of an instrument to diagnose jobs, and that it would involve collection of data from employees, from their supervisors, and from company records.

(Hackman and Oldham, 1976, p. 260)

Then, the main research instrument, the JDS, was administered

to groups of employees (ranging from 3 to 25 at a time). Before taking the questionnaire, employees were told about the nature and purposes of the research and were given the opportunity of not participating. Few employees declined to complete the questionnaire. It was also emphasized that all information obtained would be held in confidence, and that no one in the organization would have access to individual responses.

(Hackman and Oldham, 1976, p. 260)

As these two passages imply, the administration of such research instruments is likely to involve considerable skill on the part of the investigator to be admitted to the organization and to gain the co-operation of those who will provide the data. Various parties may be suspicious about the research, albeit for different reasons.

The terms 'systematically' and 'quantifiable' are deliberately linked in the foregoing account of the nature of the survey. Survey research is almost always conducted in order to provide a quantitative picture of the units in question, hence the widespread tendency to associate surveys with quantitative research. In order to attain this aim, data must by gathered in a systematic manner in order to ensure that variables on which units are deemed to differ are genuinely capable of aggregation. Thus, if a question to tap the levels of job satisfaction of people in a firm were asked in such a way that the wording differed considerably, it is doubtful whether answers could be added up since they would not be responses to the same stimuli. If they were aggregated, variations in job satisfaction could be attributed both to variations in the asking of questions and to 'real' differences in satisfaction. The account also refers to the research being conducted in relation to 'a number of variables', thereby drawing attention to the tendency for investigators to gather data on a variety of different facets of the units in question. The JDS, for example, permits the collection of data relating to a wide variety of concepts: job characteristics, GNS, job satisfaction and so on.

Finally, the account notes that the data are usually collected at a single juncture in time. This attribute should not be taken literally. In an interview survey, people may be contacted over a number of months; similarly, when a postal questionnaire survey is conducted, some questionnaires arrive by return, whereas others can take many weeks to arrive, especially when the investigator contacts non-respondents. Even though there may be such discrepancies in the timing of the data collection, respondents' answers are treated as though they were collected at an identical point in time. For example, Hackman and Oldham collected data in each organization in one to four days, but data relating to each of the seven firms were aggregated although the information would have been collected at different times. Such practices denote an important difference between the survey design and the experiment: the former permits the examination of relationships between variables which have been collected at the same time, whereas the latter entails the collection of data in relation to the independent and dependent variable(s) at different stages. Consequently, survey designs in which data are collected at a single juncture are frequently referred to as 'correlational' or 'cross-sectional' survey designs. The researcher is able to point to patterns of association among the data collected. Unlike the experimental researcher, the survey practitioner does not manipulate what is deemed to be the independent variable and then observe the consequential effects on the dependent variable. Survey researchers can only establish that people vary in relation to a number of attributes on which data have been collected (that is, variables) and analyse the co-variation that exists between pairs of variables. The inability of survey researchers to manipulate any of the variables of interest imposes important constraints in regard to their ability to generate findings from which definitive causal statements can be derived. However, this important point will be held in abeyance for further discussion later in this chapter.

Sampling

An important phase in the collection of data is the selection of the units to which the data relate. In order to facilitate the following discussion, the focus will be restricted to the selection of units for interview or self-administered questionnaire surveys. The bulk of such research entails the collection of data from samples drawn from a wider population. *Population* here refers to a universe of units which can be people, organizations, sub-units within organizations and so on. It is rare for the population to be sufficiently small for all units to be included in a survey, and more usually a *sample* must be selected from the population. It is common for textbooks to point out that researchers need not simply a sample but a *representative sample*, that is, a sample of units that is representative of the population. If one does not have a representative sample, the argument can always be levelled that the results are idiosyncratic and of unknown generality. In order to enhance the likelihood that a sample is representative, the researcher will need to engage in *probability* (or *random*) *sampling*, wherein each unit of the population has a known chance of inclusion in the sample. Probability sampling means that *selection bias*, whereby certain units are over-represented, may be largely eliminated. Of course, it is unlikely that such bias can be totally eliminated, and there is bound to be a certain degree of *sampling error*, that is, differences between the sample and the population. However, probability sampling aims to reduce the impact of such error.

Types of probability sample
The most basic form of probability sample is the *simple random sample*. With a simple random sample, each unit in the population has an equal probability of inclusion in the sample. In

order to create a simple random sample, a listing of the population, known as the *sampling frame*, is required. The sample is selected from this listing using a table of random numbers. Each unit is given a number from 1 to N, where N is the total number of units in the population. In order to select a sample of size n, a random numbers table is scrutinized until n units have been selected. Thus, if the first number in the table between 1 and N is 78, then the unit corresponding to that number will be selected, and so on until there are n units. The important point to notice with this procedure is that the human element is eliminated. If the researcher simply chose his or her respondents or relied on people being available, there is a strong chance that an unrepresentative sample would ensue, since a non-probability form of sampling would have been employed. By removing the human hand and relying on random numbers, the possibility of a systematic bias is reduced. A variation on the simple random sample is the *systematic sample*. Here the researcher samples directly from the sampling frame. Thus, if n is to be 100 and N is 1,000, implying a 1 in 10 sample, a random start of any number between 1 and 10 is made on the list, and the corresponding unit is the first to be included in the sample. Thereafter, every tenth unit is selected. If the random start indicates that the eighth unit is selected, then the eighteenth, twenty-eighth, thirty-eighth and so on will be included. Systematic sampling can only operate accurately if there is no inherent order to the listing of the population in the sampling frame. If such an order exists, there is the possibility of bias, since the structure of the sampling frame may result in the over- or under-representation of particular categories of the population.

A further type of probability sample that is often used is the *stratified random sample*. With this kind of procedure, the population is divided into strata, and simple random samples are taken from each stratum. Thus, a researcher interested in the variables with which job satisfaction among non-manual workers is associated in a firm may take the view that it is important to ensure that all functional areas within the firm are fully represented. The population of non-manual workers can then be divided into the various functional areas or strata (that is, production, marketing and sales, personnel, R & D, financial accounting and so on). By taking a simple random sample from each of these strata, the researcher can ensure that the resulting sample will accurately reflect the population in terms of functional areas. A simple random or systematic sample taken from the entire population *might* have led to an accurate representation, but the stratified random sample can enhance the likelihood of accuracy. This procedure is likely to be of particular importance when it is anticipated that the criterion on which the sample is stratified is an important characteristic that may be associated with variations in job satisfaction and the other variables of interest. Two or more stratifying criteria can be employed in conjunction. The researcher may additionally wish to stratify the population according to level (that is, upper, middle and lower management, clerical and so on). A number of combinations of functional area plus level (for example, middle management in production, sales, personnel, R & D and accounting) would ensue. Thus, five functional areas plus four levels of non-manual work would yield twenty strata from which samples would be taken. Such sampling can be either *proportionate* or *disproportionate*. In the former case, if we want a sample of 500 and there are 2,000 non-manual employees in the firm, a random sample of 1 in 4 would be taken from each stratum. However, if one of the functional areas is small (perhaps a small unit of only fifteen people as in an R & D group), proportionate sampling will produce an unacceptably small number from that area, especially if variations in job satisfaction are likely to be linked to categories of functional area in subsequent analysis. Accordingly, a larger proportion of persons working in R & D (or possibly all of them) will be included in the sample, and slightly lower proportions taken from the other strata. However, the decision about whether to stratify the population is bound to be affected by the extent to which the relevant data are readily to hand. If a firm has good records which allow persons in different functional areas and at various levels to be readily identified, the extraction of a stratified random sample is likely to be straightforward. If the relevant data are not readily available, the time and cost involved may make stratified random sampling prohibitively expensive. Similarly, when conducting survey research on organizations as such, if the information is available, a number of potential stratifying criteria can be envisaged. Cameron, Kim and Whetten employed this technique in their study of higher education organizations in the USA:

> A stratified, random sample representative of all four-year colleges and universities in the United States was selected on the basis of size (200–20,000 FTE [full-time equivalent students]), control (public/private), enrollment and revenue change (growth, decline, stability), and degrees offered (bachelor's, master's, doctorate).
>
> (Cameron, Kim and Whetten, 1987, p. 228)

Thus, this study employed four stratifying criteria ensuring a sample that was 'very close to the demographics of four-year institutions in the US' (p. 228).

The final type of sample worthy of mention is the *multi-stage cluster sample*. This form of sampling is likely to be of particular use when the researcher is seeking to investigate organizations which are widely dispersed. The procedure entails dividing a geographical region into constituent areas (such as states into counties in the USA or counties into boroughs in England and Wales). Counties or boroughs (that is, clusters) are then randomly sampled, and then organizations from each cluster are randomly sampled. The chief advantage of this approach is that, when interviews are to be conducted, interviewers will be more concentrated in particular areas, thereby saving much time and money on travel. Very often cluster sampling is accompanied by stratification, as the following· passage from a survey study of banks implies:

> The banks selected for this study were in Illinois, a state with unit bank regulations; i.e. no banks were branches of others, so each could be analyzed as a unit.
> Stratified sampling was used to select banks to represent the different economic activities of the state. The 17 economic areas of the state were grouped into . . . three groups, ranging from economically most active to least active. Four counties were randomly selected from each group, and five banks were selected randomly from each county.
> (Leblebici and Salancik, 1981, p. 585)

Thus, counties are assigned to one of three groups which are arrayed according to level of economic activity. Samples of counties are taken from each of these three clusters, and then banks are sampled from each cluster. The resulting sample was sixty (that is, three regions × four counties × five banks). The advantage of allowing stratification to accompany cluster sampling is that it permits the resulting sample to provide a good reflection of an important facet of regional diversity within a large geographical area. As its name implies, multi-stage cluster sampling can involve sampling at a number of levels. In England and Wales, electoral wards might be sampled from boroughs, so that organizations would then be sampled from wards, rather than boroughs as such. Census tracts in the USA would provide analogous clusters. Stratification could accompany any or all of the stages.

Some sampling problems in organizational research
Much of the foregoing discussion has side-stepped the problem of how large a sample should be. There are few if any definitive guidelines, but the following four considerations are worthy of mention. First, while it is probably the case that larger samples stand a greater chance of providing a representative sample, it has to be borne in mind that a law of diminishing returns seeps into sampling considerations. Once a sample of a particular size relative to its population is reached, there is a tendency for larger samples to yield increasingly small increments in accuracy (that is, in representativeness). Since cost and time constraints constitute perennial boundaries to sampling considerations, small increases in accuracy are likely to prove uneconomic. Second, the more heterogeneous the population, the larger the sample. This rule of thumb implies that when we are confronted with a highly varied population, as in the example of all non-manual employees in a firm, a large sample is required to encapsulate that variety. Otherwise, certain sections of the population may not have adequate representation in the sample or even not appear at all. With a fairly homogeneous population, it may be possible to get away with a smaller sample. Third, researchers must anticipate the kind of statistical analysis that they will perform. For example, cross-tabulation will require quite a large sample if many of the variables that will form contingency tables are capable of subsuming a large number of categories. If one variable is taken to comprise five categories and the other variable six categories, there would be thirty 'cells' in the contingency table, so that if the researcher wanted to avoid unacceptably small numbers of individuals (or even nobody) in many cells, a large sample would be required. Finally, if there are grounds for believing (for example, on the basis of a pilot study) that a large proportion of people are likely to refuse to participate in a study, a large sample may be needed in order to ensure that a sample of acceptable size, from the researcher's point of view, is achieved. It is impossible to say how far these guidelines are followed in organizational research, but the wide variety in sample sizes in respect of both individuals in organizations and organizations as such implies that few systematic rubrics are followed.

The discussion of the importance of probability sampling as a means of enhancing the representativeness of a sample should not be taken to mean that a representative sample is assured if one of the types of random sample is fashioned by a researcher. Quite aside from the possibility of sampling error, two other problems which may limit the representativeness of a random sample should be mentioned: sampling frame bias and non-response bias. Random sampling implies that there is a complete and accurate listing of the population from which the sample is selected. However, if there are inaccuracies in the sampling frame, even if a random sampling procedure is followed and there is no sampling error, an unrepresentative sample may ensue. When sampling organizations, researchers invariably rely upon directories of various kinds, but when sampling people or sub-units in organizations they usually employ company records. It is impossible to guess how accurate such sampling frames are, but the possibility of inaccuracy or incompleteness exists and therefore so too does the spectre of bias in the resulting sample.

The issue of non-response bias was touched on in Chapter 2 in the context of the tendency for interviews to engender lower levels of non-response than questionnaires administered by post and indeed self-administered questionnaires generally. Non-response is an important problem, because a perfect random sample drawn from a perfect sampling frame and with virtually no prospective sampling error can be rendered unrepresentative by a poor level of preparedness among respondents to be involved in the research. Indeed, it seems useful to distinguish between a study's *de jure* sample (that which is selected) and its *de facto* sample (that which is achieved). The problem with non-response is that those people or firms that agree to participate may differ substantially from those that do not. Those who participate are akin to the voluntary participant in experiments whose characteristics may differ sharply from those who choose not to volunteer. In Leblebici and Salancik's (1981) research on Illinois banks, which involved a careful cluster sampling procedure accompanied by stratification, forty-four agreed to participate, but three of these were dropped because they had failed to answer a significant number of questions. Thus, two-thirds (41 out of 60) of the banks sampled appeared in the *de facto* sample. There is at least the possibility that the participating banks were not representative of all of the banks in the population, even though the *de jure* sample may well have exhibited this quality. In fact, this study's response rate is in the middle of the range reported by Mitchell (1985) for survey investigations in the field of organizational research for 1979–83 (the range was 30 to 94 per cent), though over half of the studies examined failed to provide data on response (which may be a source of bias in the data on the range of response rates). It is often proposed that researchers should check to see whether there is evidence of systematic bias in their sample. In the imaginary study of non-manual employees, the researcher might be able to check fairly readily whether people in particular functional areas, or at certain levels in the organization, or men rather than women, showed a marked tendency to participate or not to participate. Leblebici and Salancik (1981) did not conduct this check, a neglect which appears to be common, since under 10 per cent of the studies analysed by Mitchell (1985), all of which were organizational research articles based on correlational designs, compared respondents with non-respondents. However, it has to be recognized that even when such checks are carried out they can rarely conduct comparisons between respondents and non-respondents in anything but the most superficial of character-istics. Less directly observable characteristics can rarely be a source of comparisons, so that even though respondents and non-respondents may appear similar in terms of face criteria (such as gender, level in hierarchy, or company absenteeism records in the non-manual employee study) deeper differences (such as attitudinal or behavioural divergences) are almost never amen-able to such analysis. It should also be borne in mind that a high refusal rate is not necessarily worse than a lower refusal rate in terms of the representativeness of a *de facto* sample; it is the systematic bias deriving from people's differential propensity to participate that is critical but which is rarely amenable to checking.

There is a sense in which much of the discussion of random sampling, non-response and so on is redundant, because there is a widespread recognition among organizational researchers that investigations using sample surveys are rarely based on probabil-ity samples. Instead, we usually find that what are often called *convenience samples* tend to prevail. A convenience sample occurs whenever a researcher gathers data on a sample of persons or firms, but the sample has not been derived from any form of probability sampling; rather, it is simply a sample that was available to the researcher. The problem of convenience samples, particularly in relation to the issue of representativeness, is twofold: are such samples representative of their populations, and what are the confines of the generalizability of the populations themselves? Taking the first issue, it is clear that relatively few instances of survey research in organization studies are based on random samples; Mitchell's (1985) analysis of articles reveals that only 17 per cent are based on random samples. It would seem that most researchers in organizational research carry out survey research on samples of respondents or of organizations that have been selected without recourse to random sampling. In many instances, there is a lack of information regarding the way in which the sample was selected, but the general impression is often that of an absence of random sampling. The issue of random sampling is of particular significance in view of the widespread use of significance testing in organizational research. Such tests, which determine how confident the researcher can be that findings deriving from a sample are likely to exist in the population from which the sample was selected, are based on the assumption that random sampling has been conducted. When a non-random method has been employed it is doubtful whether such testing is appropriate. Schwab's (1985) view is instructive in this connection:

> Of course, we all know that almost all of the empirical studies published in our journals [that is, organizational research journals] use *convenience*, not probability samples . . . Thus, if one took generalization to a population using statistical inference seriously, one would recommend rejecting nearly all manuscripts submitted.
>
> (Schwab, 1985, p. 173)

Almost equally disconcerting is the tendency to draw samples (either random or convenience) which derive from populations of relatively unknown generality. When data are collected on individuals in organizations, it is often the case that one or a very small number of organizations constitute the source of the population from which the sample is taken. Brass (1981) reports the fruits of a study of the effects of organization structure and job characteristics on job satisfaction and performance among 160 employees and their supervisors in a newspaper publishing company in the midwestern USA. A similar accusation could probably be levelled at Hackman and Oldham's (1976) initial job characteristics study; not only do the data derive from seven organizations of unknown representativeness, but also it is not clear how the 658 employees were selected for inclusion in the investigation. It is not obvious what the limits of generalizability of such research are supposed to be. Similarly, when confronted with a study of the relationship between organizational commitment and organizational effectiveness largely based upon a non-random sample of employees and their managers in a non-random sample of twenty-four organizations operating fixed-route bus services in the western USA (Angle and Perry, 1981), the reader may be concerned about the generalizability of the findings. Similarly, it is difficult to know what to make of studies of restaurants in California (Freeman and Hannan, 1983), banks in Illinois (Leblebici and Salancik, 1981), or trade sale representatives in three large organizations (Ivancevich and Donnelly,

1975). In each case, one might question the generalizability of the populations as much as that of the samples.

When research is conducted on a wide range of organizations or draws on a diverse population of people working in organizations the greater sense of generalizability that ensues frequently enhances the regard in which such investigations are held. The Aston Studies (Pugh, 1988) are a case in point. The original investigation entailed a stratified random sample of forty-six organizations in Greater Birmingham. The stratifying criteria were size (measured by the number of employees) and product or service (as indicated by Standard Industrial Classifications). The result was an extremely varied sample of manufacturing and service organizations. Of course, one might query how generalizable findings relating to the Birmingham area are (or more accurately were). In a US study which investigated similar issues to the Aston researchers and which was also based on a random sample, Blau *et al.* (1976) argued that New Jersey was taken as the region from which their sample was drawn because 'its wide variety of manufacturing firms are representative of American industry as a whole' (p. 21). A similar argument could probably have been made for the location of the early Aston research in Birmingham. What is especially striking is that the Aston research and that of Blau *et al.* have been very influential and highly regarded, and the care in the selection of, and the variety in, their respective samples is probably a factor in the esteem in which they are held.

The discussion of the procedures associated with probability sampling (like a number of other parallel discussions in this book) relates to what might be termed 'good practice', rather than to a cluster of operations that is followed on a regular basis. But why are convenience samples employed with such frequency when there is widespread awareness that they are less than ideal? The answers to this question can only be a matter of speculation, but two types of answer can be proffered. First, there may be practical reasons which inhibit the use of random samples. Firms are increasingly disinclined to allow research in their establishments. It is striking how often the contributors to a book on research in organizations (Bryman, 1988c) mention the problem of gaining access to firms. Moreover, many of the contributors expressed the view that the problems of gaining access are increasing. The initial Aston research in the early 1960s achieved a response rate of 92 per cent, but as Pugh (1988) notes, for many interviewees the investigation was a novelty. Nowadays, firms are deluged with requests for participation in research. As such, the increasing difficulty of gaining access to firms for survey research mirrors the general tendency for people to be less willing than in the past to participate (Goyder, 1988), a trend which has almost certainly been exacerbated by the growing number of surveys. Consequently, co-operation such as that received in the initial Aston research can rarely be achieved. The research by Blau *et al.* (1976) achieved a response of only one-third, for example. As a result of the problems associated with persuading firms and their members to participate in survey research, it may be that many researchers have come to feel that the difference between a *de jure* random sample that achieves a relatively poor response and a non-random sample that achieves an equally poor response rate is not great. Further, researchers may have constraints placed upon them that inhibit the possibility of random sampling of individuals in organizations. In their research on workers at a variety of levels in fifty-three US companies, Cherrington and England (1980) had to depart on a number of occasions from the random sampling of individuals 'to accommodate the production demands of the company' (p. 142).

A second reason for the employment of non-random samples may be strategic; in other words, a non-random sample may be deemed better than a random one, or a random sample may not be a feasible plan of action. A study by Daft and Macintosh (1981) which aimed to examine the relationship between the equivocality of tasks in organizations (that is, the extent to which the information required to execute tasks is capable of differing interpretations) and other aspects of those tasks (such as their inherent variety) provides an example of the former argument. The authors aimed to select a diverse sample of work units:

> The primary criterion for sample selection was to ensure that a wide range of tasks were included in the study. Rather than use variation within a single function, such as research and development, or units within a single organization, we included a variety of activities from several organizations. Selecting the sample on the basis of variation in the independent variable, rather than randomly, enables investigators to test whether independent variables are having the predicted impact on dependent variables.
>
> (Daft and Macintosh, 1981, p. 216)

Such a consideration implies that there may be tactical advantages associated with the use of a non-random approach, since it may allow certain facets of the broad domain that the researcher is seeking to emphasize to be depicted.

Random sampling is unlikely to be feasible when there is no

sampling frame or when the frame would be absurdly expensive or even impossible to construct. An interesting example is the research on top-level strategic decision-making by Hickson *et al.* (1986). The authors were interested in the nature of such decision-making and the factors that impinged on it. Hickson *et al.* were keen to maximise the amount of variety in both the types of decision they addressed and also the kinds of organization in which the decision-making process was located. They were able to gain the collaboration of thirty manufacturing or service organizations in England, which differed markedly in terms of product or service and also of size. The units of analysis were decisions, five of which per organization were selected for analysis (that is 150 decisions in total). The choice of decisions was an outcome of deliberations by both executives and the researchers in conjunction. Clearly, the process of sampling decisions was not a random one, although in the view of the investigators the sample is reasonably representative:

> It is impossible to say how representative they [that is, the decisions] are, since no one knows what sorts of decisions are taken in what sorts of organizations, but they are as diverse a coverage as has been achieved and can reasonably be taken to be the most representative to date. They certainly included every *kind* of decision that had occurred, within active memory, in each organization.
>
> (Hickson *et al.*, 1986, p. 23, original emphasis)

As this passage implies, the fact that a random sample is not feasible due to the absence of a sampling frame (or the cost and difficulty involved in constructing one) need not mean that samples with a high level of apparent representativeness cannot be contrived.

The causality problem in survey research

As the discussion of the process of quantitative research in Chapter 1 suggested, there is a strong predisposition towards findings which exhibit cause-and-effect relationships. Experimental designs are well suited to this orientation, since the investigator is able to establish a high degree of internal validity by controlling for alternative explanations of a posited causal relationship. But how well does survey research fare in this regard? Two points are particularly important to recognize. First, survey researchers do not manipulate those variables that might conceivably be considered independent. This is by no means due to a preference on the part of survey researchers. Many of the variables that survey researchers investigate simply are not amenable to manipulation; otherwise, they might prefer to use experimental research. The Aston Studies, for example, were interested in the relationship between an organization's size and its structure, and employed survey procedures to this end. However, neither of these variables is open to manipulation. We cannot make some firms small and others large, and then observe the effects of our manipulation on aspects of their structure. Second, surveys entail the collection of data on variables at a single juncture. Since notions of causality are usually taken to imply that a cause precedes an effect – something that experimental research has little difficulty in demonstrating – survey researchers are faced with a problem, since data relating to their variables of interest are collected simultaneously. In fact, survey designs can be adapted so that data are collected on the relevant variables at two or more different junctures, thereby instilling a temporal element. Such a longitudinal design will be addressed below; in the meantime, it is proposed to concentrate upon the much more familiar and more common correlational design in which data on numerous variables are simultaneously collected at a single juncture by the researcher.

One of the chief concerns of the Ohio State research on leadership, referred to in Chapter 2, was to demonstrate patterns of association between aspects of leaders' behaviour – their degree of consideration or of initiating structure – and variables such as group performance and individual job satisfaction. Although the Ohio State research suffers from a plethora of

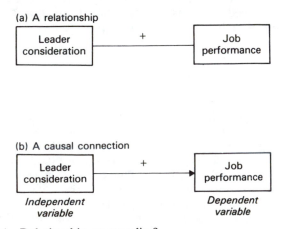

Figure 4.1 Relationship or causality?

inconsistent findings, there was a tendency for consideration to be positively associated with job performance (see Figure 4.1). This finding implies that subordinates who describe their formal leaders as considerate (in terms of the LBDQ) also perform well at work. Ostensibly this finding is simply a matter of the two variables being associated, but many commentators interpreted it to mean that leaders' consideration *caused* better performance. The problem here is that such an interpretation is highly problematic.

First, we have to be sure that the relationship is a real one, that is, that it is not spurious. By a spurious relationship is meant one which is produced because each of the two variables is associated with a third variable (often called an 'extraneous variable') which precedes them. In Figure 4.2 it is suggested that it would be necessary to ensure that a third variable like group size does not produce the relationship. It might be anticipated that leaders who are responsible for small groups are more inclined to behave considerately *and* that people prefer working in small groups and therefore perform better when in such milieux. In other words, because both consideration and job performance are affected by group size there seems to be a relationship between consideration and job performance. In order to examine this possibility it would be necessary to partition the sample of respondents into constituent batches in terms of group size (for example, small, medium and large groups) and examine the relationship between consideration and job performance in each batch. If there is still an association between consideration and performance for each category of group size, we can have some confidence that in respect of the third variable, group size, the relationship between the two variables is non-spurious. Alternatively, a procedure like

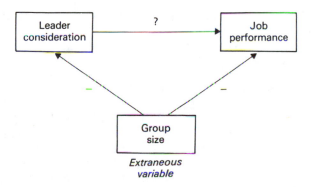

Figure 4.2 Is the relationship spurious?

Figure 4.3   Is there an intervening variable?

partial correlation might be used, whereby the correlation between consideration and job performance is examined, holding group size constant. However, in both cases it will be necessary to examine further the possibility that the relationship is spurious, since there may be other extraneous variables which impinge on it.

A further possibility is that the relationship between the two variables is not a direct one. It may be that there is an important intervening variable that has to be considered. Could it be that consideration has an effect on job performance because of a pattern such as that portrayed in Figure 4.3? This figure implies that leader consideration enhances subordinates' commitment to the organization which in turn increases people's job performance. In other words, leader consideration does not cause job performance in any direct sense. In order to discern whether the pattern stipulated in Figure 4.3 has any veracity, it is necessary to investigate whether there is an association between consideration and performance for different levels of organizational commitment. Similarly, as Figure 1.2 implies, Hackman and Oldham (1976) anticipated that 'critical psychological states' would be an intervening variable between job characteristics and the outcomes they addressed. For example, in Table 1.1 it is noted that the correlation between skill variety and internal motivation was .42, but when the effect of the intervening variable was eliminated, the correlation fell to .15. This suggests that the relationship between job characteristics and internal motivation is not a direct one. As with the test for spuriousness, administering one such test is unlikely to be sufficient, since there will be other variables which are potential candidates. In the case of job characteristics theory, further intervening variables are not implied by the theory as such.

It should be apparent that the statistical procedures for establishing whether a spurious relationship exists are the same as those involved in testing for the presence of an intervening variable. The difference between the two resides in their interpretation. In forging an interpretation, the researcher relies on hunches, deriving either from theory or from observations

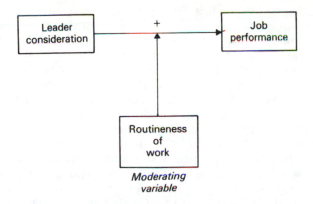

Figure 4.4 Is the relationship moderated by another variable?

about the world, concerning whether a pattern such as that depicted in Figure 4.2 (a spurious relationship) is more or less likely than the kind of pattern depicted in Figure 4.3 (an intervening variable). This is not always straightforward; in Figure 4.3, organizational commitment is presented as an intervening variable, but if the view is taken that leaders will exhibit greater consideration towards more committed subordinates, it could be considered an extraneous variable akin to group size in Figure 4.2 (and hence would constitute a test for spuriousness), since organizational commitment would be affecting both consideration and job performance. If it was found that organizational commitment did have an impact on the relationship between leader consideration and job performance, the question of whether this indicated that the relationship was spurious or that commitment was an intervening variable would have to be inferred. This would not be easy, since the two interpretations are equally plausible.

Third, the researcher must consider whether the relationship between consideration and performance holds throughout the sample. For example, we might consider the possibility that the association between the two variables is affected by the kind of work that people do, such as the amount of routine it comprises. When work is highly routine and hence lacking in variety, there may be less leeway for the leaders' behaviour to have an impact on their subordinates, as implied by Figure 4.4. The quest for such moderated relationships has been a major area of research since the early 1970s. We might find that when jobs are varied and non-routine there is a strong relationship between consideration and performance, but when jobs are routine there is little association at all. Such a finding would imply that the overall relationship between the two variables is made up of two sub-samples, one of which demonstrates a strong relationship and the other a weak one. The size of the overall relationship would have been suppressed through the inclusion of a sub-sample in which the relationship was weak. Similarly, Figure 1.2 suggests that the relationship between job characteristics and critical psychological states and between the latter variable and outcomes is moderated by GNS, for the reasons mentioned in Chapter 1. Thus, Hackman and Oldham (1976) found that the relationship between critical psychological states and internal motivation for those respondents with high GNS was .66; among those with low GNS it was .48. This contrast supports the notion that GNS moderates this relationship. In experimental research, this kind of issue would be handled by a factorial design (see Figure 3.5).

In each of these three instances, the problems associated with establishing a relationship from a correlational survey design is handled by a *post hoc* imposition of control. In so doing, the survey researcher is providing an approximation to an experimental design, that is, ruling out alternative explanations of the postulated association. Such alternative explanations derive from the inability of the survey researcher to rule them out through the combination of a control group and random assignment. However, by the standards of experimental research, the *post hoc* imposition of control is a poor approximation. First, it is only possible to control for those variables that were thought about at the outset of the research, so that the outcome is heavily influenced by the ingenuity and anticipation of the investigator. There is no virtue in recognizing as the data are being analysed that it would have been useful to have information on a particular attribute in order to examine for an alternative explanation. Further, the procedure is logically endless, confined only by the limits of the researcher's resources, patience and imagination. There is an almost limitless supply of variables that can be employed to test for spuriousness, intervening variables or moderated relationships, so that typically researchers tend to dip their toes into the water rather than dive in with gusto.

However, when it comes to a fourth problem with survey designs, relative to experimental ones, namely the problem of inferring causal direction, the *post hoc* imposition of control is less readily capable of providing a solution. The correlational survey design can only establish associations between variables; it cannot allow the researcher to impute causality. If it is found that variation in a particular facet of leader behaviour is associated with job performance from a correlational survey design, such as

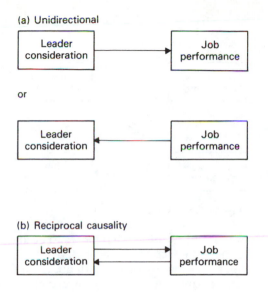

Figure 4.5 Three possible causal connections

that used by the Ohio State researchers, it is not legitimate to infer that particular kinds of leader behaviour enhance (or diminish) subordinate job performance, although it is clearly tempting to do so. While this may be a plausible explanation of a fairly strong correlation between these two variables, it is not the only one. Not only is it possible that the correlation is spurious; but even if it is found to be non-spurious, it is quite plausible that subordinates' job performance levels influence leaders' behaviour. Indeed, the relationship between the two variables may be one of 'reciprocal causality', whereby the two variables may be seen as influencing each other, albeit perhaps at different times (see Figure 4.5).

One way of testing for such possible patterns is through a longitudinal approach like a panel survey design, such as that indicated in Figure 4.6. When such a design is used at least two waves of data in respect of the same respondents are collected. In this way, data are collected in relation to the variables of interest at two different junctures, so that the causal impact of variables upon each other can be discerned over time. A study by Greene (1975) illustrates the potency of such a design, as well as the problems associated with inferring causal connections from a conventional correlational design. Greene administered the LBDQ to subordinates in three companies in order to elicit their perceptions of their leaders' behaviour. Each subordinate's job

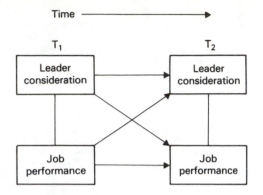

Figure 4.6 A panel design

performance was rated by his or her peers. The data on leader behaviour and performance were collected on three different occasions, each approximately one month apart. In fact, for each of the three time periods in which data were collected, Greene found very low correlations between consideration and job performance. Much of the research associated with the Ohio State instruments has been plagued with inconsistent findings (Bryman, 1986), so that the absence of strong correlations should not be too surprising. Of much greater interest was Greene's finding that over time there were strong positive correlations between consideration and performance which point to the strong possibility that the latter causes the former. Performance at Time 1 was correlated with consideration at Time 2, and likewise performance at Time 2 was correlated with consideration at Time 3. Further, performance at Time 1 was correlated with consideration at Time 3. This pattern of findings implies that when reasonably strong correlations between leader behaviour and performance are derived, it may be inappropriate to infer that the causal direction flows from the former to the latter, which has tended to be the interpretation over the years. Greene's findings suggest that leaders adjust their behaviour in line with the levels of performance exhibited by their subordinates.

Greene's research points to some of the perils associated with inferring causal statements from correlational survey designs. It also points to one way in which the conventional survey design can be adapted to permit the establishment of causal findings over time. It is not without its own problems, however. When longitudinal research of this kind is conducted, there is often a loss of respondents, either through a lack of preparedness among some initial respondents to participate at a later stage or because of mobility within the organization or even turnover. Further, panel designs are conducted so rarely that few rules of thumb to assist in decisions about the appropriate span of time between data collection phases have been developed. This is a matter of some consequence for the validity of findings, since there is evidence that the length of the time lag can exert an influence on the pattern of findings discerned. The study of leaders' behaviour when rewarding or punishing subordinates is a case in point. Panel research in this area has also shown a complex pattern of relationships between leader behaviour and subordinate performance. A punitive style has been found to be both a cause and a consequence of poor performance (that is reciprocal causality). However, as Sims and Szilagyi (1979) have demonstrated in a review of such research, the magnitude of correlations between such variables tends to be larger when the time lag between waves of data collection is short; with longer time lags, smaller correlations tend to be in evidence. Nor should it be assumed that this means that shorter time lags are superior, since it is not possible to decide a priori whether short or long intervals are preferable.

One approach to the problem of inferring causal connections from correlational survey designs is through a reconstruction of the logic of causal order. Davis (1985) has suggested that certain events tend to precede others. Thus, within the individual's life cycle, a person is likely to have gone to school before getting divorced. Consequently, if an association is found between education and propensity to get a divorce, it is fairly safe to infer that the former is the causal element. Although there may be instances in which there is a strong likelihood that one variable is causally prior to another, there are bound to be many occasions which do not readily permit a definitive attribution of causality. Consequently, researchers often seek to make clear the difficulty of inferring causality,[1] as in the following quotation from a study which was referred to in Chapter 2:

> Since static correlational analyses were employed in this study, causal relations between job dimensions [that is, characteristics of jobs] and satisfaction and motivation cannot be inferred. However, due to the substantial relations of the job dimension with satisfaction and motivation, it would be interesting to examine variation in these variables over time.
>
> (Rousseau, 1977, pp. 40–1)

On the face of it, job dimensions would seem to have a causal impact on people's experience of work, as expressed in their reported levels of job satisfaction, for example. Such an interpretation would also be consistent with the job design approach to the study of work (Hackman and Oldham, 1976). However, the author clearly feels unable to infer causal direction because of the constraints of the study's correlational survey design. Rousseau's caution is justified; James and Jones (1980), using a statistical procedure designed to investigate reciprocal causality in correlational studies, produced evidence based on a study of 642 non-supervisory employees which strongly implied that job satisfaction is a major cause of perceptions of job characteristics, as well as vice versa. Such a finding is also consistent with the study by O'Reilly, Parlette and Bloom (1980) which was cited in Chapter 2 for its finding that respondents' levels of job satisfaction can affect their perceptions of the nature of their jobs. Satisfied employees may describe their jobs in more favourable terms than those who are less satisfied. Other writers are often more cavalier, as is sometimes the case when researchers are interested in individual or organizational performance, which is often portrayed as the product of other variables. An investigation may find that firms' financial performance is associated with particular top management strategies, but the suggestion that the former is a product of the latter is a risky inference, since strategies are likely to have been affected by very recent indications of performance (cf. Snow and Hrebiniak, 1980).

Setting aside these worries about whether causality can be inferred from a correlational survey design, the researcher may propose that there are two or more independent variables in relation to a dependent variable. In order to do this it is necessary to investigate the relative contribution of each independent variable to the dependent variable. Thus, in Figure 4.7a it is suggested that job performance might be affected, not only by how much consideration leaders exhibit, but also by how far they are prepared to reward subordinates for consistently good work and how far they exhibit initiating structure. The researcher would then be concerned to establish (for example, through partial correlation or multiple regression) the unique contribution of each independent variable to job performance. Similarly, the Aston researchers (Hickson, Pugh and Pheysey, 1969) viewed organizational size and production technology as potential causes of organization structure (see Figure 4.7b), though their findings implied that size was more critical. On the other hand, Aldrich (1972) and Hilton (1972) re-analysed the same data and were able to show that other possible patterns of

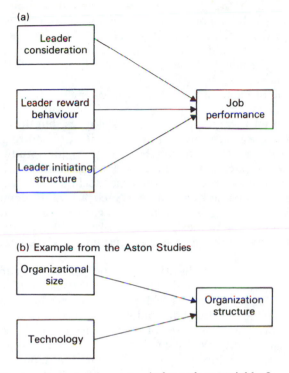

Figure 4.7 Are there two or more independent variables?

relationships between the three variables could be shown to exist, such as

$$\text{technology} \rightarrow \text{structure} \rightarrow \text{size}$$

However, *both* of the possible models (that is, 'size causes structure', as in Figure 4.7b, and 'technology causes structure, which in turn affects size') could be supported by the data. In other words, it is not easy to distinguish between the relative validity of plausible causal models with correlational survey data. The Aston Studies (Pugh *et al.*, 1969) again provide an interesting focus for some of the points raised in this section. As noted in the previous paragraph, the original research is well known for its clear finding of a relationship between organizational size and organization structure. In particular, strong positive relationships were found between size and three aspects of structure: the amount of specialization in organizations; the extent to which they rely on written documentation; and the degree to which organizations are endowed with rules. Several years after the initial study had been carried out, an 'abbreviated replication' was conducted with a much shorter version of the interview schedule (Inkson, Pugh and Hickson, 1970). Of the forty organizations that comprised the replication, fourteen had been in the original sample, thereby allowing changes over a five-year period to be examined. Ten of the organizations had declined in terms of the number of employees, but in only one of the fourteen organizations did the amount of structuring decline. In other words, even though both the original study and the abbreviated replication produced a strong positive relationship between size and structure, over time declining size and *greater* structure accompanied each other. Such a finding demonstrates the wisdom of exercising caution in regard to causal statements based on correlational designs, but it also highlights some of the interpretational problems that can undoubtedly accompany such designs.

There is little doubt that the extraction of causal connections from correlational survey designs is fraught with difficulty. The idea of relying on intuition and logic in order to determine which of two variables is the independent one has only a superficial appeal, since, as the case of the relationship between job characteristics and job satisfaction implies, real causal connections may be much more complex. The fact that a putative causal connection between two variables is implied by a theory (job characteristics theory) is not sufficient for a definitive statement about causality to be proffered. Panel designs can enhance the investigator's ability to infer causal connections, but they are relatively under-used, at least in part because of the greater cost that they incur. They also engender special problems, such as the difficulty of individuals and organizations refusing to participate in subsequent stages in the research. Bias may be introduced if this loss of respondents is differential. On the other hand, much of the research that is based upon conventional correlational survey designs could not be conducted by experimental investigations (even if researchers were so inclined), since they often relate to variables that cannot be manipulated. There are some areas within organizational research, such as job characteristics and participation studies, in which both experimental and correlational designs can be and have been used (Locke, 1986b). These areas tend to be ones which operate at the individual or group levels of analysis. Research at the organizational level is invariably less amenable to an experimental approach, because of the difficulty or impossibility of manipulating variables. However, the difficulty of establishing causality from correlational survey research does not revolve solely around the issue of causal direction. Two topics which are particularly relevant to organizational research will now be addressed briefly in terms of their implications for the elucidation of relationships – whether causal or otherwise – from correlational survey research.

Common method variance
Common method variance refers to the tendency in many studies to derive measures of different concepts from a single source, such as a self-administered questionnaire, and then to examine relationships among the subsequent measures. There is a possibility that because two measures derive from the same source the likelihood of a relationship between them is enhanced. Two sources of such spurious correlation may be considered. First, people may strive to be consistent in the answers that they give. They are likely to be aware of the tenor of the answers provided in relation to earlier answers; indeed, when a self-administered questionnaire is used they can even look up their earlier answers and the associated questions. There are reasonably strong psychological grounds for believing that such a consistency effect is more than mere speculation (Salancik and Pfeffer, 1977). Second, the format and nature of the questions asked may enhance consistency. A study like Rousseau (1977) may be a case in point. One facet of her research entailed the examination of the relationship between job characteristics (measured by the JDS) and job satisfaction (measured by the Brayfield–Rothe index). The former comprises fourteen statements (out of twenty-eight) to which respondents must indicate how accurate they think each statement is on a seven-point scale. The Brayfield–Rothe index also includes statements, but ones to which the respondents must indicate their degrees of agreement on five-point Likert scales. Since indicating whether a statement is true is not very different from saying whether one agrees with it, the common format may impose a spurious consistency on responses. The strain towards consistency may be enhanced by the presence in measures, that are supposed to tap different concepts, of questions that are not obviously very different from each other. Pearce (1981) has noted that measures of role ambiguity tend to be indicative of a deficiency in information (or the obverse). One of the most widely used scales to measure role ambiguity is that devised by Rizzo, House and Lirtzman (1970), which comprises statements such as:

- I feel certain about how much authority I have.
- I know exactly what is expected of me

As Pearce observes, it is scarcely surprising that when respondents are identified as experiencing role ambiguity they also express job dissatisfaction, since the information-deficiency component renders them almost inseparable from one another. The same point could be made of the Rizzo, House and Lirtzman measure of role conflict, which includes items like: 'I have to do things that should be done differently.' Such items are so close to statements about job satisfaction as to be almost indistinguishable from them. When there is such overlapping of item content between scales or indices supposedly measuring different concepts, the consistency problem is likely to be enhanced.

There are some possible solutions to this problem. Factor analysis is sometimes employed. If it is suspected that, for example, a scale measuring job characteristics and a scale measuring job satisfaction are likely to exhibit common method variance due to spurious consistency, the constituent items for both scales can be pooled and then factor-analysed. If a single factor or one overriding factor emerges, the case for common method variance would be considerable. However, the likelihood of extracting more than one factor is enhanced if a large number of items are pooled, so the test may not be definitive. A different tack is taken in a study of the relationship between job enrichment and job satisfaction: 'To reduce the amount of common method variance, the questionnaire was designed to measure the various dependent and independent variables in different sections of the questionnaire, usually with different kinds of scale formats' (Cherrington and England, 1980, p. 143). However, if the consistency effect has any credibility it seems unlikely that merely locating the items in different parts of the questionnaire, especially a self-administered one as in the Cherrington and England study, would suffice. The use of different formats is also unlikely to mitigate common method variance unless people are largely unaware of the meaning of the responses they provide.

The chief implication of such reflections is the need for variables to be derived from different data collection sources whenever possible. Thus, in a study of the relationship between job characteristics and job satisfaction, data relating to the former might be gleaned from structured observation, while satisfaction data might be derived from a self-administered questionnaire. A study of a broad spectrum of workers in four US organizations by Glick, Jenkins and Gupta (1986) goes a long way in this general direction. Data on job characteristics and on each of three 'outcome' variables (general work satisfaction, satisfaction with the amount of challenge in the job and effort) were gathered in three ways. First, by structured interviews. Second, during each interview session, data were collected by card sorting, whereby respondents sorted question cards into piles, each of which represented a different response category. For example, in order to gauge job characteristics, respondents were asked to indicate whether statements about their job were true or not by sorting them into four piles, from very true to very untrue. Third, data relating to all of the concepts were collected by observation. For example, in order to measure job satisfaction, observers recorded, 'how often employees smiled, laughed, daydreamed, yawned, got angry, and so forth' (Glick, Jenkins and Gupta, 1986, p. 447) and then rated them in terms of the amount of job satisfaction they thought each employee exhibited. This approach allowed the researchers to establish the extent to which the relationship between job characteristics and other variables was a 'real' relationship (as postulated by job characteristics theory) or a product of common method variance. They found that job characteristics and outcomes were related independently of common method variance, that is, the relationships could not be explained away by suggesting that they were products of common sources of data being used for pairs of variables. However, a tendency was found for common method variance to have some impact on the job characteristics – satisfaction relationships, but not in connection with the relationship between job characteristics and effort. Thus, the common method variance problem cannot be totally ignored and is fairly disconcerting when it is borne in mind that satisfaction measures are more commonly used than effort as outcomes of variation in job characteristics. On the other hand, the common method problem does not appear, from this study, to be quite as damaging as is sometimes supposed, although a limitation of the study is that it did not examine common method variance in relation to self-administered questionnaires, the most common of the data collection methods used within a correlational survey design. Self-administered questionnaires may be particularly susceptible to common method variance, because of the speed with which they can often be completed and because the respondent can scan previous answers and forthcoming questions.

Since observation can be very time-consuming, especially when undertaken in conjunction with another data collection method, structured interviews might be contemplated as an alternative for gathering data on job characteristics, with data on job satisfaction gathered by self-administered questionnaire. While this second strategy may not mitigate the common method variance problem in its entirety, it may reduce its intensity. Alternatively, if some variables are based on data deriving from other persons (peers, superiors, or customers), although collected by the same type of instrument, such as a self-administered questionnaire, the frequency of the common variance problem would be reduced, Yet another possibility is to use archival data for some variables. In each case, the aim is to reduce the reliance on individual respondents as the sources of data for all variables using one research instrument. If variables can derive from different instruments and/or different sources, the common method variance problem can be mitigated. Such solutions are likely to become increasingly commonplace, since concern about the contaminating effects of common method variance is increasing (Beyer, 1987)

Implicit or lay theories
In Chapter 2 mention was made of the idea of lay theories of social processes. Evidence was cited that implied that some measures of organizational phenomena are distorted by people's lay theories about those phenomena. However, a considerable amount of research has been carried out which goes even further and implies that many relationships between variables may be the product of similar distortions. Staw (1975) conducted an experiment in which sixty students were randomly assigned to groups of three, in which they were asked to work out the likely performance of an electronics company, based on data with which they were provided. Each group was then told whether it had done well or poorly in its calculations. In fact, these characterizations of the groups were created randomly, so that there was no prima-facie evidence for the performance rating. Each subject was then asked to fill in a questionnaire which dealt with what went on in the group, in terms of a number of characteristics, such as cohesiveness, communication, satisfaction, motivation and so on. Staw found considerable difference between the 'high' and 'low' performing group members in terms of their beliefs about the character of work and relationships within the group.

The significance of this finding is that 'mere knowledge of performance may cause an individual to attribute one set of characteristics to a high performing group and a different set of characteristics to a low performing group' (Staw, 1975, p. 428). Thus, if a person is asked to rate the leadership behaviour of his or her immediate superior, that rating might be inadvertently

influenced by the person's knowledge of the superior's performance and his or her implicit theories of how leaders who exhibit
particular performance levels behave. This notion was supported
by a study by Rush, Thomas and Lord (1977) in which students
were told of a department supervisor in a large corporation. No
other information was given, except that the supervisor's level of
performance was reported as indicating high, low, or average
performance. Subjects then completed the LBDQ to provide
descriptions of the supervisor's behaviour. Rush, Thomas and
Lord found clear differences in the descriptions according to the
supervisor's level of performance. In particular, high-performing
supervisors are deemed to exhibit greater consideration and
initiating structure than poor performers (see also Bryman,
1987); yet these divergent depictions occur in the absence of any
knowledge whatsoever about the imaginary leader's behaviour.
Interestingly, there is a fair amount of evidence to suggest that
leaders who exhibit high levels of both consideration and
initiating structure perform better than others on a number of
criteria (Bryman, 1986, p. 46). The findings on implicit leadership
theories suggest that people answering the LBDQ questions in
real settings may be affected in their assessments of leaders by
their knowledge of the leader's performance within the company
or whatever. Correlations between leader behaviour and performance may be a product of people's implicit theories about
how high- and low-performing leaders behave rather than
resulting from their actual behaviour. The accumulating evidence
about implicit leadership theories has led to considerable concern
about the meaning and validity of questionnaire-based findings
on leadership (Bryman, 1986). However, it should not be
assumed that such lay theories operate solely within the
leadership domain. Studies which examine the connection
between job characteristics and job satisfaction may also be
affected; people who are satisfied with their jobs may impute
greater skill, variety, autonomy and so on to their jobs as a
consequence of lay theories about the sort of work that satisfied
and unsatisfied individuals do.

Overview

The survey design is one in which data relating to a number of
different concepts are collected from a fairly large number of
units of analysis. The sampling of individuals, organizations, or
whatever is a prominent issue within the cluster of procedures
associated with survey research. While much of this discussion
pays lip-service to the importance of generating representative

samples through probability sampling, in practice many researchers, either by design or by force of circumstances, rely on non-probability, and hence potentially unrepresentative, samples. The common problem of non-response bias was mentioned as a particularly troublesome area in this regard. Survey research faces a number of difficulties when an attempt is made to infer causality from survey findings, because data are usually collected at a single juncture. While a number of procedures can be advocated as ways of checking whether a relationship exists between two or more variables, the problem of the direction of causality is highly intractable. Thus, survey research is usually less adept at generating definitive causal relationships than experimental designs, because of the latter's greater internal validity. In addition, two contaminating effects – common method variance and lay theories – were mentioned as areas in which difficulties associated with the establishment of relationships among variables have been identified by commentators.

Note

1 However, Becker, 1986, p. 8 has argued that a preoccupation with the canons of experimental design has made social scientists too wary of making causal statements. He argues for greater bravery in this regard, suggesting that writers are too often inclined to assert that two things are related when in fact causality could be inferred. Becker's view is consistent with that of writers like Davis, 1985, but cannot be reconciled very easily with writers who are highly critical of the derivation of causal relationships from cross-sectional survey designs, such as Mitchell, 1985.

5

Qualitative research

Qualitative research is a research design which reveals many different emphases from quantitative research. Probably the most significant difference is the priority accorded the perspectives of those being studied rather than the prior concerns of the researcher, along with a related emphasis on the interpretation of observations in accordance with subjects' own understandings. In Chapter 1, Burgelman's (1985) research in a new venture division was presented as an example of this research design. His investigation relied primarily on unstructured interviews, a research tool that will be examined in greater detail below. In order to illustrate the nature of qualitative research, a further example will be employed, but in this instance, although unstructured interviews figure in the researcher's armoury, much use is made of participant observation. With this technique, the researcher is immersed in the organization for an appreciable period of time.

Qualitative research in an insurance company

Smircich (1983) negotiated access to a firm referred to as Insurance Company (hereafter InsCo), which is one division of a large US company. She was able to spend six weeks as an observer of the top management team. She kept the same hours as they did but was not a full participant in that she did not work for InsCo. She observed the managers in a variety of contexts: staff meetings, coffee breaks, casual conversations, etc. Daily field notes were taken in connection with these observations. Near the end of her sojourn she carried out 'conversations/interviews' with each of the ten managers in the team, including the company president. These conversations were tape-recorded and dwelt on 'topics and themes which appeared to be relevant to people in the organization' (p. 57). In addition, relevant documents were perused for further information.

One of Smircich's chief concerns was to map InsCo's corporate culture, which she describes as emphasizing the importance of suppressing interpersonal differences and of not drawing attention to problem areas. The managers saw this ethos as deriving largely from the company president's personal style. Staff said of him that he 'likes to keep it cool' and 'doesn't like to hear if things are bad'. As a result,

> there was a belief that . . . 'people say what they know everyone else will want to hear.' Problems get 'buried' instead of dealt with directly because 'it's easier to handle that way.'. . . They fear that if they were to surface a disagreement they would be labelled a 'troublemaker' or accused of 'pointing a finger'.
>
> (Smircich, 1983, p. 57)

These preferences, and the staff members' responses to them, were particularly evident at the Monday morning staff meeting, which was described as having a 'ritualistic quality':

> 'We sit in the same seats, like cows always go to the same stall' said one executive. The tone of the meeting was low key, polite, calm, restrained and seemed to reflect the president's personal style of interaction which was also calm, reserved, and restrained.
>
> There was a shared belief among the staff members that these meetings were an empty formality; they consisted of 'superficial' communication. Discussion was kept at a surface level. People . . . did not 'delve as deep' into what they really felt about certain things which may be going on in their own departments or the departments of others. 'You'll never see the nitty-gritty in the staff meeting,' one executive told the researcher. 'But I think I know why (the president) does it – to keep us together.'. . .
>
> On the other hand, the president expressed the belief . . . that the staff meetings were 'a forum where we exchange information and keep up to date, on external and internal (issues) and on major decisions. They provide a forum for a little bit of important debate and discussion.'
>
> (Smircich, 1983, pp. 60-1)

The nature of qualitative research

These passages illustrate well a number of distinguishing features of much qualitative research. These features are ones which the advocates of qualitative research perceive to be prerequisites for the study of social reality; in other words, they reflect many of the goals and preoccupations of this tradition.[1] First, Smircich adopts the stance of an insider to the organization, and accordingly there is a strong accent on the interpretations offered by the managers themselves of the nature of their organization. This is not to say that a consensual portrait is arrived at, since it is apparent that the president's perception of the organization is at variance with that of his senior managers. Moreover, the frequent use of subjects' discourse reflects a concern to forge interpretations in terms of their own natural language. Second, the research gives a strong sense of context. Through the detailed description of the company's structure and of what it feels like, for example, to attend one of the Monday meetings, the researcher provides herself with a backcloth which greatly facilitates the understanding of what goes on in the organization. In addition, the reader is given a strong sense of knowing what the organization is like.

These twin strands – emphasizing subjects' interpretations and the delineation of context – served well in the understanding of a programme of action initiated by the president to deal with the substantial backlog of paperwork (claims, renewals, applications and so on) that InsCo had accumulated and which was a source of irritation to agents in the field (Smircich and Morgan, 1982). The programme was called 'Operation June 30' (OJ30), after the deadline by which the backlog was to be cleared (the starting date being 14 May). The operation was perceived as an all-out assault on the problem. The president saw the operation as a success, but it is hardly surprising in the light of the previous description of top management at InsCo that this view was not shared by members of the management team. In their view, OJ30 may have cleared the backlog but it had allowed the president to sweep the underlying problems that had led to the backlog under the carpet. Without the detailed knowledge of the varied interpretations of life in InsCo and the background context, the programme could easily have been interpreted by an outsider as a success; in fact, its value was more symbolic – a rallying cry to mobilize people's energies towards a common end.

Third, there is an emphasis on process – the unfolding of events in time. Even though Smircich was a participant observer for only six weeks (a short period in comparison with many other studies), it was possible to view a phenomenon like OJ30 as a series of interlinked events: what prompted it, what people thought of it, how they reacted to it, how it developed, its outcome and what people thought of the outcome. Fourth, Smircich's approach is very unstructured; she seems to have entered the field with little prior theoretical orientation and certainly no hypotheses. The theoretical significance of such

research is to a large extent determined during and after the
researcher's contact with his or her subjects, as when Smircich
and Morgan link their findings to discussions of the impact of
leaders on an organization's culture: 'Our case study illustrates
the importance of the leader recognizing the nature of his or her
influence and managing the meaning of situations in a constructive way' (Smircich and Morgan, 1982, p. 269). The relative
absence of structure in much qualitative research implies a
further noteworthy feature: flexibility. The researcher is able to
capitalize on chance remarks or unexpected events that propel a
new line of investigation. It is not clear from the report of OJ30
at what point Smircich learned of its impending arrival (that is,
whether before entering the firm or during her stay), but it is the
sort of unanticipated event that the researcher can use to
advantage without necessarily feeling that the line of investigation is too tangential. The very fact that it tells the researcher
something important about the organization is sufficient to
support following it through. In addition, the relative absence of
structure that pervades such investigations often denotes a
preference for minimizing the degree of distortion of the
organizational context that might arise as a result of the intrusion
of preordained research instruments.

Fifth, the investigation employed three chief sources of data:
field notes deriving from participant observation, interview/con-
versation transcripts and documents. This strategy allows data in
relation to a number of different topics to be addressed (for
example, people's interpretations of events observed by the
researcher can be tackled in an interview) and the validity of
evidence from particular methods to be checked by other
sources. Sixth, the conception of organizational reality is striking:
organizational culture at InsCo is not something that is simply
'there' waiting to be examined, but something that has been
socially constructed and is being maintained by members of the
organization. Although the culture is perceived to derive largely
from the president's influence, managers conspire implicitly in its
construction and maintenance by choosing not to challenge its
precepts. Finally, Smircich sought to obtain and retain close
proximity to the phenomena in which she was interested; she was
able to observe the flow of interaction at first hand and to
develop an understanding of what was important to her subjects
as a direct product of that proximity.

Comparing qualitative and quantitative research

These seven characteristics are important features of qualitative research. The InsCo study exemplifies some features better than others; in particular, Smircich's fairly brief sojourn means that the processual element is less evident than in many comparable studies; many exponents recommend a stay of about a year (Sanday, 1979). On the other hand, it illustrates a number of points well, and the comparatively brief period of fieldwork can be taken to demonstrate that qualitative research in which observation is a prominent ingredient need not necessarily entail a protracted period of absence from one's normal arrangements. Each of these seven characteristics can usefully be compared with quantitative research (as represented by survey and experimental investigations) to permit the distinctiveness of most qualitative research to be identified. First, the emphasis on interpretation is much less pronounced in quantitative research, wherein re-searchers typically set the parameters of what is interesting and important to them, rather than to their subjects. It does not matter to a quantitative investigation whether the features of a job denoted by 'skill variety' are relevant to respondents filling in the JDS, or whether they perceive work in this way. They answer the questions regardless of such considerations. Of course, quantitative researchers frequently study people's attitudes to various facets of the organization, but these attitudes are ones that the researcher takes to be important.

Second, quantitative studies tend to give little attention to context. For example, in studying organizations as such, the researcher is likely to take a number of abstracted variables which represent a sample of organizations (for example, formal-ization, routine, or technology); as a result, we do not get a 'feel' for those organizations, nor how those variables fit with other aspects of their functioning. Gordon (1985) administered a questionnaire designed to tap top managers' perceptions of their companies' cultures in over 500 organizations. The questions relate to a number of dimensions of culture, such as clarity of direction, integration, encouragement of individual initiative, performance emphasis and the like. Companies' scores on these dimensions were related to their levels of performance. Interest-ingly, in the light of the InsCo study, high-performing firms had considerably higher scores than low-performing firms on a dimension entitled 'openness in dealing with conflicts and criticisms'. However, two points should be registered. Although Gordon claims that he examines company cultures 'as seen through management's eyes' (p. 104), the question of what are the most important aspects of culture to the firms themselves cannot be answered. Consequently, the claim that he was looking at culture through management's eyes (ironically a phrase frequently used by qualitative researchers to describe their point of orientation) should not be taken too literally. Moreover, the research gives no sense of context: we do not know how culture connects with other aspects of the functioning of the organizations in the sample, nor what it feels like in those organizations.

Quantitative research tends to deal less well with the processual aspects of organizational reality. It often entails fairly static analyses in which relationships among variables are explored. Even when there is a before-and-after experimental study or a panel survey study, the reader derives little sense of sequences of events within the organization. This tendency means that it is rarely possible to understand organizational change in quantitative studies, although the upsurge since the late 1970s in the use of archival data has mitigated this tendency to a certain degree (see Chapter 7). Thus, while the Aston Studies (Pugh, 1988; Pugh *et al.*, 1969) revealed stable relationships between variables such as size and dimensions of organization structure, such static analysis tells us little about the dynamics of organizations.

In contrast to the loosely structured approach to data collection employed by Smircich, most quantitative research entails the rigorous preparation of a framework within which data are to be collected. In survey research, this tendency is apparent in sample selection and, to an even greater extent, in the questionnaire or schedule which specifies very precisely in advance what the researcher can and cannot find. In experimental research, the structured approach is revealed in the division of subjects into experimental and control groups and the tasks that they are set. In each case, the confines of what can be found are determined at the outset, so that there is rarely any opportunity to change the direction of the research, since the structure largely determines the course of events.

In common with many participant observers, Smircich carried out interviews and examined documents. Such additional material provides a number of benefits: the collection of data on matters which cannot be directly observed, the cross-checking of information gleaned from different sources, and the validation of her interpretation of her subjects' perspectives. By and large, quantitative research tends to use a single data source. Additional data are sometimes collected from company records, but this tends to occur in connection with particular variables that are not directly amenable to questioning, such as the widespread use of firms' financial records to provide performance measures in studies of strategic management (for example, Lenz, 1980). Indeed, the considerable concern about both the validity of many measures and the common variance problem (see Chapter 4) are reflections of these concerns. Qualitative research which derives mainly from unstructured interviews may be less able to include the element of multiple methods that Smircich's research entailed, since participant observation is not being conducted and so cannot provide a source of alternative data. However, Burgelman's (1985) research made substantial use of documents such as the long-range plans associated with the NVD and each of the ICV projects. The resulting information was compared with interview data. In addition, Burgelman (1983, p. 228) made 'occasional behavioral observations' which 'led to the formulation of new questions for further interviews'.

Sixth, quantitative research tends to present organizational reality as an inert amalgam of facts waiting to be unravelled by an investigator, much as natural scientists are often seen as laying bare the underlying laws of the natural order in their laboratories. Social reality is viewed as something external to the actor which he or she has had little or no part in fashioning. The underlying facts relating to the relationships between job characteristics and job satisfaction or between organization size and formalization are 'out there', and the job of the researcher is to devise the instruments that will allow these facts to be revealed. In contrast, qualitative research conceives of organizational reality as something which people actively devise. A possibly extreme version of this perspective on organizations is the idea developed by Strauss *et al.* (1963) of the hospital in which they conducted a qualitative investigation as a 'negotiated order' where the rules and other manifestations of social order are constantly in flux as they are negotiated and renegotiated by personnel.

Finally, the proximity of the qualitative researcher to organizational phenomena contrasts sharply with the distance between researcher and subject that much quantitative research involves. In field experiments and some survey interviewing, the researcher may have a good deal of contact with the organization and develop a fairly strong sense of how it operates, although when research instruments are mainly administered by hired assistants, the investigator's contact may be minimal. In the case of some sources of quantitative data – laboratory experiments, postal questionnaire surveys and archival data being obvious examples – the researcher may have virtually no involvement in organizations as such.

Methods of qualitative research

The three main sources of data with which qualitative research is associated are: participant observation, unstructured and semi-structured interviewing and the examination of documents. In addition to the three chief methods, researchers may use non-participant observation (where the researcher observes intermittently with little immersion in the setting), structured observation (see Chapter 8) and even questionnaires of the kind examined in Chapter 2. None the less, there tends to be a greater reliance on the three methods signalled at the outset, and these will provide the focus for the initial discussion.

Participant observation

Participant observation comprises the fairly prolonged immersion of the researcher in the context that is to be studied with the purpose of gaining first-hand knowledge of that context, primarily through observation of individuals as they go about their normal work activities. In addition to observing behaviour, the participant observer listens to what people say to each other, engages people in conversations and uses some people as informants about what is going on or to tip him or her off about events that should not be missed. The method is rarely conducted on its own, in that it is usually accompanied by some interviewing and analysis of documents. For this reason, many researchers prefer the terms 'field research' or 'ethnography' to describe qualitative research in which participant observation plays a major role. In the following discussion, 'participant observation' will be reserved for the method as such, that is, without the associated sources of data that habitually accompany it.

Participant observation allows the study of behaviour at first hand, rather than the somewhat indirect study of behaviour that much survey research affords through the elucidation of attitudes and people's reports of their behaviour. Further, it allows the researcher to peep behind the formal aspects of organizational settings and to reveal a rich, and often deliberately concealed, underlife. Our understanding of such diverse but relatively hidden features of organizational life as informal organization (Dalton, 1959), regulation of output (Roy, 1954) and pilferage (Ditton, 1977) can be largely attributed to the efforts of participant observers. Indeed, they may even be too successful for their own good in this regard, Serber (1981) reports that his qualitative study of a state agency in California for the regulation of the insurance industry quickly revealed a number of substantial departures from official policy (such as the informal processing of matters that could have led to the disciplining of companies). The identification of this realm of unofficial activities led to a substantial loss of co-operation on the part of the agency. A further advantage of participant observation is that its unstructured nature may allow the researcher to happen on promising areas of investigation that could not have been anticipated at the outset.

It is possible to distinguish three chief types of participant observer role: covert, full and indirect participant observation. Covert participant observation occurs when the researcher gains entry to the organization and observes others without anyone knowing that he or she is a researcher. The technique requires the researcher to assume a work role within the organization. The full participant observer also has a work position within the organization, but is known as a researcher when negotiating entry and will probably be known as a researcher among all or most of those with whom he or she works. The main difference from the covert role is simply that the researcher's true status as a researcher is known. Indirect participant observation occurs when the researcher is constantly in and around an organization, but does not possess a work role in it. The researcher may participate in events, such as parties and lunches, and discuss people's work with them, but does not have a formal work role. The indirect observer role is probably closest to the position of the anthropologist visiting a tribe for a period of fieldwork, since he or she rarely becomes a full member of that tribe, although an honorary status may be conferred and participation in certain ceremonies may be permitted. Much participant observation in organizations derives its impetus from the model that generations of social anthropologists have developed.

Each of the three participant observer roles carries its own advantages and limitations. Covert observation does away with two difficulties that beset the other two roles. First, the researcher does not face the problem of needing to negotiate access to the organization. As the discussion of access later in this chapter will reveal, the problem of gaining entry to an organization can be time-consuming and, more often than not, unsuccessful. Second, covert observation largely removes the problem of 'reactivity' (Webb *et al.*, 1966), which can transpire in a number of ways. Participant observers often note that subjects are wary of the researcher, especially in the early days in the field. There is also the unavoidable possibility that the observer may affect the normal flow of events or even that events are staged for effect in his or her presence. Covert observation avoids these problems by concealing the researcher's true status.

On the other hand, covert observation exhibits some important limitations. First, it tends to be highly controversial because of the suggestion in many quarters that it is an ethically dubious practice (Bulmer, 1982b). The ethical grounds on which it tends to be condemned are: it is an invasion of privacy, there is a lack of informed consent on the part of those studied, people are deceived, and there is the possibility that harm could come to those studied (Bulmer, 1982a). Thus, anyone who conducts covert observation is likely to become embroiled in a dispute of some magnitude, regardless of his or her own position on these issues.

There are forms of covert observation that are much less likely to occasion such hostile reaction. For example, when the researcher retrospectively writes up material collected at an earlier date, when the prospect of a publication had not been envisaged, the activity seems somewhat more acceptable. Cavendish (1982) worked on an assembly line in a pseudonymously named firm in order to gain insights into the experiences of women's manual work. She was hired in the normal way for the kind of job she wanted to perform; and although she worked at the firm for seven months, the prospect of a longer, even permanent commitment was in her mind. The decision to write a book occurred at a much later stage in her deliberations about the experience. However, there are other limitations to the covert role other than its ethical status. The ability to use other methods such as interviews is likely to be curtailed, since one cannot reasonably produce an interview guide without revealing the truth about one's role. It is likely that documents can be consulted and that conversations can be steered in particular directions so that they are virtual interviews, but the opportunity for a systematic integration of methods is likely to be restricted. Indeed, the anxiety of having his or her cover blown is likely to act as a considerable barrier to the researcher's confidence in the field. Further, participant observers rely a great deal on recording as many of their observations as quickly as possible, by writing notes which record events or remarks of importance. This procedure is difficult to accomplish for a covert observer, who cannot scribble notes all the time, but must write them up at a later juncture (for example, Cavendish, 1982, p. 7). A delay is clearly undesirable, since important points may be forgotten or distorted with the passage of time. Ditton's report of his attempt to conduct covert observation in a bakery is salutary:

> Right from the start, I found it impossible to keep everything that I wanted to remember in my head until the end of the

day . . . and so had to take rough notes as I was going along. But I was stuck 'on the line', and had nowhere to retire to privately to jot things down. Eventually, the wheeze of using innocently provided lavatory cubicles occurred to me. Looking back, all my notes for that third summer were on Bronco toilet paper! Apart from the awkward tendency for pencilled notes to be self-erasing from hard toilet paper . . . my frequent requests for 'time out' after interesting happenings or conversations in the bakehouse and the amount of time that I was spending in the lavatory began to get noticed. I had to pacify some genuinely concerned work-mates, give up totally undercover operations, and 'come out' as an observer – albeit in a limited way. I eventually began to scribble notes more openly, but still not in front of people when they were talking.

(Ditton, 1977, p. 5)

In other words, regardless of the morally dubious nature of covert observation, this role seems to be associated with a number of tactical difficulties in the field. It is relatively rarely employed in organizational research, although it is not always easy to detect from an author's account of the research process whether a covert role was employed. It should also be borne in mind that the distinction between covert observation and the other two roles can be a matter of degree. Even when participant observers are open, it is unlikely to be the case that all persons with whom they interact will be aware that they are researchers. Further, participant observers often create 'fronts' which only partly reflect their real goals and motives for their investigations, in the context of both gaining access and getting on with people in the organization.

Participant observers in the full and indirect roles do not face these problems, but they are likely to encounter the difficulties of access and reactivity that covert observation deals with fairly readily. Aside from the problem of access, reactivity may occur, implying that subjects' behaviour may be affected by the observer's presence. However, many participant observers argue that this problem becomes less pronounced as the researcher becomes increasingly accepted and part of the scenery. Equally, observers have to minimize the degree to which they themselves intrude in the natural flow of events, for fear that what is observed may be unduly contaminated. Cole (1971) was a full observer (working as a manual worker) in two Japanese manufacturing firms. In one of these – Takei Diecast Company – he found that many of his subjects identified with him and envied his role as an observer during a period that was very trying for his co-workers. At one juncture, there was a major clash between management and the union (as well as within the union itself), which split the workers into different camps in terms of their attitude to the parties to the dispute. The various factions saw Cole as 'a third-party observer who must be won over to their side' (p. 47), a role which he was at great pains to avoid because of the potential for contamination. In the end, Cole suggests that his impact in this affair was marginal: 'Since everyone knew that as a participant-observer I was there for only a limited time and was entirely without power, it is highly unlikely that my presence affected the course of developments' (p. 47), although he also notes that the affair was a valuable source of information. Such problems are likely to be less acute for the covert observer, though this role would not have been feasible for Cole as a Westerner in a Japanese factory.

Most participant observers adopt either the full or indirect roles, the studies by Cole (1971) and Smircich (1983) being examples of these two roles respectively. An interesting insight into these two roles can be gleaned from a discussion by Rosen (1986b), who has acted as a full observer in a small investment banking firm and as an indirect observer in an advertising agency. In the latter study, he spent ten months in the agency during which time he spent up to three weeks with each of various personnel at different hierarchical levels:

> I would sit in a member's office and listen to their phone conversations and business meetings, follow them down the hall to a conference or outside to lunch, and so on. I played softball with their intramural team, went fishing on week-ends . . . and drank beer on some evenings. I was ignored on some occasions and treated like a member of the agency on others . . . People knew that my primary role was as a researcher. I could therefore collect data openly. I mostly did so with a pen and notepad, recording conversations by writing quickly.
>
> (Rosen, 1986b, p. 67).

In addition, he collected an assortment of documentary materials, such as reports, public relations material and memos. In the other study, Rosen became a registered stockbroker, learned about investment banking and participated fully in a range of activities which made up the firm's business, such as facilitating the process of going public for a number of companies and selling stock. He felt that this role would provide him with a deeper understanding of the organization and of what it was like to be one of its employees. On the other hand, although it would appear that the full participant role is preferable, not least because of its greater leverage on the ability to interpret from the perspective of those who are being studied, Rosen encountered some special difficulties. For example, because of his identification with management in the bank, he found it much harder to get non-managerial personnel to discuss matters with him; also, his status of employee, rather than of stranger, meant that individuals were less inclined to impart information that was potentially damaging to them. Further, when he asked people questions in the bank, he found that he became a source of confusion as he attempted to switch from being an employee to a researcher. One might also speculate that it would not have been easy to record data with the same degree of immediacy that was possible in the advertising firm because of work pressures, thereby occasioning problems of memory loss and distortion. However, there can be little doubt that the role of full participant allowed access to layers of understanding about the bank that would not have been readily gleaned from a slightly more removed stance.

Unstructured interviewing

The kind of interviewing normally carried out by qualitative researchers differs considerably from that associated with survey interviews. Whereas the latter tend to be structured, often with closed-ended questions, and standardized, qualitative research interviews are relatively loosely structured. The aim is to elicit respondents' ways of thinking about the issues with which the qualitative researcher is concerned, so that there is usually a preference for minimizing the degree to which they are constrained. While the tendency so far has been to refer to unstructured interviewing, qualitative research exhibits a range of approaches which vary in terms of the degree to which the asking of questions is structured.

Truly unstructured interviews are not guided by a pre-existing schedule; at most, interviewers use an *aide-mémoire* which reminds them of the topics they want to cover, while giving respondents considerable latitude over what they want to say and how they say it. The interview is often started by some general questions, and the *aide-mémoire* topics are activated only to ensure that everything is covered. If the respondent goes off at a tangent or chooses to speak about issues that he or she believes to be important the researcher goes along with the drift of the discussion, often asking questions that seem to be of interest. Gouldner's (1954, p. 248) research in a gypsum mine seems to have employed interviews of this kind: 'after setting the interview on its course we allowed it to go pretty much wherever the respondent wanted it to'. Similarly, Whyte's co-worker – Edith Lentz – used a casual, responsive style of interviewing in the context of an action research project in a hotel, a study that will be examined in Chapter 6 (Whyte and Hamilton, 1965). The following passage, in which Lentz is interviewing a maid – Agnes – about work conditions and relationships, provides a flavour of aspects of predominantly unstructured interviewing:

> AGNES: For one thing they might do something about shelves for glasses. We have usually one shelf for glasses and bottles. . . Don't you think that would be an easy thing to fix?
> LENTZ: Seems so, doesn't it?
> AGNES: That's my idea. Maybe it's not such a good one, but that's my suggestion.
> LENTZ: It sounds like a practical one, and I'm glad to get your idea.
> AGNES: . . . Lorraine [the floor supervisor] says we shouldn't visit on the floor. Well, I can see that, it wouldn't do for us to spend our time talking to one another. We have too much work to do . . . But on the other hand, I don't see why this place should be run like a prison either, do you? Why shouldn't I stop to say hello to the other girls on the floor? What's wrong with that? . . . I don't know, this is a funny place. You are supposed to work alone all day and eat alone, it isn't human . . . Well that's all the suggestions I can think of. Do you like this work?
> LENTZ: Oh, it's a lot of fun, Agnes. I like to talk to people and get their slant on things. One thing I'm supposed to get an understanding of is why we have so much trouble getting good girls and keeping them. It is so discouraging when they stay a day or so and then quit.
> AGNES *(filling up with tears, speaking with great earnestness):* Lorraine brings all the girls to me for their training and I think that's wrong. How can I train them and do my work too? . . .
> LENTZ: How do they arrange it now, Agnes? Like yesterday, for instance, how many rooms did the girl work with you?
> (Whyte and Hamilton, 1965, pp. 224–5)

It is striking that the interview is more like a conversation than the kind of formal question-and-answer format of the survey interview. In fact, only two of the four interventions by Lentz are really questions. Her second intervention generates a stream of gripes and suggestions, of which the remarks about Lorraine are only a part. Lentz is perfectly prepared to allow Agnes to talk for almost as long as she wants about the things the latter finds interesting, but there is the suggestion in Lentz's penultimate intervention that she wants her respondent to address a particular topic. On the other hand, most of Lentz's questions are directly prompted by things that Agnes has previously said, whereas in survey interviewing the interviewer usually simply moves on to the next question. Moreover, Lentz is involved in the interview. She lets Agnes know that she approves of her idea of doing something about the glasses when asked her view. In survey research, interviewers are often instructed not to respond to such prompts from respondents.

Such relatively unstructured interviewing is usually contrasted with semi-structured interviewing, whereby the investigator uses a schedule but recognizes that departures will occur if interesting themes emerge from what respondents say and in order to get their version of things. In Sutton's investigation of dying organizations, general questions were asked and prompts for the interviewer were provided. For example:

> 8 Now I'd like to ask you about the decision to close the organization. Please describe how the decision to close the organization was made. (Prompts: Who participated? How big was the group? Was it secretive? What pressures was the group or individual facing? What information was used? How many different points of view were represented? What were the reasons that the organization was to be closed?. . .)
> (Sutton, 1987, p. 568)

Interviews that are closer to the semi-structured end of the continuum probably risk not gleaning information about what the subject deems to be important about the issues being examined. However, such interviews often give considerable latitude to respondents and are more responsive to lines of answering initiated by respondents.

Documents
The point has been made on a number of occasions that the collection and examination of documents are often an integral element in qualitative research. In his research on eight dying organizations, which was based primarily on interviews, Sutton (1987) used a number of documentary sources. The following account of the sources used in the context of a hospital provides a

flavour of the kind of material that can be employed:

> Budgets, internal correspondence, financial viability study by consulting firm, marketing research on the attitudes of physicians, patients and community members, newspaper articles, press releases, company newsletters, closing plans, closing announcements, and union-management contracts.
> (Sutton, 1987, p. 569)

Such sources of data can fulfil a number of functions for the qualitative researcher. They can provide information on issues that cannot be readily addressed through other methods; they can check the validity of information deriving from other methods; and they can contribute a different level of analysis from other methods (such as the gap between official policy and practice).

Mintzberg (for example, Mintzberg and McHugh, 1985) has conducted a number of investigations on company strategy using a similar research approach within a common framework. Documents are more intensively employed than in most qualitative research. He conceives of strategy differently from the conventional view that it is something that is formulated and then implemented. Instead, he suggests that many intended strategies do not come to fruition, while realized strategies may not always be the products of pre-formulated strategies; that is, strategies may come about without there being a full recognition of their emergence. This conception implies that strategy is something that must be 'tracked' over long periods of time. The investigation of the National Film Board of Canada (NFB) from 1939 to 1975 by Mintzberg and McHugh (1985) serves as a good example. The research approach comprised four stages. First, basic data were collected from archives to trace decisions and actions taken by the NFB, to pinpoint environmental changes and to provide performance measures. Where these documentary sources (such as annual reports and film catalogues) were insufficient, interviews were conducted to provide the necessary information. For example, realized strategies in terms of various characteristics, such as finance, number and length of films, and staffing, were inferred and examined. Second, decisions and actions were chronologically arranged to infer strategies over time. Six distinct time periods, each reflecting a distinct strategic orientation in the NFB's history, were inferred from this chronological arrangement. Third, interviews were conducted with long-standing employees, and reports were examined to explore the reasons behind major changes in strategy. Finally, there was a theoretical analysis of the materials in order to interpret the various periods and themes. For example, one of the most consistent motifs running through the NFB's transitions was a desire to take advantage of and build on established skills and knowledge.

Although they are widely employed by qualitative researchers, documents are rarely used on their own. In most cases, documents are used to provide additional data and to check on the findings deriving from other sources of data. Mintzberg's research is unusual in the degree of its reliance on such materials. Turner's (1976) qualitative study of the organizational concomitants of disasters is even more unusual in its total reliance on documents. The use of documents will receive more attention in Chapter 7.

Types of qualitative research

In this section, a tentative classification of types of qualitative organizational research will be attempted. The previous discussion of the methods used by qualitative researchers provides a backcloth to the classification, because most of the studies to be described employ various combinations of these approaches to data collection. Like all classifications it should be interpreted as a heuristic device, rather than a perfect representation of its subject matter. On the other hand, unlike many comparable classifications, it focuses exclusively on qualitative research conducted in organizations.

Although qualitative research can be differentiated in terms of a number of characteristics, an important component seems to be the degree of participation in the organization(s) in which the research is conducted. Variations in researchers' levels of participation have implications for their closeness to the organization and its members and the kind of data that are acquired. Rosen's (1986b) research in an agency and a bank reflects this distinction in that his participation in the latter organization was greater by virtue of his being a full participant observer. Moreover, these differences had implications for his experiences as a researcher and for the kind of information he was able to glean in each context. Table 5.1 suggests four types of qualitative organizational research which are arrayed from high to low in terms of the amount of participation in the organization that appears to be in evidence. Each type is described in the table, and some examples of each type are provided. The examples are chosen on the basis of their receiving mention in this book, or being regarded as 'classics' in the field, or being recent studies that have generated considerable interest. A useful exercise for the reader would be to examine how readily instances of

Table 5.1 Types of qualitative organizational research

	Participation		
High ◄——————————————————————————————————————► Low			
Type 1 Total participant	Type 2 Semi-participant	Type 3 Interview-based	Type 4 Multi-site
Researcher is full or nearly full (or covert) observer in one or two organizations. There is an emphasis on participant observation, usually coupled with some interviewing and examination of documents	Researcher is an observer in one or two organizations, but is in an indirect role. Such research is usually accompanied by interviewing and examination of documents	Chief emphasis on interviews in 1–5 organizations, along with examination of documents. Observation may occur, but if it does occur it tends to be in periods between interviews	Chief emphasis on interviews with, or observation of, individuals in 6 or more different organizations, but usually more than 10, and there is usually some examination of documents. Interviewers usually do some observation and observers some interviewing
Burawoy (1979) Cavendish (1982) Cole (1971) Dalton (1959) Ditton (1977) Lupton (1963) Pinfield (1986) Ritti and Silver (1986) Rosen (1986b – investment bank study) Roy (1954, 1960)	Barley (1986) Finlay (1987) Pollert (1981) Powell (1985) Rohlen (1974) Rosen (1986a, 1986b – advertising agency study) Smircich (1983; Smircich and Morgan, 1982)	Bresnen (1988) Bryman et al. (1988) Burgelman (1983, 1985) Collinson (1988) Gouldner (1954) Jackall (1983) Johnson (1987) Pettigrew (1985) Serber (1981) Whyte and Hamilton (1965)	Bennis and Nanus (1985 – 60 chief executives) Goss (1988 – 29 printing firms) Isenberg (1984 – 12 senior executives) Kotter (1982 – 15 general managers from 9 companies) Sutton (1987; Harris and Sutton, 1986 – 8 organizations)

qualitative organizational research not mentioned in the table can be subsumed under the types that are detailed.

Type 1 (total participant) studies

With Type 1 studies the researcher is likely to be a participant observer who is a member of the organization, as either a covert or a full observer. Additional data are often collected through interviews and the examination of documents, but the bulk of the evidence tends to derive from participant observation. Of the research previously mentioned in this book, the studies by Cavendish (1982), Cole (1971), Ditton (1977) and Rosen (1986b – the investment bank study) are clear examples. The opportunity to be a full member of the organization can occur in a number of ways, of which covert entry is one. Pinfield (1986) was seconded for two years from his university to a senior staff group in the government of Canada, which afforded him the opportunity of examining decision-making processes at first hand. He was a member of a small task force charged with the responsibility of developing an 'Executive Resourcing Strategy' which would provide a personnel policy framework for the government bureaucracy. In addition to being a member of the task force he conducted interviews with interested parties and senior bureaucrats and examined organizational archives for documentary material. By contrast, Silver (Ritti and Silver, 1986) was integrally involved with the Bureau of Consumer Services (BCS) in Pennsylvania at the time that he conducted his participant observation research on this agency. Shortly after its inception in 1977, the BCS contacted Pennsylvania State University regarding the design of a computerized information system. Silver was working for the university at that time and was appointed project manager to the system. He was subsequently employed by the BCS. Ritti and Silver (1986) detail the agency's manipulation of symbols in creating a framework that would facilitate its growth and survival. The evidence on which the work is based derives from Silver's recorded observations in connection with the agency's contacts with other organizations, interviews and documents relating to its goals and inter-organizational relationships. Members of the BCS were fully aware that Silver was writing up various materials, so he was a full rather than a covert participant observer.

Type 2 (semi-participant) studies

Qualitative studies subsumed under this heading differ from those in the previous section by virtue of the researcher not being a member of the organization. These studies are ones in which the researcher is an indirect participant observer, such as Rosen's (1986a, 1986b) advertising agency research and Smircich's (1983) InsCo investigation. At the very least, the researcher spends a substantial amount of time in the organization, interacts a great deal with members of the organization and relies extensively on the recording of observations, rather than the greater emphasis on interviews that characterizes the Type 3 studies (see below). Powell's (1985) research on how decisions are made by publishing houses about which books to publish is an example of a study in which a great deal of time is spent in the organization (in this instance two), but which is not quite as intensive as the kind of participant observation carried out by Rosen in his advertising investigation. One of the two organizations in which Powell carried out fieldwork is referred to as Apple Press. The initial and main period of fieldwork lasted five months, during which the firm was visited one day per week. The research is described as follows:

> I listened to people describe their work and explain the details of the specific projects with which they were involved. A typical day would find me sitting in someone's office, reading manuscripts that had been submitted, going through editors' correspondence with authors, and looking at sales records. During this time the person would carry on with his or her business more or less as usual, with the exception that about fifteen minutes out of every hour would be spent answering my questions.
>
> (Powell, 1985, p. xxviii)

After this initial period, Powell visited Apple Press much less frequently. He tended to visit people for fairly brief sessions in order to interview them in connection with particular topics about which he had formulated hypotheses.

The chief difference between total and semi-participant studies is largely one of whether the researcher is fully integrated as a member of the organization. Semi-participant studies vary considerably in the amount of participation exhibited. In her study of mediators in two mediation and conciliation services, Kolb (Van Maanen and Kolb, 1985) was treated by the people she was observing as though she were a trainee, and so was able to learn what an apprentice would learn. Accordingly, she was steeped in the cases with which the mediators were concerned and discussed a host of issues about the cases with them. This active involvement is different from the apparently more passive stance that many indirect participant observers practise (for example, Smircich, 1983). Unfortunately, it is not really feasible to effect a subclassification of Type 2 studies along these lines, since researchers do not always provide sufficient detail about their activities to permit such a distinction.

The decision about whether to adopt a total or a semi-participant approach is not a matter of whim or of the researcher's own preferences. First, many organizations will allow a researcher to be around but will not entertain the prospect of having someone work for them. Second, many jobs require specialist training, so that the researcher is effectively debarred from covert or full participant observation. For example, Barley (1986) was an indirect participant observer in two community hospitals in the USA during the year that each introduced its first whole-body computed tomography (CT) scanner and was able to show that this new technology produced quite different organizational arrangements in the two organizations, a finding of considerable significance for the examination of the technology–structure link (Rousseau, 1983). The requirement of learning the technical skills associated with radiology would effectively eliminate the option of conducting a total participant study even if he had been so inclined.

Type 3 (interview-based) studies

Type 3 studies rely much less on participant observation than Type 1 or Type 2 studies; instead, they tend to employ unstructured or semi-structured interviews and documents as sources of data. To the extent that observation occurs, it is largely non-participant, with the researcher being very much on the periphery of interaction, and is undertaken in a somewhat unstrategic manner. Such observation is usually supplementary and something that is carried out in the spaces between interviews or at meal-times.

Burgelman's (1985) research on a new venture division, which relied primarily on unstructured interviews and the examination of documents (see Chapter 1), is an example of an interview-based study. Bryman *et al.* (1988) report the results of a study using semi-structured interviews which sought to examine the perceptions of leadership among individuals in managerial and supervisory positions on three construction projects in the UK. One strand in the investigation was the kinds of factor that is perceived by managers as affecting the styles of leadership that they need in order to enhance project performance. The bulk of research on leadership effectiveness has tended to emphasize the role of broad categories, such as task structure or leader's position power, as situational factors that must be taken into account in seeking to maximize performance (Bryman, 1986). Bryman *et al.* found that their respondents emphasized factors that were fairly specific to the construction industry. For example, because construction projects are temporary, time perspective plays an important role in leaders' decisions about the most effective style. As one respondent put it:

> I think a fast job, when there's no room for messing about, you get a much more directive style of management. I think if you get time on the job, it's a more consultative style of management, you are more willing to get blokes in to sort the thing out, be together, you've got time for a joint approach. On a really fast job, you can't afford that.
>
> (Bryman *et al.*, 1988, p. 22)

This study involved very little non-participant observation. When such observation occurs in interview-based studies, its role is mainly to augment interviews and documentary materials (for example, Collinson, 1988; Jackall, 1983) and often assists in the formulation of interview questions (for example, Burgelman, 1983). Gouldner (1954) found that the interviewing of miners was made easier by periods of observation, since it enhanced his ability and that of his research team to talk meaningfully with their respondents about the work.

While the studies in the interview-based group tend, as their name implies, to emphasize interviewing, a study by Pettigrew (1985) of organizational change in four divisions and the head office of Imperial Chemicals Industries (ICI) in the UK made considerable use of documents. In this research, Pettigrew looked in particular at the intervention and effects of organization development (OD) consultants. The research was specifically concerned to elucidate processes over time, so an explicitly longitudinal approach was designed. Over the period 1975 to 1983, Pettigrew interviewed 134 ICI employees (some more than once). The interviews were semi-structured and derived from Pettigrew's reading of the relevant literature and from conversations with some ICI employees to produce 'a very open and flexible set of themes and questions' (1985, p. 40). Some 500 hours of tape-recorded interviews were produced. Crucial documents concerning the company were scrutinized (such as documents relating to company strategy, to organizational changes and to the training and use of OD consultants), while informal conversations and some observation in factories and offices provided additional data. The period covered by Pettigrew's research was 1965 (the year in which OD work got under way) to 1982. Thus, some of Pettigrew's data derive from retrospective questioning of key figures (covering the period 1965 to 1975), but from 1975 the data are (as he puts it) in 'real-time'. A broadly similar approach can be discerned in Johnson's (1987) study of strategic change at Foster Brothers, a menswear retail chain. Through the combination of retrospective and concurrent interviewing over a number of years and past and present high-level documentary evidence, these studies constitute a form of interview-based qualitative study in which an explicit longitudinal emphasis is thoroughly exploited.

Type 4 (multi-site) studies
Type 4 studies entail the collection of qualitative data in a number of different organizations, unlike research subsumed under the other categories, which rarely involves the collection of data in relation to more than two organizations and in any case not in excess of five. The methods are fairly varied; Isenberg (1984) and Kotter (1982) employed a combination of observation and interviews, Sutton (1987) interviews and documents and Bennis and Nanus (1985) and Goss (1988) interviews alone. Because of the researcher's involvement in a number of organizations, the amount of time spent in each is generally considerably less than that exhibited by the three other types. Isenberg (1984) spent a mode of two and a half days with each of the dozen executives he investigated. Sutton (1987) carried out a maximum of eight interviews in each of the dying organizations he studied.

Kotter's (1982) research entailed a number of different methods of data collection. He observed fifteen general managers (GMs) in a largely unstructured manner for a total of 500 hours. He spent nearly 100 hours interviewing them and 200 hours interviewing people with whom they worked. In addition, relevant written documents were accumulated and two question-naires were administered, the latter largely to provide data on background and personality. To provide a flavour of the observational evidence collected by Kotter, the following record from a conversation between one GM (Thompson) and two of his subordinates (Dodge and Smith) is provided:

THOMPSON: What about Potter?
DODGE: He's OK.
SMITH: Don't forget about Chicago.
DODGE: Oh yeah. (Makes a note to himself.)
THOMPSON: OK. What about next week?
DODGE: We're set.

THOMPSON: Good. By the way how is Ted doing?
SMITH: Better. He got back from the hospital on Tuesday.
(Kotter, 1982, p. 89)

This passage, which has been extracted from a much longer conversation, is utilized by Kotter to illustrate that many of the conversations he witnessed appear highly chaotic, but in fact were extremely efficient. Four tasks were achieved in a matter of seconds:

1 He learned that Mike Potter has agreed to help on a specific problem loan. That loan, if not resolved successfully, could have seriously hurt his plans to increase the division's business in a certain area.
2 He reminded one of his managers to call someone in Chicago in reference to that loan.
3 He also learned that the plans for next week, in reference to that loan, are all set; these included two internal meetings and a talk with the client.
4 He learned that Ted Jenkins was feeling better after an operation. Ted worked for Thompson and was a reasonably important part of his plans for the direction of the division over the next two years.

(Kotter, 1982, p. 90)

These passages illustrate well the potential of the kind of data that derives from the use of observation (usually a 'fly-on-the-wall' approach) in multi-site studies. When interviewing is conducted, it is usually to provide information about a focal individual (for example, Kotter) or about organizations (for example, Sutton). Further, inferences are made across individuals or organizations; the GM, Thompson, is taken to exemplify a pattern or tendency common to most of the GMs he observed. Although multi-site studies could be viewed as veering in the direction of survey research, the search for common features is consistent with Van Maanen's (1983, p. 257) suggestion that 'qualitative work is more concerned with commonality and things shared in the social world than it is with differentiation and things not so shared'.

Comparing the four types
All social research is subject to trade-offs; even when researchers do their hardest to dovetail research problem and research method or design, it is rarely possible to avoid certain pitfalls or disadvantages in the choice(s) made. In reality, much research

entails an attempt to maximize 'damage limitation'. Similarly, the four types delineated thus far allow the concerns of qualitative research to be realized in different ways and degrees. The seven distinguishing features of qualitative research encountered earlier in this chapter can serve as a framework. These features are a matter of considerable importance to qualitative researchers, many of whom have seen their tradition as a movement to challenge the orthodoxy represented by quantitative research (see, for example, Morgan and Smircich, 1980).

First, while all four types display a concern to forge interpretations in actors' own terms, the degree to which this occurs varies considerably. Van Maanen (1982) has observed that while the insider/outsider distinction is often employed to distinguish qualitative and quantitative research, it can also be used *within* the qualitative tradition. An outsider perspective in qualitative research is likely to occur when 'the framework selected by the researcher to interpret what is observed is not one that would be thought obvious, natural, or probably very interesting by those studied' (Van Maanen, 1982, p. 18). The reliance on interviews in interview-based and some multi-site studies might be taken to indicate that the degree of penetration of, and fidelity to, the perspectives and interpretations of those studied is less pronounced (since the researcher's participation and involvement in the organization are less marked) than in total and semi-participant studies. Except in the case of the most unstructured interviews, some kind of guide or schedule is produced which is bound to reflect the preconceptions of researchers, even though they may try very hard to detect and follow up subsequently those matters that are of particular concern to their interviewees. However, the outsider element can be discerned in other study types. Pinfield's (1986) total participant study involved an attempt to test and evaluate two views of the decision-making process: the structured perspective that views it as a rational, orderly sequence and the anarchic perspective that views decision-making as a much more random, haphazard activity. However, this way of thinking about decision-making probably departs quite considerably from participants' perspectives. Therefore, although there may be a tendency for total and semi-participant studies to exhibit greater fidelity to members' interpretations, there can be exceptions.

The contextual emphasis tends to be less pronounced in the multi-site studies than in the rest. The requirement of developing common themes across a number of cases often entails a sacrificing of the contextual nuances that are usually evident in the other types. Third, there does not seem to be anything inherent in any of the types that inhibits the infusion of a processual element, but it tends to be handled in different ways. In total and semi-participant studies, processes, in the sense of interconnections of events over time, tend to be observed as they happen; in interview-based and multi-site studies, processes are usually inferred from documents and retrospective questioning of informants. Pettigrew's (1985) ICI research is an exception in that aspects of change could be established through ongoing interviewing. An example of retrospective questioning leading to clear inferences about processes is Sutton's (1987) study in which a model is produced that depicts the interpretation shifts that occur as members of dying organizations initially view their organizations as permanent but struggling, then as dying and then recognize that death has occurred. The role of leaders in bringing about these interpretation shifts is articulated within this process model.

Fourth, multi-site studies are probably the most structured of the four types, because of the need to draw reasonably comparable data across different cases. Interview-based studies tend to be somewhat more structured than total and semi-participant studies, whose broadly unstructured approach means that they usually exhibit greater flexibility. On the other hand, in his interview-based study of one of five construction projects, Bresnen (1988) notes how some chance remarks in a pub which implied some conflict between senior and junior management which he had not picked up previously prompted a new line of inquiry.

Fifth, virtually all of the studies that have been examined employed more than one data source, so that the use of multiple methods of data collection does not seem to be associated with a particular study type. Sixth, total and semi-participant studies probably display a greater emphasis on the notion that organizational reality is something constructed by individuals rather than a prior entity that is independent of people. Barley's (1986) study of the introduction of CT scanners emphasizes that the contrasting social structures of the two radiology departments in which he was an indirect participant observer could be attributed to the different patterns of reaction to the new technology as experienced by those personnel affected by it. The social structures were not simply 'there'; they were an outcome of the way in which the technology was integrated into the contrasting social arrangements of the two departments. However, a multi-site study like Sutton's is able to show how organizational definitions of the state of health of dying organizations are substantially affected by leaders' attempts to alter members' perceptions, suggesting that other study types can incorporate this aspect of qualitative research. On the other hand, interview-based and multi-site studies generally seem to place less emphasis on this feature. Finally, total and semi-participant studies generally exhibit much greater proximity to, and first-hand involvement with, the flow of interaction. In interview-based and some multi-site studies, the reliance on interviewing removes the researcher somewhat, creating a layer between researcher and subject.

In summary, studies in which there is a substantial amount of participant observation – as in Types 1 and 2 – probably exemplify the general characteristics of qualitative research better. These are precisely the characteristics on which the proponents of qualitative research have sought to emphasize the uniqueness of their enterprise (for example, Morgan and Smircich, 1980; Rosen, 1986b). However, not all topics and contexts lend themselves equally to a total or semi-participant approach: it is difficult to imagine using such an approach in connection with the long time-spans covered by Pettigrew (1985), for example. Further, interview-based and multi-site studies carry their own special advantages, such as the greater opportunity for studying a number of organizations (and hence potentially greater generalizability) offered by multi-site research.

Some problems in qualitative research

In this section, a number of difficulties in the practice of qualitative research, as perceived by many of its practitioners, will be explored. One particular problem is not covered – the difficulty of generalizing from a single case or a very small number of cases. This topic will be covered in the next chapter when the issue of case study generalization will be examined.

The access problem
One of the most vexed areas for many researchers is quite simply getting into organizations. In much the same way that survey research can engender uncomfortably low response rates, qualitative researchers often report considerable difficulty in getting access to organizations for in-depth studies. Jackall (1983) carried out an interview-based study in four US companies but was also denied access by thirty-six companies. Sutton (1987) initially contacted twenty dying organizations, but was refused access by twelve. Both of these authors remark that the experience of refusal is not always entirely negative, in that it sometimes affords the possibility of collecting some relevant information. Further, there are few rules of thumb to assist in gaining access,

as confirmed in the remark that entry to most organizations 'involves some combination of strategic planning, hard work, and dumb luck' (Van Maanen and Kolb, 1985, p. 11). The following points can be borne in mind when seeking access.

First, intending researchers should not be chary about employing an opportunistic approach. Sometimes, friends or relatives may be able to smooth access. Hoffman (1980) was originally unsuccessful in her attempts to interview the elite members of hospital boards of directors in Quebec, but when she sought respondents on the basis of social ties (for example, known to her or to a member of her family) she enjoyed much greater success. Similarly, Buchanan, Boddy and McCalman (1988) report, in the context of their research on the impact of new technology, that they have tended to be more successful when friends, relatives, or former students have been able to facilitate access.

Researchers differ about whether access should be sought at the top of an organization. Crompton and Jones (1988) recommend this strategy, arguing that trying to secure access through a lower level may mean that much time is spent in negotiations only to be turned down at the last minute by those with the ultimate authority for such decisions. Buchanan, Boddy and McCalman argue that it is sometimes better to seek access through lower levels. This can certainly be advantageous if the researcher is able to interest a manager in his or her prospective research, who will then act as a sponsor. In this context, it is useful to bear in mind Van Maanen and Kolb's (1985) general recommendation regarding the advisability of gaining the support of sponsors who act as go-betweens in relation to organizational gatekeepers. One potential problem with entry solely through top management is that of subsequent identification with this group and hence resistance by other parties (such as trade unions) to the research (Beynon, 1988). In such circumstances, entry through both groups may need to be negotiated (Kahn and Mann, 1952). There seem to be few clear recommendations to make about the issue of the level at which access should be attempted, but if one has a contact it may be useful to secure entry through this route; if not, entry through top management may be best, since access often has to be approved at this level in any case.

Third, offering a report can often facilitate access. The desirability of this strategy is mentioned by Buchanan, Boddy and McCalman and a number of contributors to a collection of articles on issues relating to access (Brown, De Monthoux and McCullough, 1976). Indeed, organizations are increasingly taking the initiative in this regard when researchers attempt to negotiate access (Beynon, 1988). The provision of a report is not always required, as found by Smircich (1983) and by Van Maanen and Kolb (1985) in the context of their research on the police and mediators. It is necessary to realize that offering a report carries risks; it may place the researcher unwittingly in the unwanted role of consultant and it may invite restrictions on the dissemination of the researcher's findings if they are not to a firm's liking. However, it may be better to face such risks than the prospect of not securing entry in many cases.

Finally, clear explanations about the researcher's intentions and a preparedness to deal with the firm's reservations and worries (such as over how the information will be used and confidentiality) are essential, as writers like Buchanan, Boddy and McCalman (1988) and Crompton and Jones (1988) have suggested. However, even when entry has been achieved, the access problem is not over because the researcher needs access to people, many of whom will worry about why he or she is 'really' there or whether he or she is 'really' going to evaluate their work. Such worries are common, particularly during the early days in the field (Beynon, 1988; Bresnen, 1988; Buchanan, Boddy and McCalman 1988). Further, the researcher's activities may be restricted by management. Rosen (1986b) was not permitted access in the advertising agency to meetings at which corporate secrets (for example, company strategy) were discussed. Serber's (1981) activities in the state regulation agency were curtailed when his early findings engendered the displeasure of senior managers. There is little that can be offered to assist the researcher in dealing with the political problems that may be encountered (though see Buchanan, Boddy and McCalman and Crompton and Jones), but an awareness of such difficulties may allow obvious mistakes to be avoided.

The problem of interpretation

The qualitative researcher's empirical focus is largely determined by the emphasis upon seeing through the eyes of one's subjects. This invites a consideration of how it is possible to know whether this has been done correctly; how can we be sure that the qualitative researcher really has interpreted organizational reality through the eyes of his or her respondents? Is it not possible that the qualitative researcher has substituted his or her own understanding, one which would be fairly alien to the subjects themselves? This potential problem is heightened because, on the few occasions that anthropological researchers (who provide the paradigm for much qualitative research) have conducted re-studies of tribes and villages, they have frequently failed to agree about how these social worlds should be interpreted (Bryman, 1988a). For example, when Lewis (1951) re-studied a Mexican village that had previously been investigated by Redfield (1930), his findings departed markedly from those of his predecessor; where Redfield had found harmony and co-operation, Lewis encountered conflict and dissensus. Of course, one reason for such disparities may be the passage of time (seventeen years in the case of Lewis). Indeed, re-studies within the context of quantitative research produce similar problems of interpretation (Bryman, 1989). However, the possibility that the two researchers provided different accounts of how their subjects viewed social reality cannot be discounted. Such re-studies do not occur within the context of qualitative organizational research, though when Burawoy (1979) became a machine operator at Allied Corporation he discovered that he was in the same department as that in which Roy (1954, 1960) had been a participant observer thirty years earlier. Obviously, too many years had elapsed for Burawoy to treat his material as a re-study of Roy's research; instead, he used Roy's research in order to chart changes in work practices. Qualitative researchers usually recognize that they cannot provide a definitive account of their subjects' perspectives, a view expressed by two exponents when they write:

> The fieldworker's understanding of the social world under investigation must always be distinguished from the informant's understanding of this same world. . . . To argue that we have become part of the worlds we studied, or that we understand them in precisely the same way as those who live within them do, would be a grave error.
>
> (Van Maanen and Kolb, 1985, p. 27)

In the light of such a recognition, a more helpful way forward would be to concentrate on ways of bringing the researcher's and subjects' perspectives into closer alignment. One approach is through *respondent validation*, whereby researchers provide subjects with an account of their findings for assessment. Buchanan, Boddy and McCalman (1988) fed back interview transcripts to respondents to check information and also reports of their findings 'to check for factual and interpretive accuracy' (p. 65). The latter exercise simultaneously fulfils the requirement of producing a report that is often a pre-condition of access. Unfortunately, it also involves the same risks which were mentioned in the context of the discussion of access, since the exercise may invite censorship. In fact, Buchanan, Boddy and

McCalman report that they have not encountered this problem, but were it to occur censorship would seriously impair the researcher's ability to provide an untainted account of the investigation and might even inhibit publication of the findings.

The fact that qualitative researchers rarely report that respondent validation exercises have been conducted should not be taken to denote that investigations deriving from this tradition are questionable. First, even when respondent validation is undertaken, it is necessary to remember that subjects are not able to validate the inferences that are drawn for the researcher's academic audience. Researchers are rarely content simply to relay their subjects' interpretations, but are invariably concerned to relate such evidence to the concerns of organization studies. Respondent validation is unlikely to assist at this stage where the researcher's conceptual and theoretical skills come into play. Consequently, even if verisimilitude is established, a further tier of interpretations is required as the findings are made available and relevant to other researchers. Second, bearing in mind that much qualitative research involves the deployment of more than one technique of data collection, the opportunity for checking interpretations through different sources presents itself; for example, the interpretation of the meaning of patterns of observed behaviour can be checked through interviews. Third, qualitative researchers' proximity to the people they study makes them less inclined to impute motives and meanings than with other methods. Indeed, the opposite problem can occur: the researcher may become too involved and may experience difficulty in straying from subjects' perspectives, thereby making it difficult to generate a theoretical analysis of the material for an academic audience. Certainly, the disinclination of some qualitative researchers to extract themselves from their data and the tendency to provide an analysis that lacks theoretical concerns have been a source of concern and of difficulty in getting qualitative material published (Daft, 1985). Thus, while the problem of interpretation is not to be taken lightly and it may be advantageous to employ tactics such as respondent validation, the problem should not be exaggerated. On the other hand, as the previously quoted qualifications provided by Van Maanen and Kolb (1985) imply, the capacity of qualitative researchers to see through the eyes of their subjects should not be taken literally.

The problem of data analysis
Many qualitative researchers refer to the experience of being overwhelmed by data (for example, Whyte, 1984, p. 225). This tends to occur because of qualitative researchers' dislike of a

structured approach to data collection and a preference for not sealing off potential issues at a possibly premature stage. In total and semi-participant studies, so much of the field being observed is potential 'data' that there is a problem of knowing what to record, or if almost everything is recorded, what it all means. In interview-based and multi-site studies, the reliance on interview transcripts and documents tends to generate a huge amount of information. As a result of his research on pilferage in a bakery, Ditton (1977, p. 9) had accumulated 'a total of over 4560 hours of participant observation and thirty-four taped and typed interviews', which represents a vast amount of material to explore. While rich and detailed, qualitative data are often seen as an 'attractive nuisance' (Miles, 1979). Unlike the analysis of quantitative data, there are few generally agreed rules of thumb for the analysis of qualitative material. Further, the preference for grounding qualitative studies in subjects' interpretations constitutes a constraint on the kind of analysis that can be undertaken.

When the researcher has a fairly explicit focus, as in the case of Pinfield's (1986) study of the relative utility of two perspectives on decision-making, there is a semblance of structure within which the data can be organized and tentatively conceptualized. Many qualitative researchers prefer a *tabula rasa* approach, whereby they delimit the area they are investigating as little as possible and wait for interesting themes to emerge. The stages at which these themes are handled vary; some researchers prefer this phase to occur at a very late stage in the data collection process (or even at the end) to prevent a premature closure. Ditton's (1977) emphasis on pilfering occurred after his data had been collected. In Ritti and Silver's (1986) research on the Bureau of Consumer Services (BCS), a large amount of collected data resulted in an analysis which was 'presented to the principal actors . . . to verify the accuracy of the observations and to uncover the BCS members' interpretative framework for these key events' (p. 29), that is, a respondent validation exercise. Their observations suggested that 'distinct patterns of interaction' could be discerned, which revealed themselves *inter alia* in relationships with other organizations perceived to be central to the operations of the BCS. In its early years, the BCS was concerned to achieve an air of legitimacy, which was apparent in its relationships with other organizations. In particular, it sought to extend its domain of activities by making a contribution to areas beyond its official mandate. In addition to developing a conceptualization of these inter-organizational relationships as largely ceremonial (that is, established in order to convey a sense of importance), Ritti and Silver related their research to the emerging 'institutional' framework for organizational analysis which postulates that organizations adopt structures and practices to achieve legitimacy in the eyes of the surrounding environment rather than necessarily to solve technical problems.

This example points to a common approach to the analysis of qualitative data, whereby patterns or themes are elaborated and afforded a conceptual coherence, and are then further extended to a wider theoretical domain. The idea of *grounded theory*, advocated by Glaser and Strauss (1967), provides a contrasting approach. This approach seeks to generate theory which is grounded in data and entails a constant moving backwards and forwards between data and emerging theoretical notions. Initially, the researcher elaborates 'categories' that correspond to the data fairly well, undertaking further data collection to refine the categories until confident about their relevance and boundaries. The researcher then seeks to extend these categories by asking what kinds of phenomena can be subsumed under them and by exploring possible connections with other emerging categories. Hypotheses are developed about the links between categories; then the researcher seeks to establish empirically the extent to which the connections and the hypotheses relating to them pertain in a variety of contexts.

Sutton's (1987) study of dying organizations employed many of the main phases recommended by Glaser and Strauss. This tendency is particularly evident in a report of 'parting ceremonies' in such organizations:

In general, our method [of analysis] entailed continually comparing theory and data until we had developed adequate conceptual categories . . . Before and during data collection, we met every week to discuss the emerging theory. Our earliest meetings focused on constructing a rough theoretical framework . . . Subsequent meetings entailed comparing the emerging framework to new evidence from the field study and the organization studies literature; adjusting the framework to allow for new facts and new ideas; and planning to collect new evidence. One week, for example, we noted that former members of dying organizations usually receive invitations to parting ceremonies. We developed hypotheses about the functions such invitations serve. Plans were made to call back an informant and ask him if former members of his defunct organization had been invited to parting ceremonies. Finally, we urged the two other members of the research team to ask informants about such invitations . . . We used this method to

generate a theory about the functions that parting ceremonies serve for displaced members and to identify functions that such ceremonies serve for the management of dying organizations.
(Harris and Sutton, 1986, pp. 10–11)

Examples of the application of grounded theory are growing in number (see Martin and Turner, 1986), but many instances seem not to involve the back-and-forth movement between data collection and theorizing that the foregoing description implies. In some examples, the data are collected and their conceptual elaboration occurs at a later stage. Further, it is striking that Harris and Sutton chose to develop a rough theoretical framework prior to the initial data gathering. While this approach is consistent with Miles's (1979, p. 591) view that qualitative research that eschews a prior framework runs into difficulties at the analysis stage, it is at variance with the preference to postpone theoretical reflection expressed by Glaser and Strauss (1967) and by Whyte (1984). Each way of approaching the analysis of data has its own advantages and the choice of either strategy is likely to be affected by the aims of the researcher (such as the degree of explicitness of the topic being investigated), as well as by his or her preferences regarding fidelity to the ethos of qualitative research.

Overview

Qualitative research is in many respects an oppositional strategy which has gained in popularity since the early 1970s, at least in part as a result of some disillusionment with quantitative research. In addition to being perceived as an alternative to quantitative research, the qualitative style of investigation comprises its own parcel of methods and practices. It should also be clear that qualitative research is not simply quantitative research without numbers; it stands for a quite different set of beliefs about how organizations and their inhabitants ought to be studied. The emphasis upon the interpretations of the subjects being studied is probably its most central motif. Nor does it make much sense to describe quantitative research as scientific and qualitative research as non-scientific. It is certainly the case that many quantitative researchers have sought to exhibit the trappings of the natural sciences in their work, but two points must be registered. First, there is considerable discussion about what constitutes a science, and many writers would balk at a definitive attribution of quantitative research as scientific (see Bryman, 1988a; Keat and Urry, 1975). Further, in the modern world to label something as non-scientific is to imply lack of rigour, of objectivity and of reliability. In fact, none of these three descriptions could be unambiguously applied to qualitative research, and indeed some quantitative research is lacking in these respects. In Chapter 6 the possibility of combining the two approaches will be examined.

Notes

1 This list of characteristics has been drawn from the writings of a number of proponents of qualitative research, such as Morgan and Smircich, 1980, and Van Maanen, 1982, 1983, and of writers concerned with the differences between quantitative and qualitative research, such as Bryman, 1988a.

6

Case study and action research

The case study sits neatly between the research designs that precede and follow it in this book: qualitative and action research respectively. Most qualitative research is in fact a form of case study, though some Type 4 (multi-site) investigations are exceptions. Indeed, some writers treat 'qualitative research' and 'case study' as synonyms. However, not all case studies can adequately be described as instances of qualitative research, since they sometimes make substantial use of quantitative research methods. Similarly, most action research is based on case study investigations, so that the case study, which is examined later in this chapter, overlaps with a number of other designs. Indeed, when survey research or structured observation or field experiments are conducted in just one or a very small number of organizations, there is ostensibly little to distinguish the case study from such quantitative investigations.

Case study research

Some of the classic studies in organizational research have derived from the detailed investigation of one or two organizations, for example, Blau (1955), Gouldner (1954), Roy (1954, 1960) and Selznick (1949). However, the case study went into decline in the 1960s, as the quest for a scientific study of organizations propelled many researchers in the direction of experimental and survey investigations (Daft, 1980). A major reason for the loss of faith in case studies was a prevailing view that it was not possible to generalize the results of research deriving from just one or two cases. In the study of organization structure, this view led to the corollary that it was necessary to focus on samples of organizations, from which generalizations to wider populations of organizations could be derived. This shift in orientation can be discerned in the intellectual passage of Peter Blau from his early study of two public bureaucracies (1955) to later investigations of large samples of organizations (such as Blau *et al.*, 1976). Case study evidence came to be seen as idiosyncratic, since it derived from one or two potentially untypical organizations and seemed to capture less well the scientific approach with its search for universal laws.

The issue of the generalizability of case study research will be examined below, but some attention needs to be given to the nature of the case study. First, what is a case? The classic studies cited in the last paragraph all took the site, such as an organization or a department within an organization, as constituting 'the case'. Blau studied a department in each of two public bureaucracies; Gouldner's research was located in a gypsum plant; Roy conducted his research in a machine shop in a steel-processing plant; and Selznick's research was concerned with the Tennessee Valley Authority. Events and activities can also be viewed as the units of analysis in case studies: an example is the detailed investigation of the decision-making processes leading up to a firm's resolution to purchase electronic data-processing equipment (Cyert, Simon and Trow, 1956). The 'case' can also be a person; the investigation by Gronn (1983) of the ways in which a school principal employed talk as a means of achieving control with teachers is an example. However, places or sites as such usually provide the focus of investigation, and further references to 'case' in this chapter can be taken to refer to places unless otherwise indicated.

Second, 'case study' seems to imply the study of one case, but many examples of such research focus upon two or more sites. A large number of case studies have been based on two sites, such as Barley (1986), Blau (1955), Cole (1971), Lupton (1963) and Powell (1985), while Chandler (1962) in his historical analysis of strategy and structure in corporations, Dalton (1959) in his study of managers and Sutton and Callahan (1987) in their investigation of stigma among bankrupt organizations conducted their research in four organizations. The reasons for including a second case (or more) are usually twofold; the generalizability of the research may be enhanced, and comparisons allow the special features of cases to be identified much more readily. Lupton (1963) conducted two case studies for his research on output regulation among manual workers. One organization did not exhibit output regulation to a marked degree, but the second firm did, and the contrast between the two organizations allowed him to draw out some important themes regarding the environmental and internal organizational factors that are likely to promote regulation. Similarly, Barley's (1986) study of two radiography departments (see page 155), allowed the different organizational consequences of the introduction of CT scanners to be identified. Much larger numbers of sites are feasible. The dying organizations that provided the data for Sutton's (1987) research are described as being 'eight case studies' (p. 544), while Yin's (1979) examination of innovation is based on 'nineteen case studies' (p. 12). When such larger numbers of cases provide the data for an investigation, the distinctiveness of the case study approach becomes questionable, especially since the emphasis on the unique context that is a feature of the case study is easily lost, though this is not to deny the importance of such investigations.

Third, case studies can and do exhibit the whole gamut of methods of data collection. Many examples involve a number of methods within one investigation, and in this connection a later section in this chapter will examine the mixing of quantitative and qualitative methods within a single study.

Fourth, case studies usually comprise a number of emphases, which distinguish them from much quantitative research in particular. There is a strong emphasis on context; readers feel that they know what it is like to be in the organization being studied, and this slant provides a frame of reference for both researcher and reader to interpret events. The usually prolonged involvement of the researcher means that interconnections of events can be traced over time, so that processes can be inferred. It is striking that attempts to provide process models of organizations (models which chart sequences of elements and which are often deemed to be underemployed – Mohr, 1982) almost always derive from case studies (for example, Burgelman, 1983; Sutton, 1987). In the examination of the impact of policy, case studies are increasingly recognized as having an important role (in contrast to the quasi-experimental research that pervades this sub-field), since they are able to illuminate the effects of implementations on everyday activities (Patton, 1987).

The problem of generalization is often perceived as the chief drawback of case study research; indeed, many practitioners adopt an almost apologetic stance when presenting evidence and feel it incumbent upon them to justify their reliance on a single study, as when Burgelman (1985, p. 42) writes: 'Field studies in one setting raise questions about the external validity of the findings.' On the other hand, there is a growing recognition that some of the accusations about the limited generalizability of case studies may be based on an erroneous application of statistical notions which treats the case as a sample of one. Of course, nobody believes that a single case can be representative of a wider population, although within multiple case studies a conscious attempt to increase the range of types of organization investigated may mitigate this point somewhat, as in the studies by Sutton (1987) and Yin (1979). As both Mitchell (1983) and Yin (1984) have argued, case studies should be evaluated in terms of the adequacy of the theoretical inferences that are generated. The aim is not to infer the findings from a sample to a population, but to engender patterns and linkages of theoretical importance. Thus, in the context of his research on new corporate ventures, after noting the apparent problems of external validity, Burgelman writes:

> Living with these concerns [about the external validity of findings] may be a necessary cost of providing new insight in as yet incompletely documented management processes in complex organizations . . . The purpose of such efforts is primarily to generate new insights that are useful for building theory.
> (Burgelman, 1985, p. 42)

This passage makes two points. First, case studies are often useful for providing an understanding of areas of organizational functioning that are not well documented and which are not amenable to investigation through fleeting contact with organizations. Second, the author was concerned to build theoretical insights, such as the process model presented in Burgelman (1983).

But what if GAMMA is totally unrepresentative of firms which have corporate venture activities? Surely this would mean that the theoretical insights that have been induced are questionable? Yin (1984) argues that the theory should be tested in comparable contexts to see whether it fits other cases; if it does not, it is likely that the conditions under which the theory operates will need to be specified more precisely. Yin calls this approach a 'replication logic' and argues that it is a more appropriate framework within which to judge the generalizability of case study evidence than in terms of sampling notions. Case study research which examines more than one site often comprises its own replication logic. Thus, in their research on the stigma of bankruptcy, Sutton and Callahan (1987) indicate whether each of the various themes that they identified was strongly or only modestly supported in each of the four firms. The theme 'denigration via rumour', which refers to the spreading of knowledge about the firm's bankruptcy by outsiders (such as former employees and competitors) in order to disparage it, received strong confirmation for three of the organizations, but only moderate support in the fourth. Further, because of their reliance on a number of informants and of methods of data collection, the degree of fit between each theme and the data for each organization could be gauged.

In addition to permitting the generation of theory, case studies can serve a number of other purposes. First, they can be employed in a somewhat exploratory manner in order to achieve insights into a previously uncharted area. Powell (1985) conducted his research into academic book publishing and was concerned with three questions:

(1) How do editors decide which few manuscripts to sponsor, out of the hundreds that flood their desks?. . .
(2) What is the nature of the editorial task? In short, how do editors ply their trade?. . .
(3) What are the specific ways in which scholarly houses are embedded in a larger social context?

(Powell, 1985, p. xix)

The questions with which he started out are very general and do not seem to have been motivated by a strong desire to build theoretical ideas out of his evidence. This is not to say that he was unconcerned with theoretical issues; for example, he shows how his evidence on decision-making has implications for approaches like the 'garbage can' model (Cohen, March and Olsen, 1972) which views organizational decision-making as much more haphazard and non-strategic than is usually implied by approaches which emphasize rationality. While Apple Press exhibited the characteristics of the garbage can model, the second case study – Plum Press – was closer to the tenor of rational models of decision-making. This difference prompts a consideration of what factors might account for such differences among apparently similar firms, which led to a discussion of the contrasting ways of organizing the editorial task at each of the two presses. This point illustrates the uses to which a replication logic for examining the generalizability of findings might be put. It is also striking that the use of the case study in this exploratory manner and the conception of the case study as a means of generating theory are very close to the view of science as a voyage of discovery (Selye, 1964).

Case studies can be used in order to test theories. This view stands in marked contrast to the idea that they mainly allow new ideas to be generated. Pinfield's (1986) study of a senior staff group in the Canadian government bureaucracy permitted a test of the two approaches to the study of decision-making with which Powell (1985) had been concerned. He found that they were each appropriate to some contexts but not to others; for example, when there was consensus about goals the rational approach was appropriate, but when a lack of consensus existed the garbage can model worked better. Equally, both were inadequate in some respects, for example, because each neglects the role of environmental factors in decision-making.

Third, case studies can allow the findings from other studies to be confirmed. Several studies have demonstrated the capacity of individuals to invest increasing amounts of time and resources in administrative ventures that evidence suggests are unlikely to come to fruition. In other words, people sometimes allow their commitment to projects of action to escalate regardless of rational assessments of the likelihood of success or failure. The research on this topic has highlighted a number of variables that lead either to escalation or to withdrawal. Although some stable findings have been established, the research has largely derived from laboratory studies, much of which has been based on students (for example, Staw and Ross, 1978). Since the external validity of such research has been questioned by some writers (see Chapter 3), corroborating evidence from another source would reduce such doubts. In this connection, Ross and Staw (1986) examined Expo 86 in Vancouver as a possible manifestation of the escalation pattern. A variety of documents constituted the chief data source, and some interviews with reporters and staff personnel were conducted. By and large, the phases in the process of escalation and the forces which promote it were confirmed by this case study. The advantage of this case study is that it confirmed the results of research whose applicability to the real world was inhibited by its grounding in laboratory research.

Combining quantitative and qualitative research in case studies
Case studies provide one of the chief arenas in which quantitative and qualitative research can be combined. Most case study research involves more than one method of data collection, but this derives from the tendency for qualitative research, which typically employs two or more sources of data, to be intensively used. The combination of quantitative and qualitative research offers further possibilities. One of the most obvious advantages of deploying the two in tandem is to check the validity of findings using very different approaches to data collection, as suggested by the research reported by Faules (1982) and Jick (1979). The former study, which was concerned with issues relating to performance appraisal, was conducted in a local government agency in the USA. Data were collected by survey questionnaire and semi-structured interviews. The questionnaire comprised fifty-one items concerned with contentious aspects of appraisal (such as goals, feedback, and judging its importance) and was administered to 250 employees in the agency, of whom 138 responded. The semi-structured interviews were conducted with sixty-two individuals and dealt with what people talk about in

connection with appraisal and with 'stories' about performance appraisal in the agency. Stories have become a topic of increased interest as a result of the emergence of organizational symbolism and culture as important areas of investigation (Dandridge, Mitroff and Joyce, 1980). Faules concentrated on two areas: the functions of appraisal and the perceived quality of the system. Areas of convergence were found, for example, with both sets of data pointing to a questioning by employees of the relationship between performance ratings and job performance. Also, the questionnaire data provided evidence of differences in the responses of supervisors and subordinates, which was supported by the analysis of stories. However, divergent findings emerged as well. The stories picked up a phenomenon referred to by Faules as 'change in evaluation', which occurs when an initial appraisal by a person's superior is changed by someone else; this practice was seen as unfair by subordinates, but deemed acceptable by supervisors, who believed in the importance of comparing people's ratings and of ensuring that they were not excessively skewed. However, this element had not been included in the questionnaire and so was not addressed by this method. Further, although Faules believes that the results were broadly consistent, the nature of the information gleaned was often divergent; the questionnaire provided data on general attitudes, while the stories allowed access to the issues of why particular views are held and how people make sense of the appraisal process.

This example suggests that, in addition to allowing the cross-checking of data, the use of quantitative and qualitative research in conjunction may often allow access to different levels of reality. Precisely because quantitative research and qualitative research have their own strengths and weaknesses, it is not difficult to envisage that each will be relevant to some issues but not to others. A study by Schall (1983) takes this principle to an extreme. She was concerned to establish how far a 'communication-rules' perspective could provide a viable approach to organizational culture. This perspective draws attention to the 'tacit understandings (generally unwritten and unspoken) about appropriate ways to interact (communicate) with others in given roles and situations' (p. 560). The research was undertaken in a large investment company and focused upon two interfacing groups. Her concern was to distinguish the groups' communication rules. The study was conducted in five phases. Initially, following an orientation meeting of both groups with the researcher, a questionnaire to determine individuals' styles of influencing others in each group was devised. In phase 2, documents (such as annual reports and speeches) were scrutinized to discover officially sanctioned rules for influencing people within the organization. The resulting influence rules were assessed by a corporate executive and revised accordingly. In phase 3, three approaches to data collection were in evidence. Schall was a participant observer for one month in each group. She conducted unstructured interviews with each group member, asking such questions as: 'How do people here generally go about getting what they want or need? What works best?' Schall carried out two card-sort exercises at the end of each interview. In one exercise, a deck of thirty-eight cards, with each card carrying information about a compliance strategy, was sorted by each respondent in terms of whether the strategy was likely to be influential in the individual's group. The three sets of data were examined for patterns which could be taken as indicative of informal rules. In phase 4, a 'workplace rules' questionnaire was developed and administered. This questionnaire comprised sixty statements, and respondents had to indicate whether the statement was operative and ethical. Fifty of the statements derived from the phase 3 exercise and ten from phase 2. Five descriptions of each of the two cultures were built up from the various data collection exercises (two from the influence styles questionnaire, one relating to formal rules and two deriving from the workplace rules questionnaire) and submitted to members of the two groups to establish how far the descriptions captured their own perceptions. The data deriving from phase 4 (which reflects the communication-rules approach) fared best, suggesting that it provided a superior account to one based solely on the influence styles questionnaire or one based on top management's formal rules. Schall's study demonstrates the utility of employing quantitative and qualitative methods at different stages of the research process and in relation to different facets of the topic being investigated (see also Gross, Giacquinta and Bernstein, 1971, for a further example).

Overview
There has been a slight renaissance for the case study since the late 1970s, as predicted to a certain degree by Daft (1980). This renaissance can in part be attributed to the increased use of qualitative research, since the two often go hand in hand. These changes should not be exaggerated, in that quantitative research still prevails in organizational research. A major problem for the case study has been the accusation of limited generalizability. In this chapter, the view that this accusation entails a misunderstanding of the nature of case study research has been examined.

The arguments of Mitchell (1983) and Yin (1984) suggest that it is the purpose of the case study to permit the generation of theory, not to be considered a sample of one. Indeed, when it is borne in mind that much survey research and field experimentation are based on one or a very small number of organizations, the uniqueness of the case study's disability is less striking. On the other hand, Yin's notion of a 'replication logic' approach to the generalizability of case study research is not entirely convincing. It works fairly well in the context of research across a number of sites carried out by an investigator (for example, Sutton and Callahan, 1987). As a prescription for programmes of research in which subsequent investigators carry out replication tests, it works less well. First, replication is often deemed to be a low-status activity and is frequently difficult to publish (these two points are related). Second, the results of case re-studies are notoriously difficult to interpret, because, if a subsequent researcher attempts to test the theoretical ideas deriving from an earlier case study and finds a lack of correspondence, there are numerous reasons for this eventuality: the theory is wrong; the place is different; the time period is different; the researcher's values may have had an impact; or different approaches to data collection. Multiple case studies go some of the way towards removing these worries, but when large numbers of cases are involved, such as nineteen in Yin (1979), some of the distinctiveness of case study research is lost. However, case studies may sometimes be more attractive to practising managers, since their closeness to detail and familiarity with ongoing organizations can be more meaningful to them than the preoccupation with often abstract variables that characterizes much quantitative research.

Action research

Action research can reasonably be conceptualized as a research design which entails a particular framework within which the relationship between researcher and subject takes place. There are a number of different versions of the precise constituents of action research (Ketterer, Price and Polister, 1980; Peters and Robinson, 1984), but it is possible to infer some essential ingredients which are roughly common to the various traditions (Hult and Lennung, 1980). Action research is an approach to applied social research in which the action researcher and a client collaborate in the development of a diagnosis of and solution for a problem, whereby the ensuing findings will contribute to the stock of knowledge in a particular empirical domain. The emphasis tends to be upon the need to understand a total system in conducting such an analysis, so that many action research projects are in fact special kinds of single case study, though there are examples of multiple case study projects (Seashore, 1976). The whole gamut of research designs and approaches to data collection can be and have been deployed in action research; indeed, in suggesting that action research is a type of research design, the point is really being made that it has a distinctive approach to the purposes of research and to the relationship between researcher and subject, since it can entail the various research designs (and research methods also) covered in this book. Susman and Evered (1978) go even further in viewing action research as a distinct epistemology which they contrast to the prevailing positivist ethos of much organizational research.

The term 'participative' is often used as an adjective to describe certain forms of action research, and indeed is increasingly being employed (Whyte, 1984). The term is used to distinguish action research in which senior members of an organization have almost total control over the definition of a problem, as well as over reflections on its solution, from a participative approach which entails the following features:

> (1) The professional researcher is responsible not simply to organizational heads, but structures relations so as to be accountable also to lower-level officials and the rank and file. In industry, this may be done particularly by working with and through a union.
> (2) Organization members at various levels participate in the project design and research process including reporting findings.
>
> (Whyte, 1984, p. 168)

Some early action research did not exhibit this participative quality. Whyte's own research in a hotel (Whyte and Hamilton, 1965) was originally written up as an exercise in action research, but is now referred to as 'research in an organization development framework' (Whyte, 1984), presumably to distinguish it from participative action research. The element of participativeness does not seem to be a necessary ingredient of action research; while many definitions stipulate that action research is collaborative, this collaboration generally denotes the nature of the relationship between researcher and client. Since 'the client' can simply be represented by senior managers, the involvement of a large constituency within the organization is not a necessary feature.

As some of the preceding discussion implies, what is and is not

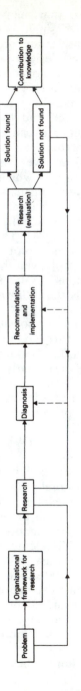

Example (based on Pasmore and Friedlander, 1982)

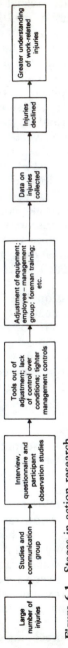

Figure 6.1 Stages in action research

action research is a definitional problem of considerable magnitude. The top diagram in Figure 6.1 is an attempt to detail some
of the chief characteristics. The figure implies an iterative process
which moves from problem recognition to data collection to
diagnosis to formulation of action to implementation to evaluation. If an action programme is unsuccessful, the process may be
reactivated at one of a number of points. The figure should be
seen as a model which captures many central ingredients and
processes associated with action research, but from which
numerous departures can be anticipated when examining specific
instances.

In order to expound the chief characteristics of action research
it is proposed to proceed by an illustration from Pasmore and
Friedlander's (1982) report of a participative action research
programme. An attempt is made in Figure 6.1 to relate features
of this study to the model of action research. The research site
was a plant employing 335 people in the production of consumer
electronics items. The authors describe the plant as imbued with
a strong production orientation which largely emanated from the
plant manager. Most jobs were simple and repetitive. The plant
manager approached the authors to solicit their assistance in
connection with a pervasive problem of work-related injuries, in
that a large proportion of employees suffered from 'damage to
muscles in the wrist, forearm and shoulder' (p. 345), a condition
later identified as tenosynovitis. In some cases, the condition was
very serious. The problem was worsening. Five years prior to the
authors' involvement only two or three injuries per year were
reported; two years later, there were almost forty; and at the
time of the approach, the number of injuries was approaching
eighty. The plant manager had commissioned a number of
environmental studies of the plant and physiological examinations of the employees, but had never sought the employees'
views of the causes of the problem. These studies were not very
conclusive, but a number of patterns in the data (for example,
some shifts were affected, but others were not) led to the
conclusion that employees' reactions to work were more
instrumental in the injury problem than the work itself, a view
that prompted the manager to turn to social scientists for help.

Pasmore and Friedlander assembled various personnel (five
employees, two foremen, a manager and themselves) to form the
Studies and Communication Group whose function was 'to direct
the investigation and convey results and recommendations for
change to employees and management' (p. 348). The group
formulated a number of data collection strategies which were
based on their delineation of various hunches about possible

causes of the problem. The chief strategies were: open-ended interviews administered to employees, containing questions about their work, the climate of the firm and aspects of their injuries if they had experienced them; a questionnaire survey of employees, covering attitudes to their work and management, stress, working conditions, participation in decision-making, etc.; and participant observation by members of the group. These various studies helped the researchers to identify a constellation of factors that are summarized in the following passage:

> First, the necessary repetitive hand movements associated with tenosynovitis injury were present, compounded by tools out of adjustment, which caused victims to exert more pressure than they normally would. Second, the self-pressuring workforce [victims were found to be more conscientious and responsible than their peers] was unable to feel in control of its working conditions because of the organization's structure and management methods. Demands to increase productivity and unnecessarily tight supervisory control probably caused the tension that produced the initial injuries. Then, mass psychogenic contagion reactions occurred that resulted in large increases in stress and in the number of people affected. Injuries slowed production, which resulted in management's imposing even tighter controls and greater demands for production.
>
> (Pasmore and Friedlander, 1982, pp. 353, 354, 355)

On the basis of these findings, the Studies and Communication Group composed sixty-one recommendations for change, most of which were accepted by the plant manager. The data were fed back to all employees in conjunction with a list of actions that were to be introduced immediately to deal with the problem, including: continued adjustment of equipment; the continuation of the group; the establishment of an employee–management group to test possible work redesign changes in jobs which had been particularly prone to injuries; and the introduction of foreman training. Some months after the intervention had begun, two unforeseeable events occurred. The group concerned with work redesign discovered that the metal used for welds was of poor quality, and the employment of better quality materials enhanced the plant's productivity and product quality. Second, both the plant manager and supervisor of operations were replaced by new personnel. Pasmore and Friedlander argue that these changes may have been attributed to the action programme, and may have fostered a view that these new personnel would be more sensitive. The action research programme, in tandem with these unanticipated events, had a material impact; four years after the point at which the action research started, injuries were at a rate of only two or three per year. Further, materials usage and labour efficiency were enhanced.

Of course, the research lacks conventional standards of rigour in a number of ways. We do not know which particular changes had a beneficial impact on injuries, nor how far they would have had an impact without the unanticipated changes (although there was a clear decline in injuries prior to the occurrence of these unforeseeable events). Further, there is always the possibility that, in a situation in which there was widespread concern regarding an apparently intractable problem about which those affected were not consulted, *any* participative approach to problem-solving would have worked. On the other hand, as the authors note, more rigorous methods might have been a good deal less effective because they probably would not have involved the employees themselves in the search for a solution to the same degree.

This study exemplifies a number of characteristics of action research. The investigation is explicitly concerned with problem-solving, but also contributes to our understanding of industrial injuries and the effects of organization structure and job design on the experience of work. The research was carried out in a participative climate, in that the employees identified hunches and participated in the design and administration of the research instruments. Thus, action research contrasts with a consultant–client relationship, in which employees may have little or no participation in the nature and direction of the research effort, and in which there is little interest in the possible contribution of the investigation to the stock of knowledge. Further, the implementation stage is crucial, in that the fruits of research and proposed recommendations are rapidly introduced and their effects analysed. Unlike much so-called applied research, action research comprises a framework for the application of findings (Cherns, 1969). Further, Pasmore and Friedlander's report illustrates the tendency for much action research to reveal a concern for the understanding of the whole system, rather than the specific problem itself (Hult and Lennung, 1980), since the research broadened into an understanding of the plant's organization structure and climate.

Pasmore and Friedlander's investigation provides an example of action research that operates largely within the framework of quantitative research. A number of action researchers have conducted investigations which are much more consonant with the qualitative approach depicted in Chapter 5. The afore-mentioned hotel study by Whyte and Hamilton (1965) is an example of such an investigation. Whyte gave a talk at the Hotel Tremont on his previous research in restaurants which was attended by the hotel's vice-president and general manager, Mr Smith. The latter was impressed by the presentation and asked Whyte to recommend someone trained in human relations for the post of personnel manager at the hotel, a position that had been occupied by three previous incumbents in just over a year. This level of turnover appears to have prompted warning bells to sound in Whyte's head, and he proposed that, if Smith would accept and finance an action research project in the hotel, Whyte would be able to recommend a personnel manager and a researcher. The proposal was accepted, and Meredith Wiley and Edith Lentz respectively took up these positions. On the face of it, these beginnings seem to belie the notion, explicitly suggested in Figure 6.1, that action research is problem-driven. On the other hand, the turnover of personnel managers could be interpreted as a symptom of underlying human relations prob-lems within the hotel. Further, early probings by the researchers pointed to a constellation of interpersonal and organizational problems. Supervision was very autocratic, and senior managers were remote and indifferent to the needs and suggestions of lower-level employees, such as waitresses. When things went wrong in the hotel's functioning, individuals, rather than procedures, tended to be blamed. Consequently, the hotel tended to resist the introduction of changes. In addition, Whyte and Hamilton found high levels of turnover in many jobs, conflict between factions and unclear lines of authority. It seems likely that Smith was aware of the personnel problems that his organization faced, although he probably did not perceive them in the same terms. He had not articulated these problems to Whyte at the outset, although the turnover among personnel managers was recognized.

Whyte and Hamilton employed a combination of unstructured interviews and direct observation in various sections of the hotel. The general procedure was for Lentz to collect information which would then lead to some proposals about the reorganization of work. Since there was a strong autocratic climate within the hotel, proposals had to be handled diplomatically so that they were not perceived as usurping the authority of the various supervisors. The approach that the investigators often took was for Wiley to discuss with supervisors the desirability of holding group meetings in which work and interpersonal problems could be aired. Lentz attended these meetings and discussed with various employees their responses to them. This information provided Wiley with feedback, some of which was passed on to the supervisors, who were appraised of how well the group meetings were going. In addition, information about grievances and problems that was being gleaned from the group meetings was funnelled upwards to Smith, in order to mitigate his remoteness from the workflow.

The first department in which this framework was used was the coffee shop, which serves well as an illustration. This section had the second highest level of turnover within the hotel. Lentz carried out in this section an intensive study which involved 'observations at various hours of the day, the rush periods and the recovery ones, and also interviews with all personnel beginning with the supervisor' (Whyte and Hamilton, 1965, p. 40). Among other things, the interviews revealed that the waitresses were irked by the many complaints they received from customers regarding their failure to keep the water glasses full. According to the waitresses, the problem was a result of there not being a water spigot that was accessible without their having to walk long distances. The waitresses were also annoyed that there were no rubber mats on the steps leading to the kitchen, since this meant that they often slipped while carrying dishes and was viewed as further evidence of management's indifference to their welfare. These were two among a number of grievances about the physical environment in which they worked. They also complained of the autocratic and punitive style exhibited by various supervisors, and there was considerable conflict with the kitchen staff. Group meetings of coffee shop staff were started, and soon afterwards a new spigot and rubber mats appeared. However, the long-standing tension between the waitresses and the kitchen staff was still simmering, and it was decided to hold a coffee shop meeting to which the chef was invited:

It was quite a meeting. At first the waitresses, politely but plainly, told the chef of the troubles they were having. For one thing they were having trouble getting fruit juices. The pantry girls didn't want to be bothered pouring it out glass by glass. For another thing, the cooks played favorites and that got everyone upset . . . The chef [who had to be coaxed to attend after initially failing to turn up] answered them calmly, asking for suggestions on such things as the fruit juice crisis. The waitresses suggested that the juices be poured into pitchers so they could pour out glassfuls themselves as needed, and he agreed to so order it. There was remarkable give-and-take at this meeting, and by the time it came to a close the chef had the girls asking him for advice where at first they had had only criticisms.

(Whyte and Hamilton, 1965, p. 51)

In addition to the alleviation of these specific problems, the general atmosphere within the coffee shop improved. The spigot and rubber mats, for example, were 'symbolic of a new relationship between top management and the employees' (pp. 52–3).

The framework within which this investigation occurred was broadly similar to the model depicted in Figure 6.1. One stage that is strikingly absent is the setting up of an organizational apparatus that parallels Pasmore and Friedlander's Studies and Communication Group. In part, this tendency reflects the absence of the involvement of lower-level employees in the hotel in the formulation of the research problem, in the development of research questions and methods and in the interpretation of the findings. Where this participative element is omitted, the setting up of an organizational framework is likely to be missed out as well, as implied by the extra loop in Figure 6.1 that skips this stage. The involvement of such personnel is highly desirable so that the action researcher does not become an instrument of management which is indifferent to the needs of all members of an organization. Cherns (1975, p. 28) has observed that all action research which aims to introduce organizational change smacks of manipulation; this suggestion is likely to be even more pro- nounced when lower-level employees are not involved. But ethical problems associated with action research do not end here. Rapoport (1970) raised a number of ethical questions such as whether the goals of the organization (such as a tobacco company) are relevant to decisions about taking on an action research study. Clark (1976) raises the problem of knowing how to respond when a firm vetoes the action researcher's proposals for generating data. He reports the example of a firm that requested assistance in dealing with problems of low morale, conflict and sabotage. The management preferred a survey study of worker morale and also insisted on the right to accept or reject the project's findings. The researchers preferred experimental studies of autonomous work groups, but this direction was refused, as was a request to allow the researchers to seek the permission of the unions. Indeed, there is always the possibility that a firm will refuse to implement proposals because it does not like the researcher's findings, for example, because they are implicitly critical of the management. Thus, there are a number of ethical and political dimensions to action research which, while not unique to it, certainly appear in sharp relief. On the other hand, it has considerable support among some researchers because it constitutes an ethical alternative to consultancy, it can be carried out within a framework of making a contribution to knowledge and it provides a route for the rapid application of social scientific knowledge.

Overview

In action research, the investigator virtually becomes part of the arena being studied with the purpose of solving organizational problems. This orientation appears to involve a surrendering of detachment, and it is not surprising that many practitioners display concern about the ethical bases of their enterprise. However, action research is explicitly concerned to develop findings that can be applied in organizations, a position that contrasts with the peripheral relevance to organizations that much organizational research exhibits. Although the basic ideas relating to action research have been around since the 1940s, it has never achieved widespread acceptance; for many researchers it is too close to a consultancy role, while the taint of manipulation and an excessive managerialism has done little to endear it to others.

7

Archival research and secondary analysis of survey data

This chapter examines two similar but analytically separable sources of data employed by organizational researchers. First, archival research, in which the investigator analyses existing documents, statistical sources and other media, will be examined. In such research, new data are not created, though a great deal of detective work may be required to generate the necessary information. As a category of research, it subsumes a wide variety of different kinds of investigation. Second, the secondary analysis of existing social survey data will be explored. Here, the researcher analyses survey data collected by someone else. While secondary analysis of previously collected data can be undertaken in relation to the product of most of the methods encountered in this book, it tends to occur most frequently in connection with survey data deriving from interviews and questionnaires, in part because data deriving from such investigations are often lodged in 'data archives', such as the Economic and Social Research Council Data Archive in the UK and the International Consortium for Political and Social Research in the USA.

Archival research

The use of documentary evidence has been encountered in previous chapters, particularly in the context of its deployment in conjunction with other methods of research such as interviews or questionnaires, but will receive a more explicit treatment here. The materials employed in archival research comprise a number of different types of information: written materials, such as letters, reports to shareholders, memorandums and chief executives' speeches; statistical materials, such as company records which provide data on absenteeism, profitability and size; and compilations of information which provide data on a variety of characteristics of firms, such as *Moody's Industrial Manual, Standard and Poor's Register of Corporations* and *Fortune Plant and Product Directory*, from which statistical evidence can be

Table 7.1 Types of archival research

Type of Data	Method of analysis	
	Quantitative	Qualitative
Recent	*Type I* Bettman and Weitz (1983) Brown (1982) Freeman and Hannan (1975) Grusky (1963) Hinings and Bryman (1974) Kamens and Lunde (1988) Lieberson and O'Connor (1972) Meindl, Ehrlich and Dukerich (1985) Rumelt (1974) Staw, McKechnie and Puffer (1983)	*Type II* Hirsch (1986) Mintzberg and McHugh (1985) Ross and Staw (1986) Turner (1976)
Historical	*Type IV* Barnett and Carroll (1987) Carroll and Delacroix (1982) Carroll and Huo (1986) Delacroix and Carroll (1983) Hannan and Freeman (1987) Meyer *et al.* (1988) Tolbert and Zucker (1983)	*Type III* Chandler (1962) Dunkerley (1988) Staples (1987)

collated. Moreover, the materials may be either relatively recent or historical.

A simple classification of types of study employing documentary evidence can be constructed (see Table 7.1) in terms of (1) whether the data are analysed quantitatively or qualitatively and (2) whether the materials relate to relatively recent events (at the time that the research was being conducted) or are historical. These distinctions yield four types. A number of studies are cited in each cell to provide examples of each type. The studies have been chosen on the basis of their being good and often well-known examples of each type and by virtue of being discussed in this book. When studies cover long time periods which merge with the recent past, such as Carroll (1984) and Carroll and Delacroix (1982), both of which span 1800 to 1975, the research is treated as relating to historical data. In describing a study as involving a quantitative analysis, Table 7.1 does not distinguish between the analysis of already quantified data and the analysis of data which are quantified by the researcher. Further, the classification relates only to research which relies almost exclusively upon documentary materials; studies which make substantial use of other sources of data are excluded, though they will be touched on in the following exposition.

Type I studies: quantitative/recent
In terms of the number of studies that could fill this box, this category is probably the largest. Four major groupings can be distinguished. First, studies of the effects of leadership succession on organizational effectiveness can be subsumed in this category. Early research on this issue concentrated on sports teams (for example, Grusky, 1963) and used records of turnover of personnel like team coaches and managers. Turnover was then examined in relation to subsequent team performance. As Carroll (1984) has observed, the choice of sport as a context for such research was inspired, because measures of performance (such as points, percentage of games won and league position) are readily available and relatively unambiguous. A more recent study (Brown, 1982), examined National Football League (NFL) teams during the period 1970–78; the percentage of games won was related to turnover of coaches, while some organizational variables (for example, number of middle-management officials) were employed to test for conditional and other effects. By no means all of such research has concentrated on sport. Lieberson and O'Connor (1972) conducted their investigation in relation to large US corporations. Data on leadership succession were derived from the annual publication, *Poor's Register of Corporations, Directors and Executives*, for changes in presidents or chairmen of the board between 1946 and 1965. Indicators of performance were taken from sources such as *Moody's Industrial Manual*. The results of these studies have tended to be inconsistent (Bryman, 1986, pp. 194–7); sometimes an effect is observed, sometimes not; sometimes leadership succession precedes better performance, sometimes it precedes poorer performance. In certain respects, such research demonstrates a major problem with the quantitative analysis of documents: how to interpret the ensuing results. For example, this literature concentrates exclusively on succession but with only one or two exceptions says nothing about what leaders do when in office, because the data cannot shed light on this issue, whereas research on leader behaviour has sought to highlight the importance of what leaders do (Bryman, 1986).

Second, much of the research on the relationship between organization size and the administrative component (the ratio of administrators to production personnel or the percentage of administrative staff) has derived from documentary evidence (see, for example, Freeman and Hannan, 1975; Hinings and Bryman, 1974). Many organizations and agencies routinely collect data on numbers of personnel in different occupational positions. Such data have been a fertile source for researchers interested in the ways in which the administrative component is affected by both growth and organizational size. The area has been plagued with definitional problems; different organizations may not always mean the same things when designating employees as 'administrative' or 'clerical', so that an investigation which examines a sample of firms may not be analysing genuinely comparable data.

Third, a number of investigators have content-analysed documents such as chairmen's speeches, newspaper and magazine articles and reports to shareholders. A content analysis entails the quantification of themes in such materials in order to establish their frequency and how variation is related to other variables. Meindl, Ehrlich and Dukerich (1985) analysed both the *Wall Street Journal* and articles in business periodicals for references to leadership and related annual counts of such references to changes in the US economy. Staw, McKechnie and Puffer (1983) analysed letters to shareholders in annual reports to examine 'self-serving attributions', that is, companies' attempts to take credit for success and to deflect blame for poor performance. Letters relating to eighty-one large companies were examined for 1977, forty-nine of which experienced an increase of 50 per cent or more in regular earnings, the remainder a decline of at least 50 per cent. Letters were coded for such topics as whether performance was described as due to the company or to environmental factors. In addition, data on subsequent stock performance were collected; so too was information (also from documentary sources) on the age, tenure and salary of each chief executive who wrote the letters. Self-serving attributions were found to have a positive impact on stock prices, although senior managers often sold stock themselves after prices had increased. A very similar study has been conducted by Bettman and Weitz (1983). Questions are often raised about the reliability and validity of the measures that are derived from content analyses such as these. Investigators often carry out tests of inter-coder reliability but little else. Staw, McKechnie and Puffer used two coders and computed the 'relative incidence of each coding across all causal events noted in a shareholders' letter' (p. 590) for each coder. They then correlated the two sets of codings. While the authors seemed satisfied with the results, the intercorrelations seem disconcertingly low in some instances. For the category 'explicit causes', which denotes whether explicit or implicit reference was made in letters to the causes of performance, the correlation was .11, and for 'industry attributions', which refers to the locus of performance causation in aspects of the industry, it was .23. It is difficult to dismiss the possibility that such low levels of correlation indicate that the measures are of questionable validity.

A fourth area is a major strand of research on strategic management inaugurated by Rumelt's (1974) influential study of the relationship between firms' diversification strategies and their performance. Drawing on the early insights of writers like Chandler (1962 – see below for an account of this work), Rumelt examined data relating to *Fortune* 500 companies (the largest US industrial companies, as listed by *Fortune* magazine) in order to classify firms in terms of their diversification strategies and organization structures and to relate these two variables to financial performance. A sample of 100 firms was taken for each of the years 1949, 1959 and 1969, but because some firms appeared in more than one year the ensuing overall sample size for all three years was 246. The relevant data were culled from a variety of sources, including company annual reports, prospectuses, *Moody's Industrials*, books and articles. Rumelt indicates that the classification of firms in terms of their diversification strategies proved difficult. In order to ascribe companies to categories, he needed data on such matters as what he calls their 'specialization ratio', that is, the proportion of a firm's revenue attributable to its largest discrete product activity. He found company prospectuses to be the best source of information in this respect, because the legal requirement to include all relevant information in these documents 'often produced quite a different view of the firm from that presented in annual reports' (p. 42). Such an experience points to the need for caution in an excessive reliance on one data source, especially one like annual reports which is designed to have a particular impact on various audiences. None the less, annual reports were used extensively to allow firms to be classified according to categories of organization structure. As Rumelt noted, an annual report for a single year may not be very informative in regard to understanding a firm's structure, but a twenty-year sequence can often provide telling information, although the resulting classification of a firm can only relate to one of the three years pertaining to the research. Ten measures of financial performance were employed, such as rate of return on both capital (ROC) and equity (ROE). Rumelt's research has been one of the most important initiators of systematic research into strategic management, and the array of sources used is impressive. However, one of the legacies of the approach for strategic management research has been an excessive preoccupation with very large firms; the intensive use of the *Fortune* 500 or 1,000 as a sampling frame has led to findings which may have limited generalizability to firms in general. Even when their research is not based solely on archival sources, such as when interview or questionnaire surveys are conducted (for example, Hitt, Ireland and Stadter, 1982), the *Fortune* lists are often employed by strategic management researchers.

Type II studies: Qualitative/Recent
Two studies which have been examined in previous chapters – Mintzberg and McHugh (1985) and Ross and Staw (1986) – fall within this category. So too does Turner's (1976) analysis of official reports of three disasters in Great Britain which were used to develop a model (using grounded theory) of the errors of perception and judgement that administrators exhibit which may be major contributors to such phenomena. Hirsch (1986) studied the vivid language that often abounds in 'hostile takeover' contests in the USA. He examined the coverage of such events between 1965 and 1985 in three business periodicals: *Wall Street Journal, Fortune* and *Business Week*. Transcripts of congressional reports and hearings on take-overs were also scrutinized. He also conducted sixty interviews with individuals directly involved in take-over activity (either CEOs or 'deal-makers' with investment banks). The three data sources were used to cross-validate each other. The language and ideologies of the take-over focus

> on such settings as the western, in which the ambush and shoot-out replace the offer made and actions taken; the love affair and/or marriage; warfare, replete with sieges, barricades, flak, and soldierly honor; mystery; and piracy on the high seas, with raiders and safe harbors. Generic formulations also entail the frequent appearance of mercenaries or hired guns (investment houses to which most of the negotiating is delegated) and black and white knights (culled from tales of chivalry in which the distressed damsel is either undone or rescued) . . . In virtually all formulations, the acquiring executive is macho and the target company is accorded the female gender ('sleeping beauty' or a bride brought to the altar); reference to rape also emerged early on.
>
> (Hirsch, 1986, p. 815)

Hirsch shows that the imagery associated with the language of take-overs has changed over time, as the hostile take-over has become both more frequent and routinized. He argues that these linguistic frames serve a number of functions, such as helping participants and observers to make sense of events, or reducing the stigma of being taken over. Hirsch's emphasis on cross-validating findings and inferences does much to assuage doubts that the materials are being incorrectly interpreted.

Type III Studies: qualitative/historical
Studies in this category are ones which bear a strong resemblance to standard historical research. Chandler's (1962) research on the emergence of the multi-divisional form of organization structure in the USA is probably the best-known example within organization studies. Initially, Chandler analysed the business records of a large number of the biggest industrial companies in the USA from the early twentieth century to the 1950s. He employed company reports, articles in periodicals, biographies and various other documentary sources. The hub of his work was detailed studies of four major companies – General Motors, Du Pont, Standard Oil (New Jersey) and Sears, Roebuck – which derived from 'internal company records – business correspondence, reports, memoranda, minutes of meetings, and the like. These historical documents were supplemented by interviews with men who had participated in the organizational changes' (Chandler, 1962, p. 4). Out of these case studies, Chandler showed that population changes, technological developments and shifts in consumer income provided the four firms (albeit at different junctures and in different markets) with new opportunities and imperatives for change that led to a strategy of diversification. This trend in turn put pressure on the co-ordination of the overall organizational effort which existing centralized, functional structures coped with very poorly. Out of these problems the decentralized, multi-divisional structure was born. These phases are charted in all four cases and lead to a general formulation of the role of strategies in fashioning organization structures.

Qualitative/historical studies have been used by a number of writers working within a Marxist perspective. Staples (1987) used parliamentary papers, newspaper and business publications and a previously published business history to elucidate changes in the social organization of work at a British hardware firm, Kendricks, during the period 1791 to 1891. He shows how a patriarchal authority structure gave way in the 1860s to a paternalistic apparatus and how this shift can be attributed to social and economic forces. Staples is cautious not to overgeneralize from the study of a single case, but argues that such case studies can be aligned with similar exercises conducted by other researchers to delineate the variety of forms that capitalist production has generated.

The decision to use historical documents is not one that the non-historian should take lightly. Dunkerley (1988) describes how his planned study of the Royal Naval Dockyard in Plymouth went through a number of changes, which in part reflected a failure to appreciate fully certain types of problem. He had originally intended to examine census enumerators' books since 1851, since they were known to be kept at the Public Record Office at Kew. In fact, he found that much of what he had intended to use was no longer available or was 'obscurely catalogued' (p. 86). Also, working on census materials proved more difficult than he had anticipated. Consequently, the general thrust of the project was reassessed and refocused.

Type IV studies: quantitative/historical
This final category has become much more prominent since the late 1970s. One factor behind this trend is the emergence of two broad theoretical perspectives which prompt a consideration of long-term changes in organizational practices and structures: the population ecology and institutional approaches. The research that will be discussed can usefully be considered in terms of these two approaches.

The population ecology approach sees organizations and their forms as linked to the environmental niches in which they operate. Organizations are seen as inclined towards inertia, as a result of factors like tradition and internal politics which lead to resistance to change. They are viewed as surviving or dying as a result of the adequacy of the fit between the environmental niche and organizational form (that is, a cluster of goals, activities and structures). This broad orientation implies a need for the study of organizations and their environments over long spans of time and particularly emphasizes the requirement of long-term investigations of environmental characteristics that are associated with the birth and death of organizations. The theory operates at the level of populations of organizations sharing common environmental niches, but not all researchers have operated at this level of analysis. Research on the newspaper industries of Argentina and Ireland (Carroll and Delacroix, 1982; Delacroix and Carroll, 1983) has been undertaken at the organizational level. None the less, this research illustrates the link between the orientation of the ecology perspective and Type IV studies. Carroll and Delacroix collected data on the timing of births and deaths of all newspapers in Argentina from 1800 to 1900 and in Ireland from 1800 to 1975. They show that death is a common event in a newspaper's early years. They then examined economic and political events over each time period for the two countries in order to assess their impact on organizational mortality. For example, they created a dichotomous variable which indicates the presence or absence of political turmoil. Their analysis shows that newspapers which are born in years of political turbulence are vulnerable to early demise; those born in years of stability are more likely to survive. This effect was much more pronounced in Argentina than in Ireland, a pattern that the authors have considerable difficulty in explaining. A number of studies have been undertaken using this broad perspective and similar types of data (for example, Barnett and Carroll, 1987; Hannan and Freeman, 1987).

Institutional theory is also concerned to illuminate the relationship between organizations and their environments, but emphasizes the normative pressures that the latter exert on the former. Organizations are depicted as seeking to incorporate organizational practices and structures that are esteemed within the wider society, thereby achieving legitimacy in the eyes of the environment and enhancing their chances of survival. This pressure on organizations to conform means that their practices and structures do not necessarily reflect, and become uncoupled from, their primary tasks. A major study in this tradition is Tolbert and Zucker's (1983) investigation of the introduction of civil service procedures in municipal governments in the USA between 1880 and 1935. Such reform involved a system of written examinations for appointees and sought to reduce the potential for political influence on officials by introducing tenure. The data derive from a number of sources, but most especially from reports by the Civil Service Reform League. Tolbert and Zucker examined 167 cities, 74 of which had a legal mandate to introduce reform prior to 1930, but the remaining 93 did not. As expected, in cities with a legal mandate, reform was introduced rapidly; in the rest, it was slow to be instituted, but after a certain point the pace of adoption of reform accelerated. In the earlier period, the adoption of reform was related to demographic characteristics of the cities in question. For example, cities with larger percentages of immigrants tended to adopt reform, a pattern which can be attributed to a desire to keep foreign-born persons out of municipal office by establishing educational criteria that they were unlikely to fulfil and thereby mitigating patronage among immigrant-dominated cities. Thus, in this early period, voluntary adoption was a rational response to internal pressures to do with the enhancement of technical performance. Tolbert and Zucker argue from their data that in the later period the voluntary introduction of reform was unrelated to such internal pressures; they take this finding to mean that reform had become an indicator of legitimacy and that therefore reform was voluntarily introduced in order to convey a sense of the municipal authority being authentic and professional. During the earlier period, cities were responding to the fulfilment of the requirements of their core functions; thereafter, reform was adopted because it had come to be seen as invested with considerable symbolic virtue, whereby it was deemed to be an essential ingredient of an efficient, rationalized organization.

Some studies within the institutional tradition span the implicit periods referred to by the distinction between Type I and IV. Meyer *et al.* (1988), for example, employed state-level statistics on organizational changes in the public education system in the USA for the period 1940–80. Other investigations within the institutional tradition should more properly be considered Type I studies (for example, Kamens and Lunde, 1988). Also of interest is a study by Carroll and Huo (1986) of organizational births and deaths in the newspaper industry in a Californian region from 1850 to 1980, which used a variety of published sources and employed concepts drawn from both the population ecology and institutional approaches.

Prospects and problems in using documentary and archival material
The potential of the data sources employed in this section is considerable. Since the materials are non-reactive (that is, they are not the product of investigations in which individuals are aware of being studied), the possible biases which are often recognized to derive from interviews and questionnaires are removed. Second, the data can cover much longer time spans than are typically feasible using most of the approaches to data collection previously encountered in this book, and therefore the factors that impinge on organizational change can be elucidated. This advantage is considerable, since organizations are manifestly changeable entities, but very often the time-restricted methods which are normally used do not tap this important ingredient. Third, documentary materials can provide access to information about individuals who are normally fairly inaccessible to conventional approaches. For instance, while it is possible to interview senior executives (for example, Pettigrew, 1985), documentary and archival materials can provide much more ready access. Thus, research on letters to shareholders (such as Staw,

Mckechnie and Puffer, 1983) provides indirect access to such people, as do such compilations as *Who's Who* (for example, Smith and White, 1987).

It is important to be aware of some of the limitations of such sources of data. When considering the accuracy of such materials as documents – letters, memos, reports, company records – it is useful to bear in mind the checklist of criteria suggested by Gottschalk, Kluckholm and Angell:

1 Was the ultimate source of the detail (the primary witness) *able* to tell the truth?
2 Was the primary witness *willing* to tell the truth?
3 Is the primary witness *accurately reported* with regard to the detail under examination?
4 Is there any *external corroboration* of the detail under examination?

(Gottschalk, Kluckholm and Angell, 1945, p. 35)

This is a very stringent cluster of tests, but it is useful in drawing attention to some of the possible pitfalls in an unquestioning treatment of such evidence. Documents are rarely neutral entities (as the research on self-serving bias in letters to shareholders implies), so that they need to be cross-checked wherever possible. Also, documents do not always survive the passage of time, so that the researcher conducting a historical investigation must be cautious about the representativeness of the surviving materials. The link made between concepts and data is often a matter of concern, since it is difficult to translate the tests for validity and reliability that have been developed in the context of interview and questionnaire measures (see Chapter 2) to the environment of archival materials. When content analysis is conducted, some assessment of inter-coder reliability tends to be carried out, but as suggested above, the results of these tests can be disconcerting.

When the data are in statistical form, the accuracy of the data needs to be borne in mind. For example, when comparing data across organizations or time, care has to be taken that the unit of analysis is identical; do organizations mean the same thing when they define someone as a clerical worker and do their definitions change over time? Folger and Belew (1985) have pointed to the considerable variety that exists in firms' procedures for recording absence from work:

> Some firms require that employees fill out a time card daily (or even several times a day), whereas others give employees a

card to complete only once per pay period. Still others require managers to keep a track of who is absent. Some are blatant about taking attendance (e.g., public roll call), whereas others conduct surreptitious spot checks.

(Folger and Belew, 1985, p. 141)

Such recording differences can easily be a source of bias within and between firms, as well as over time. Further, there are other sources of bias with these methods, such as friends filling in cards, forgetfulness and differential checking of 'trouble-makers' by managers. The latter may even have a vested interest in a particular level of reporting (for example, an excessively high level might be taken to mean the manager cannot get on with subordinates). Yet data on absenteeism from company records are widely used (for example, Hackman and Oldham, 1976), while parallel problems may afflict similar sources of statistical data.

Finally, the findings deriving from archival studies may be prone to a variety of interpretations. Of course, archival research is not unique in this respect. However, because the researcher has little control over what data are available in archival investigations, information on critical variables or issues may not be possible; researchers have to make do with what they have. The collection of further data or testing interpretations in a comparable context may not be viable options for the archival researcher. The difficulty Carroll and Delacroix (1982) experienced in interpreting the different effects of political turmoil in Argentina and Ireland is an example; although attempts were made to test different interpretations, the authors admit that they are not definitive. Similarly, Tolbert and Zucker's (1983) research on the adoption of civil service reforms views later reform as indicative of ceremonial conformity and a quest for legitimacy. However, as Scott (1987a), in the context of a reassessment of the institutional approach, has observed: 'it could well be that later city officials confronted different types of governance issues – giving rise to a different set of internal problems – to which civil service reform was seen as a general solution' (p. 504). The absence of a means of gaining empirical leverage on competing explanations, while not unique to the data sources discussed in this section, is particularly pronounced in some archival investigations.

Secondary analysis of survey data

In this section, the analysis of databases deriving from social survey research by researchers who were not involved in the collection of data will be explored. The secondary analyst examines data which have already been collected and analysed by the creator of the database (and indeed which may already have been analysed by other secondary analysts). Such secondary analysis is most likely to occur in the context of research that has achieved a reputation for generating interesting and important findings and which comprises a large number and range of variables. Secondary analysis may be undertaken for a number of reasons. One possible reason is that a secondary analyst may wish to consider an alternative interpretation of a set of data from the original researcher. The researchers associated with the Aston Studies (Hickson, Pugh and Pheysey, 1969; Pugh *et al.*, 1969) became particularly well known for their finding that organization size is a more important correlate of organization structure than technology, a variable that had been emphasized by other investigators such as Woodward (1965). The findings of the Aston researchers suggested that organizational functions that are more remote or distant from the workflow are less likely to be affected by it. Hickson, Pugh and Pheysey also suggested that the impact of production technology on structure is likely to be greater in small firms, in which the technology will be more pervasive, than in large firms. When Aldrich (1972) and Hilton (1972) re-analysed the same data, using a different statistical technique (path analysis, which allows a particular model of possible relationships among variables to be tested), they found that technology could be shown to have a more pervasive impact upon organization structure than the Aston group had originally allowed. Other possible reasons for the analysis of someone else's data can be envisaged. High-quality research can be a useful context in which to elaborate methodological points; a re-analysis of the original Aston research by Bryman and Pettitt (1985) allowed some statistical anomalies resulting from the use of short scales (that is, ones which comprise a rather small number of indicators) to be highlighted. Further, the data may offer the potential for analyses that the original researcher did not report, or new ideas or perspectives associated with the study of organizations may suggest new avenues for analysis which the collectors of the data could not have envisaged. These two areas of potential can be discerned in the following discussion of the New Jersey study by Blau *et al.* (1976).

The New Jersey manufacturing plants research

In Chapter 4 mention was briefly made of the study in 1972 of a random sample of 110 firms in New Jersey employing 200 or more individuals by Blau *et al.* (1976). The unit of analysis was the operating unit, not the parent company (only eleven of the firms were not owned in this way). This research followed similar procedures to the Aston researchers in collecting data by structured interview with key informants. Like the Aston researchers, Blau *et al.* found little association between production technology and structure, but were not able to support the findings of Hickson, Pugh and Pheysey *et al.* (1969) regarding the moderating effect of size. The chief focus of this research was upon issues associated with a contingency perspective (Lawrence and Lorsch, 1967), so that the research emphasized the constraints that organizations face regarding the kinds of structure that they are able to adopt.

Hull and Hage (1982) re-analysed the New Jersey data for a different though related purpose. Drawing on the work of Burns and Stalker (1961) they noted that organic organizations (that is with few rules, a lack of close job definitions, overlapping tasks, decentralized decision-making and so on) are typically seen as more innovative than their mechanistic (that is, bureaucratic) counterparts. First, they reconceptualized the Burns and Stalker pairing in such a way as to permit two organizational forms in addition to mechanistic and organic types (that is, four types in total including a 'mixed' one). Second, they translated some of the characteristics on which mechanistic and organic organizations are supposed to differ into variables along which firms could be arrayed. Each of these variables could then be correlated with innovation (operationally defined as the number of patent applications in 1967–72). In this way, centralization of decision-making could be related to innovation, for example, and following the Burns and Stalker dichotomy a negative relationship would be anticipated. Data from all firms on the required variables were not always available. Only 92 firms had provided sufficient data for classifying firms in terms of Hull and Hage's fourfold typology, and innovation data were available on 101 firms. This re-analysis allowed a number of themes central to Burns and Stalker's influential work to be tested and enhanced.

Hull, Friedman and Rogers (1982) employed the New Jersey study to test Blauner's (1964) influential work on the effects of technology on alienation. In this latter research an inverted U-curve relationship was discerned between technological progress and alienation, suggesting that greater technological complexity heightens the experience of alienation among manual workers, but advanced technology as exemplified by process industries (for example, petrochemical) reverses this trend. Thus, as we move from craft to assembly-line production alienation increases, but with the advent of automated process production the degree of alienation declines. Hull, Friedman and Rogers classified the New Jersey plants in terms of their prevailing production technology in a manner similar to the scheme employed by Blauner. However, Blau *et al.* (1976) had not collected information on work experiences which would have been relevant to Blauner's thesis, since their interviews had solely been carried out with senior managers. As a surrogate measure of alienation, Hull, Friedman and Rogers used data that had been collected on turnover rates, arguing that there is 'a general relationship between quit rates and job dissatisfaction' (p. 35). By and large, Blauner's inverted U-curve thesis was supported. However, as the authors recognize, Blauner conceived of alienation as a multi-faceted concept in relation of which turnover data can only reflect a small portion. Other re-analyses by Hull of the New Jersey research can be found in Hull (1988) and Hull and Collins (1987).

A re-analysis by McKinley (1987) of the New Jersey data provides another example. The starting-point for this work is an observation that past researchers have frequently found positive relationships between administrative intensity in organizations (the proportion of personnel in administrative positions) and both technical and structural complexity. Technical complexity usually refers to the degree of technological sophistication, following Woodward (1965). Structural complexity refers either to the amount of horizontal or vertical differentiation within firms or to the degree to which the firms' members are spatially dispersed. Using the New Jersey data, McKinley measured structural complexity in terms of the number of plant divisions or sub-units. To a large extent, the empirical relationships among these variables were examined by Blau *et al.* (1976), but McKinley sought to extend this analysis by seeking to establish whether the character or degree of the relationships differed according to whether firms were growing or declining in size. It was possible to examine this possibility since data had been collected on the number of employees in both 1967 and 1972 for sixty-seven plants. McKinley found that whether firms were growing or declining did moderate the complexity–administrative intensity relationships; as McKinley (1987, p. 101) puts it, 'this study suggests that complexity of production technology and complexity of structure will be correlates of administrative expansion in growing organizations, but not in declining ones'. This is an important finding which suggests that studies which are based on samples which contain growing and declining organizations (which is usually the case) may produce misleading results if the results are treated as pertaining to the sample as a whole.

The PIMS database

A particularly interesting database is the PIMS (Profit Impact of Market Strategies) programme. The idea for the programme originated with an internal study conducted by the General Electric Company in the early 1960s and which gradually expanded to include other companies when the administration of the programme was taken over by the Harvard Business School. In 1975 its administration was taken over by the Strategic Planning Institute, an independent body. Data are collected from companies on their business lines, that is, products or services. In 1974 over 50 major firms contributed data on around 600 businesses (Schoeffler, 1977), but the respective figures grew rapidly to 200 firms and 2,000 business lines (Hambrick, 1983). Each business line is reported on annually in respect of some 100 items of data. These data relate to the strategy surrounding each line, the business environment, its market share and other aspects of competition and performance. The emphasis is 'on what people *do*, not on *why* they do it' (Schoeffler, 1977, p. 110, original emphasis). Ostensibly, such microeconomic data are unlikely to be of great interest to organizational researchers, but the emphasis upon strategy within the database has enhanced its potential by virtue of the growing recognition of the importance of this aspect of organizations. However, it is clear that the bulk of studies using PIMS have exhibited a marked orientation to fields such as marketing, business policy and strategic management (Ramanujam and Venkatraman, 1984), although this last field often converges with organization studies in a number of respects. The basic structure of PIMS is that the performance of a business line is determined by a number of independent variables. The main performance measure is return on investment (ROI) – a common indicator in much research on strategic management. In addition to the problems associated with this kind of measure of performance (see Chapter 9), the excessive reliance on this criterion has been the source of some criticism (Anderson and Paine, 1978). Data relating to strategy, business environment and so on are seen as constituting the independent variables.

A study by Hambrick (1983) provides an example of a secondary analysis of the PIMS database which has some relevance to organizational research. The focus for this study is a typology of organizational strategies developed by Miles and

Snow (1978) from their research in four industries. The typology specifies three types of strategy which reflect the degree to which a company changes its products or markets: *defenders* (which are involved in very little change in these areas); *prospectors* (which are prone to considerable change); and *analysers* (an in-between group that inaugurates some changes, but less frequently than prospectors). As Hambrick notes, because the classification is not industry-specific, it can be used in a variety of sectors and is therefore well suited to the PIMS database which draws on a considerable diversity of settings. Hambrick was interested in the link between strategy type and performance under different conditions. In his analysis, Hambrick focused solely upon defenders and prospectors since he wanted to emphasize extremes of strategy. Following Miles and Snow, he operational- ized strategy in terms of actions carried out by businesses relative to their competitors: 'The classifying variable was the percent of sales derived from new products for this business minus the percent of sales derived from the new products for the three largest competitors' (Hambrick, 1983, p. 14). High scores on this measure were taken to be indicative of a prospector strategy, low scores a defender strategy. Business lines exhibiting intermediate scores were eliminated from the analysis, yielding 649 defenders and 201 prospectors. It was found that a defender strategy generally yields superior performance, especially when ROI was the indicator. The effect of strategy on another performance measure – change in market share – was affected by the environment in which the business operated. In innovative industries (as reported by respondents), in which new products account for over 5 per cent of the revenues of the three largest competitors, prospectors fare better in terms of change in market share.

Such findings provide something of a flavour of the measures that make up the PIMS database. Unfortunately, the data do not provide information that might have been of particular interest to many organizational researchers. For example, Miles and Snow found that the three strategic types differed in terms of their organizational structures and management styles, such as greater decentralization being evident among prospectors than defend- ers. However, in spite of the interest shown by researchers on strategic management in such variables (for example, Lenz, 1980), it is not possible to examine issues to do with structure and style, since the PIMS data do not include such information. As with many databases which have been constructed with a particular focus in mind (in this case marketing and micro- economic issues), secondary analysts are likely to be constrained by the absence of data appropriate to their specific requirements. In addition, the absence of longitudinal data is bound to be a disadvantage for the investigation of certain topics such as innovation or decline; this probably accounts for the lack of attention to such topics among researchers using PIMS (Ramanujam and Venkatraman, 1984), though the accumulation of more and more annual data is likely to mitigate this difficulty. Further, the absence of longitudinal data renders the causal structure that underpins PIMS somewhat dubious. It is also unclear how far findings relating to the business lines in the database can be generalized to smaller firms, since the contributors to PIMS are mostly large market leaders. Lubatkin and Pitts (1983) have also questioned the degree to which the findings deriving from a varied sample of lines operating in diverse industries produce what they term 'universal truths' that pertain irrespective of industry. Taking longitudinal data from the US brewing industry 1952–1974, they compared the model that underlies PIMS with a model developed by Thiel (1978) which was specifically devised in relation to the US brewing industry. While the PIMS model fared well, in that it explained over 60 per cent of the variation in performance, Thiel's industry-specific model did even better, with over 80 per cent. Lubatkin and Pitts also found that the PIMS model was much more effective in explaining the performance of large national brewers than regional brewers, confirming the suggestion that findings deriving from the PIMS data and model may be biased towards large national corporations.

It is not feasible in a short section to cover all of the many contexts in which secondary analysis might take place (see Dale, Arber and Proctor, 1988, for a detailed exposition). Two types of database have been considered in this section: the secondary analysis of an *ad hoc* survey (the New Jersey and the first Aston study) and of a semi-official ongoing research programme (PIMS). In spite of the fact that only two types of secondary analysis of survey data have been considered, the benefits and costs of such an exercise can readily be seen from the illustrations cited. The advantage of not having to engage in the time-consuming and costly activity of conducting a survey (particularly one generating data of high quality) is counterbalanced by the prospect of not having data on key variables of interest. PIMS reveals the problems for the researcher of a database that derives from a specific model and from a restricted range of variables, but which has attracted a great deal of attention from secondary analysts concerned with organizational and related issues.

Overview

This chapter has examined forms of research which exhibit considerable variety. The opportunities and limitations of both archival studies and secondary analysis of survey data have been examined. Although there is an affinity between the two, in that in both types of study the investigator is not generating new data, there is one important difference between them. Whereas archival sources, as noted above, are non-reactive, survey data are reactive. The secondary analyst of survey data must recognize this potential source of bias in the material being analysed.

8

Structured observation, simulation, language studies and other methods of data collection

The purpose of this chapter is to provide discussions of three sources of data which have been employed quite a lot by organizational researchers and a somewhat concise treatment of methods which are little used but worthy of mention. There is a fairly strong compatibility between the three main methods discussed – structured observation, simulation and language studies – in that each exhibits considerable attention to the observation of behaviour, albeit in different ways. However, whereas structured observation and simulation have been used for many years, language studies are of more recent origin.

Structured observation

A data collection technique which has attracted a good deal of attention in organizational research since the early 1970s is structured observation (Martinko and Gardner, 1985; Mintzberg, 1970), sometimes called systematic observation (McCall, 1984; Weick, 1968). This method entails the direct observation of individuals in field settings and the recording and encoding of observations according to a previously formulated schedule. Like a forced choice questionnaire or interview schedule, the researcher decides in advance the items of interest and prepares the observation schedule to reflect these predetermined foci. Most research based on this technique tends to be undertaken along the lines of the quantitative research process, although, as the discussion will establish, there are some ambiguities about the ways in which structured observation can be (and is) interpreted.

In order to examine the nature and potential of structured observation, Mintzberg's (1973) highly influential study of managerial work can be taken as an example. In this research, five CEOs from different settings were studied for a period of five working days each. Data were collected in terms of three different types of record. First, there is the *chronology record* which details the times and basic activities that punctuate the executive's day. The beginning and end of each activity are separately recorded (for example, desk work, scheduled meeting, call, unscheduled meeting) along with its duration. These items of information provide an indication of the structure of the executive's working day. Second, the *mail record* chronicles the nature of the mail received and generated by the executive. The items of information recorded are: the form of the mail (for example, memo, letter or report); the source; the purpose; the manager's attention to the item (whether read or skimmed); and the action taken. Finally, the *contact record* provides details of the meetings, calls and tours undertaken by the manager which make up the chronology record. The data recorded are: the participants; the purpose of the activity (such as whether the manager gives or receives information); who initiated the activity; and its duration. Mintzberg was able to record the time spent by each manager in different activities and the proportion each took up, as well as numerous other items of information relating to each manager's mail and the content of meetings. Anecdotal information was also collected. On the basis of his data, Mintzberg generated an often-cited classification of ten managerial roles which could be grouped into three headings: interpersonal (managers as figureheads, leaders and providers of contacts outside the organization); informational (monitoring information about the organization, disseminating information from outside and as spokesperson who transmits information about the organization to outsiders); and decisional (as entrepreneurs, disturbance handlers, resource allocators and negotiators). This classification was established after the previously described data had been collected.

Mintzberg's research has been highly influential. In a survey of structured observation studies of managers by Martinko and Gardner (1985) only four pre-dated the major publication to emerge from Mintzberg's research (in 1973), but fourteen came after it, many of which used identical or similar schemes to his. One of the chief reasons for the popularity of this research is that his findings seemed to contrast sharply with the image of managerial work that is frequently conveyed in the literature. Rather than an emphasis on order, rationality and planning, Mintzberg's findings suggested that much managerial work is fragmented, lacks planning and entails reactive responses to immediate events. Further, in its use of structured observation, it was possible for managerial work to be studied without the aid of questionnaires and interviews. In particular, research on leadership, which relies a great deal on questionnaire measures, has been influenced by Mintzberg's research because of its capacity to address what managers or leaders (the two are often used interchangeably) do, rather than what their subordinates say they do (as with the LBDQ) or what managers themselves say they do. Consequently, studies have been carried out which replicate or extend or seek to modify his work in various ways. Ironically, Mintzberg's research and most of the investigations which have followed in its wake differ from the few structured observation studies preceding it in two important ways (Martinko and Gardner, 1985). First, unlike the early studies, Mintzberg's research and subsequent investigations have derived their data from very small numbers of individuals. Excluding one study of forty-three managers, the mean number of subjects is five, with a range of one to sixteen. Second, again unlike the pre-Mintzberg investigations, most research has followed Mintzberg in describing managerial behaviour, without assessing how effective managers behave. This tendency is surprising in view of the marked preoccupation with this kind of issue typically exhibited by organizational research.

The work of Luthans (Luthans and Lockwood, 1984; Luthans, Rosenkrantz and Hennessey, 1985) and Martinko and Gardner (1984) has countered these trends, thereby bringing structured observation much closer to survey research in both style and focus. Martinko and Gardner (1984) report the development of an observation schedule which records the timing of events, persons involved and their characteristics, location, medium of communication and so on and which was used to observe fourteen high- and seven moderate-performing educational managers (school principals). Although their approach to the recording of events was broadly similar to that of Mintzberg, one interesting innovation was to depart from his convention of treating events as mutually exclusive (that is, only one event carried out at any one time) and to allow a coding of principals' behaviour such that they could be treated as being involved in multiple events. The subjects were differentiated in terms of performance by five criteria (two examples of criteria were superintendents' performance ratings of both the schools and the principals themselves). Each principal was observed for a mean of 6.7 days. As a result of their design, it was possible to compare the behavioural differences between the two groups of managers. High performers were more likely than moderate performers to initiate a greater proportion of contacts with teachers, spend more time in unscheduled meetings with teachers and use a task-oriented style in dealing with teachers and students. It is also striking that when structured observation research is employed in this way, essentially the same research design as that used by many survey researchers (see Figure 4.1a) is employed.

Luthans and Lockwood (1984) report some data deriving from the Leader Observation System (LOS), an observation schedule which was derived from 440 hours of unstructured observation of forty-four leaders. The resulting schedule permits the coding of behaviour into one of twelve categories (for example, planning/co-ordinating, staffing, decision making/problem-solving, processing paperwork and managing conflict) and the 'behavioural descriptors' associated with each category. An example of behavioural descriptors for one LOS category is as follows:

11 Managing Conflict

   (a) managing interpersonal conflict between subordinates or others
   (b) appealing to higher authority to resolve a dispute
   (c) appealing to 3rd-party negotiators
   (d) trying to get cooperation or consensus between conflicting parties
   (e) attempting to resolve conflicts between subordinate and self.

Each manager was observed for a randomly selected ten-minute period every hour for two weeks. Luthans *et al.* (1985) distinguished a sample of fifty-two managers in terms of their success (based on an index relating to promotion) and, like Martinko and Gardner, examined the behaviour of successful and less successful managers. The former were found to engage in more conflict management, socializing/politicking, interacting with outsiders and decision-making, and were less concerned with staffing, motivating/reinforcing and monitoring activities, than their less successful counterparts.

The approach to the use of observers differed greatly between the studies encountered. Mintzberg acted as the observer in his research, whereas Martinko and Gardner used doctoral students and two professors as observers. The observers were trained in two-day programmes in which the recording approach was learned and difficulties were encountered and gradually dealt with. The recording of behaviour by the LOS was undertaken by 'participant observers', that is, employees of the organizations in which the research was carried out who had consistent contact with the person being observed. In most cases, the observer was the manager's secretary or a key subordinate. Twenty per cent of the observers acted in relation to more than one manager (usually two). Observers were required to undertake substantial training.

As with the use of questionnaires and interviews, structured observation often engenders considerable concern about the validity and reliability of the ensuing measurement. In large part, this concern derives from the researcher's awareness that the method is highly obtrusive (and possibly intrusive) and that the observer's presence may inhibit managers or result in the staging of certain events. Mintzberg argues that people get accustomed to being observed, so that reactive effects will diminish after a while, although the short periods of time for which many subjects are observed (such as five days per subject in the case of Mintzberg's research) imply that managers are often not given much time in which to become acclimatized to the researcher's presence. Further, he suggests that much of a manager's work cannot change simply because of a researcher's presence. Many meetings are scheduled in advance, and much activity is too urgent and important for the presence of a researcher to constitute a major influence. In the case of the LOS research, Luthans, Rosenkrantz and Hennessey argue that intrusiveness is reduced by using members of the organization as observers. Mintzberg cites a number of other difficulties in respect of structured observation: one can only listen to one end of a telephone conversation, managers' evening work and meetings away from the organization cannot be observed, and some meetings are likely to be missed. He argues that some missing data can be ascertained by seeking out information to fill such gaps, for example, by asking managers specifically about missed meetings or what was said by the other person in a telephone conversation.

Both Martinko and Gardner and Luthans and Lockwood report the results of reliability testing of their respective schedules. The former examined test/retest reliability by numbering each day of observation for each principal and dividing into odd- and even-numbered groups and then computing the relationship between the two groups of observations. With structured observation, a major reliability concern is the degree to which observers accurately record what they see. The training programmes are designed to maximize accuracy, but, especially when observers are hired, the potential for errors cannot be ignored. Consequently, there is often concern about the degree to which different observers can agree over the ways in which their observations are recorded. The following was one among a number of checks used by Martinko and Gardner (1984, p. 150): 'All observers have a second observer spend at least one day with

them observing a principal. The interobserver agreement percentage is calculated from the field notes of the two observers.'
Similarly, Luthans and Lockwood report the intermittent use of
outside observers to check the recording carried out by the
'participant observers', which point to considerable interobserver reliability. Luthans and Lockwood also detail a number
of validity tests that were carried out. For example, the LBDQ
was administered to the managers' subordinates to provide
measures of consideration and initiating structure. The LOS
categories were collapsed to provide indicators of these same
concepts, for example, managing conflict was taken to be
indicative of consideration. These various tests failed to provide
strong evidence of validity. However, it is extremely difficult to
interpret such tests. Since the LBDQ is itself a problematic
measure (see the discussion of lay theories in Chapter 2), it is not
obvious what a lack of correspondence means, a problem which
is compounded because the LOS was not devised to measure
consideration and initiating structure. A comparable exercise
which contrasted a structured observation approach to job
characteristics with a self-administered questionnaire study of the
same jobs is similarly ambiguous (Jenkins *et al.*, 1975).

Snyder and Glueck (1980) have raised an interesting query
about Mintzberg-style research. They argue that Mintzberg's
failure to locate a planning role in what managers do is a function
of his tendency to examine discrete activities or events. A
replication of Mintzberg's approach was conducted in relation to
two chief executives, but in addition to structured observation
subjects were asked to explain what they were doing and why
they were doing it. This additional technique of data gathering is
extremely similar to the creation and analysis of verbal protocols
(see discussion later in this chapter). This additional probing
permitted Snyder and Glueck to see much more pattern to their
subjects' activities, and as a consequence they proposed that in
fact managers spend a considerable amount of time in planning.
As Snyder and Glueck graphically put it, in concentrating on
series of discrete activities rather than programmes of action
'Mintzberg is not seeing the forest, only hundreds of different
trees' (p. 75). The authors' experience is highly consonant with
that of educational researchers. Structured observation of
classrooms has been a prominent technique in educational
research, but has been criticized, *inter alia*, for an excessive
emphasis on overt behaviour and insufficient attention being paid
to underlying intentions (for example, Delamont and Hamilton,
1984). Of course, writers like Mintzberg additionally collect
anecdotal information, but it is not clear precisely what such

materials comprise nor what role they play in the analysis of the observational data. Buttressing structured observation data with another method is clearly a solution to these problems. In addition to the deployment of protocol analysis, the collection of ethnographic data may be considered as a means of providing leverage on gaps in findings (see Bryman, 1988a, for some examples).

Sampling issues tend not to be given a great deal of attention by structured observation researchers. Martinko and Gardner (1985, p. 686) note that the tendency towards small samples precludes 'formal hypothesis testing with inferential statistics', but sampling problems do not pertain solely to this issue, since the generalizability of 'actors, actions, settings, and occasions' is also affected (McCall, 1984, p. 270). Not only is the representativeness of the individuals who are observed rarely given a great deal of consideration, but also the generalizability of what goes on in the settings that are focused upon is given scant attention. For example, researchers frequently choose to observe managers on particular days, but the representativeness of those days is rarely given much thought. Certain activities may vary in incidence during particular days of the week; even more likely, phases in an organization's year may have a considerable impact on managers' behaviour. The prevalence of scheduled meetings may be highly affected by the organization's annual cycle. Greater attention to such sampling issues is necessary, although survey research, which is often treated as the model to which structured observation should aspire, is not without problems in this arena too.

One of the chief arguments in favour of structured observation is that it gets away from the excessive reliance on questionnaires and interviews as sources of information about organizational behaviour. Since there has long been a debate about whether there is a close correspondence between what people say they do and what they actually do (LaPiere, 1934), the advantages associated with the ability to obtain information about behaviour as such cannot be understated. On the other hand, structured observation is not without problems, although this section has pointed to a number of areas which are capable of solution. There is much to recommend Luthans's approach of using unstructured observation as a precursor to the preparation of an observation schedule, since it will minimize the distortion that might be caused by the imposition of an inappropriate scheme. Further, the dovetailing of structured observation with other techniques to address issues at the cognitive level has clear advantages.

Simulation

There is some indication that simulations are finding increasing favour among organizational researchers. Organizations are complex devices that may not always be amenable to the more common techniques of data collection encountered in earlier chapters, so that there may be a strong temptation to devise representations of such settings to allow certain facets or processes to be examined. Precise definitions of what constitutes a simulation are somewhat elusive, but a simulation can be seen as an attempt to represent a sphere of reality by abstracting variables of direct interest to a cluster of research questions and creating a setting wherein the operation of those variables can be observed. Many laboratory experiments make use of simulations in that subjects are induced to carry out tasks that are meant to be near replicas of work settings. The Day and Hamblin (1964) laboratory experiment, which was employed as an example of an experiment in Chapter 3, is an instance of laboratory simulation in that an industrial work setting was created and subjects were requested to carry out tasks that were similar to assembly-line work. However, the use of simulation in organizational research is not restricted to the experimental context, in which there is substantial control over the activities and direction of participants' activities. Simulations can give participants a much freer rein than the experimental framework necessarily entails (Fromkin and Streufert, 1976), and it is upon this kind of simulation that it is proposed to dwell in this section.

Simulating work: the in-basket test

The in-basket test provides a pertinent example of an approach to the simulation of work. It is a simulation technique that was originally developed as a device to assist in the assessment of the potential of prospective managers (and hence their recruitment) as well as in their subsequent appraisal. It is often one among a cluster of techniques forming part of the 'assessment centre' approach to the prediction of management potential and effectiveness (Thornton and Byham, 1982). The test is supposed to simulate aspects of a manager's job and takes a number of slightly different forms, although the basic idea is fairly standard. In one form appraisees have to imagine that they must stand in for a plant manager who has just died and must deal with the outstanding contents of the manager's in-basket. Usually, the appraisee is told to complete the task in two or three hours. Individuals are rated in terms of which materials they choose to handle and how they do so. Their approaches are coded in terms of a number of categories and characteristics of interest to assessors, such as requesting more information, discussing issues with others and initiating a framework for the work at hand. There is some evidence that those who do well at the test tend to be successful in their subsequent managerial careers (Bray, Campbell and Grant, 1974).

Brass and Oldham (1976) scored the test, which was administered to seventy-one foremen, in terms of a scheme for classifying leadership activities. This scheme posits six activities: personally rewarding, personally punishing, setting specific goals, designing jobs with greater challenge for subordinates, placing subordinates in challenging jobs and providing subordinates with feedback. One potential problem with a technique like the in-basket test is how far the results are affected by idiosyncratic coding. Brass and Oldham found a fair degree of agreement among those responsible for rating individuals in terms of the leadership categories. This finding mirrors that of other researchers who have found a high degree of agreement between coders (Thornton and Byham, 1982). Brass and Oldham asked the superiors of the foremen to rate them in terms of a number of effectiveness criteria and found that the first four of the leadership activities cited above were associated with effectiveness.

Shapira and Dunbar (1980) report using the test as a means of collecting data on managerial roles and in particular following up Mintzberg's work on this theme. They note that Mintzberg's research suggests that managers perform ten analytically separable roles which can be brought together into three groups: interpersonal, informational and decisional (see previous section). The in-basket test was adapted so that subjects could be rated in terms of whether and how far they carried out each of the roles. Two sets of subjects were used: MBA students and managers. Although the two groups differed somewhat, they were similar in that instead of the three clusters suggested by Mintzberg, Shapira and Dunbar found that the roles could be grouped into two: one concerned with 'information generation and transmission' and the other with 'the active formulation and execution of decisions' (pp. 93, 94). As the authors recognize, the degree to which the in-basket really can simulate the job of management is a matter of empirical research. However, like other simulation methods and projective techniques, the in-basket test is a source of unease in at least two respects. As Shapira and Dunbar acknowledge, the degree to which such techniques reflect the phenomena that they are supposed to stand for is bound to be a matter of conjecture until convergent validity is established. Second, the coding of people's responses is in need of continual attention, since such techniques place considerable emphasis upon the ability of coders to rate accurately the material with which they are presented.

Simulating organizations

McCall and Lombardo (1982) note that a great deal of research on leadership derives from questionnaires rather than the observation of leaders in action. They devised a simulation of an organization – referred to as Looking Glass Inc. – within which the behaviour of leaders could be observed. The simulation, which lasts roughly six hours, comprises a fairly large 'manufacturer' and is based upon site visits, interviews with managers and a variety of documentary materials. Thus, although not 'real', the organization has been constructed from evidence that makes it a logically possible entity. In each session, twenty participants (always practising managers) are assigned to top management roles and are told to run the company. On the evening prior to the start of the session, participants are acquainted with the nature of the work that the simulation entails and the organization itself. There are nearly 160 management problems that participants may deal with or possibly ignore (for example, production capacity problems and a lawsuit with a customer). Further, the company comprises three divisions which vary in the degree of uncertainty of their respective external environments. Like the in-basket test (which is a component of the overall Looking Glass programme), the simulation is used as a training tool, though in the eyes of McCall and Lombardo it offers many research possibilities also.

The simulation allows the effect of variation in the degree of uncertainty associated with the external environment on leader behaviour to be investigated. Since the participants are allocated to a variety of top management roles, the implications for leader behaviour of different functions and levels in the hierarchy can be assessed. In addition, various organizational processes can be examined as they occur; and because data on these processes from a number of sessions can be gathered, it becomes possible to explore variations between them. For example, in some sessions divisions may become autonomous, whereas in others they may exhibit interdependence. Consequently, the implications of such naturally occurring variations in interdependence for other aspects of organizational functioning can be evaluated. Similarly, because at the end of each session a questionnaire is administered to participants in which variables such as organizational climate are measured, the sources and consequences of variation in such variables can be addressed as data from sessions are accumulated. In addition to being able to examine the implications of these naturally occurring variations in sessions, McCall and Lombardo observe that it is possible to manipulate facets of different sessions in order to observe their effects. For example, they point out that it may be interesting to know whether experienced and inexperienced managers deal differently with the settings which are created for them; accordingly, some sessions could be run with experienced managers on some occasions, inexperienced ones on other occasions. Also the introduction of a major crisis into some sessions may allow the researcher to observe the consequences such a major event may have for managers and their organizations. The introduction of interventions brings the simulation much closer to an experimental study.

Cameron and Whetten (1981) drew upon an organizational simulation created by Miles and Randolph (1979) to examine changing criteria of effectiveness over the life cycle of organizations. This simulation entails a small production unit comprising four divisions, each of which has two departments. The organization has to solve anagrams to produce words and to solve word puzzles to produce sentences. An overall co-ordinator sells anagrams or puzzles, which must be solved within a single session, to departments. The simulation comprises six sessions each of which is of roughly one hour's duration. There is a short break between each session during which the organization's performance is assessed and resources are distributed to it in accordance with its performance. Unlike Looking Glass Inc., participants are undergraduates at US universities. At the end of each of the six sessions, a questionnaire was administered to tap participants' perceptions of the relative importance of various criteria of effectiveness. In this way, Cameron and Whetten were able to examine how far criteria of effectiveness change at different stages in an organization's development. The 'organizations' gradually changed from a structureless entrepreneurial style to formalized bureaucratic organizations at the end. Accompanying these changes were various alterations in participants' criteria of organizational effectiveness. For example, participants' early emphasis upon individual performance tended to be superseded by a growing concern for organizational effectiveness. Further, as the organizations developed, the emphasis on attaining desirable levels of output increased, relative to the importance of two other criteria of performance: obtaining inputs and resources and maintaining satisfactory internal processes. By contrast, the assessment of performance in terms of obtaining inputs tended to decline with time. According to the authors, one of the most important implications of these findings is that organizations tend to emphasize different aspects of effectiveness at different stages in their life cycle. This implies that research which aggregates samples of organizations at different stages of development, in order to examine the variables that affect performance, may be masking a great deal of variation in firms' priorities. The findings also imply that different models of organizational effectiveness (see Chapter 9) may be appropriate to organizations at different junctures in their development, rather than being absolutely true or false.

A note on computer simulation

In addition to experimental and free simulations, there is the computer simulation, a technique that has received some attention from organizational researchers, but which has only had a minor impact. A useful definition has been supplied by Smith:

> Computer simulation is a methodology for building, testing, and using computer programs which imitate . . . system behaviour. Numbers or symbols representing a system and its parts are stored in computer memory and are manipulated by a *simulation program* written in a suitable computer programming language.
>
> (Smith, 1985, p. 143)

A computer simulation of the behaviour of a department store buyer by Cyert and March provides an early example. The authors studied the price and output decisions of approximately twelve departments in a large retail department store in the USA. One of these departments was chosen for detailed investigation, and in particular one buyer in that department (the manager) was studied. Cyert and March observed the decision-making processes involved in buying decisions. For example, they noted that the buyer made sales estimates in line with the department's sales goals and tried to establish a set of routine procedures for advance ordering in this light. The authors examined the decision-making process under different conditions, such as when the sales target for the buyer's department was not being achieved. In this situation, he might seek to enhance his department's promotional budget and/or mark a number of items down. Alternatively, he might seek to buy in goods cheaply which could be sold at standard mark-ups, for example, when a supplier was in financial difficulty and needed rapid access to cash. The various facets of the buyer's decision-making were modelled by the authors, and a simulation program was created to allow predictions of the buyer's behaviour in a variety of circumstances to be calculated. When a good deal is known about the domain to be simulated (as in the case of the buyer on whom a great deal of information has been collected), a computer simulation is feasible; when the domain is uncertain or complex, other forms of simulation are likely to be preferred (Inbar and Stoll, 1972).

Overview of simulation
Why simulate? Simulations can make a large amount of data fairly readily available. While it is possible to observe a large number of managers in many organizations, problems of time, cost and access are considerable, whereas a simulation like Looking Glass Inc. makes such research a practical possibility. Even if one were to conduct a similar study of managers in 'real' organizations, it is unlikely that the researcher would be given a *carte blanche* to tinker regularly with firms' operations in order to examine the effects of such interventions. Simulations can permit access to issues that are not readily amenable to observation in real life. Cameron and Whetten would have had to study organizations over long periods of time to draw out the points they wanted to address. There are notable studies of organizations over long spans of time (for example, Mintzberg and McHugh, 1985), but such research relies extensively on documentary evidence which may not allow the kind of inference sought by Cameron and Whetten to be made. Further, it is often suggested that simulations are useful for formulating hypotheses which can subsequently be tested in the field (Inbar and Stoll, 1972). As Cameron and Whetten point out, this benefit is of considerable importance to organizational researchers, for whom research and negotiating access are time-consuming and costly, so that simulation offers the prospect of investigating hypotheses that are more likely to be important.

On the other hand, simulations are invariably subject to the charge of artificiality, implying that findings deriving from them may not be valid. Indeed, the very idea that findings from simulation studies need to be treated as hypotheses is indicative of this view, since it implies that such findings must be treated as tentative. Many of the arguments levelled against the laboratory experiment which were encountered in Chapter 3 (for example, people are forced to work in short-term *ad hoc* groups, or using students as subjects as in the Cameron and Whetten study) are relevant to such considerations. McCall and Lombardo's Looking Glass Inc. manages to dispel a number of worries by using real managers as subjects and by having derived the framework for the simulation from a great deal of fact-finding research about the world of managers. However, the simulation seems to have a strong training component built into it, and it is doubtful whether firms would be prepared to allow their managers to be participants for such a long stretch of time if the simulation was purely for research. Further, as Weick (1965) has pointed out, researchers must take great care to ensure that they have created a realistic representation, because even apparently quite insignificant design errors can remind subjects that they are only in a laboratory and not encountering real-life problems.

Doubts about the validity of simulations can be assuaged to a fair degree by validity testing. The predictive validity of assessment centre simulation tests like the in-basket is often examined by tracking executives to see how they progress in their careers (for example, Thornton and Byham, 1982). Indeed, the in-basket test fares quite well in this respect. McCall and Lombardo (1982, p. 547) suggest that a similar approach could be used in connection with Looking Glass Inc. They also report that there is a fairly good correspondence between findings deriving from the behaviour of managers in the simulation and data deriving from diary and observation studies with managers in the field. However, as Cameron and Whetten recognize in their discussion of their simulation of changing conceptions of organizational effectiveness, there are no obvious validity tests for their study 'because comparable "real" data are not available' (1981, p. 539). On the other hand, they point to favourable comments on Miles and Randolph's (1979) simulation by participants at a management institute, which imply that the executives in question took the exercise very seriously and thought it to be realistic. However, since Cameron and Whetten's subjects were undergraduates, it is not obvious what relevance these comments have for their study. Cyert and March were able to conduct a number of validity tests. For example, they tested the ability of the computer simulation to predict price decisions on the basis of information about mark-ups that had been introduced into the computer program. They drew a random sample of invoices and used the cost and classification of each item as input data for the simulation. The question was how well the predicted price coincided with the actual price on the invoice. In fact, 188 of the 197 predictions were precisely correct. Clearly, simulations have a good deal to offer, possibly as a way of trying out preliminary ideas and particularly when based on a considerable amount of prior research to create a realistic and meaningful setting.

Studying language

In the last fifteen years there has been a growth of interest in the detailed analysis of cognition, communication and culture in organizations. These are not new topics for organizational researchers, but the formulation of the issues concerned has altered, and with this shift interest in language and discourse in organizations has grown. For example, whereas interest in organizational communication previously centred on themes such as the causes of communication breakdown or how messages come to be distorted, researchers are increasingly concerned with the content of communication and how people interpret it (Krone, Jablin and Putnam, 1987). The study of cognition in organizations, by contrast, has come to the fore much more recently (see Sims and Gioia, 1986). Ostensibly, much qualitative research reflects an interest in language, as implied by the frequent quotation of transcribed passages. However, some researchers exhibit an interest in language as such – how it is used and with what consequences in organizational life. It might appear that the study of language is not a method but a substantive topic, but researchers who conduct language studies appear to conceive of their work as denoting a particular way of studying organizations and work. On the other hand, the study of language does not constitute a single method, since there are many different approaches to it (Donnellon, 1986; Potter and Wetherell, 1987). In this section, the distinctions between these different approaches will be glossed over, and the main thrust will be to provide some examples from this area. It might also be thought that this section would fit better in Chapter 5, as a form of qualitative research. However, while some examples of research on language would sit well in a discussion of qualitative research, not all would. Moreover, many students of language see their work as constituting a separate domain of inquiry which links with, but should not be subsumed under, qualitative research (Dingwall and Strong, 1985). Most language studies entail the detailed examination of transcripts of speech. Normally, these transcripts derive from the audio- or video-recording of naturally occurring contexts, in which the researcher is totally uninvolved. Sometimes, language studies can derive from transcripts which are a product of participant observation or of unstructured interviewing or from documentary materials.

One theme to emerge from studies of language is how language is used in organizations – how it is employed as a device to effect certain outcomes. Some examples of this theme will be used to provide illustrations of its characteristics. Johnson and Kaplan (1980) focus upon the transcript of a conversation in a university computer centre between a programmer and a 'user' who had just found that a previously submitted job had failed to work. The user was processing data through the *Statistical Package for the Social Sciences (SPSS)*, the major suite of computer programs for statistical analysis (Nie *et al.*, 1975). The authors show how the programmer is keen to impute responsibility for the failure to the user, who, in turn, tries hard both to disclaim the impending attribution and to show that he is not a novice in such matters. The programmer, for example, says: 'You could have miscounted your cards. The data cards are right in there, supposedly' (p. 356). The user then tries to display his competence by suggesting a solution but is headed off by the programmer, who finds a host of other errors. Johnson and Kaplan argue that an important component of this interaction is that both parties perceive the programmer to be an 'agent of the machine' with specialized technical knowledge about the computer. Thus, the programmer is less concerned to help the user to understand where he went wrong and to minimize the risk of a recurrence of the failure (the user clearly does not comprehend the programmer's explanation) than to display his technical knowledge, thereby reinforcing existing status differences in respect of knowledge about the computer. Johnson and Kaplan see in this interchange an attempt by the programmer to protect his domain and therefore to ensure that users do not become so knowledgeable that programmers become redundant. A congruent study which examines the linguistic styles employed by professionals concerned with the classification and referral of children with difficulties and how their discursive repertoires are tailored to convey a sense of their expertise and authority on decision-making committees can be found in Mehan (1983).

A further example draws on written, rather than spoken, language. Huff (1983) examined documents produced over an eight-year period in connection with the formulation of strategy for a university business school in the USA. Two years after his arrival in 1970, the new dean produced a long document of fifty-one pages which outlined a strategy entitled 'Philosophy and Thrust'. In her analysis, Huff emphasizes the rhetorical expression of the document. She notes the dean's declarative style (for example, 'the climate that compels changes . . . is . . . critical', p. 171), which implies that facts rather than opinions are being conveyed. A number of themes can be discerned in the document: a need for the *commitment* of everyone in the school; *unity* will be necessary; a quest for *excellence*; the need for *relevance* in research and teaching; and so on. Within this plan the school's doctoral programme appeared to lose out, which prompted a number of documents from individuals associated with the programme to provide a defence of their position. The initial responses used much of the dean's vocabulary and a similar style, while deploying some of his themes in new arguments (for example, doctoral dissertations place 'value on *relevance*', p. 176) and injecting some new themes (such as *quality*). Huff draws a number of general ideas from these materials. For example, she suggests that her findings point to the capacity of leaders to use language as a resource for 'framing' the ways in which issues that they see as important are conveyed. People who wish to contest leaders' ideas must respond in the leaders' own terms, so that the tone and the agenda of the issues have been set in advance. Similarly, Gronn's (1983) examination of a school principal's work shows how much administration is accomplished through talk. In particular, Gronn shows that talk is an important vehicle for the affirmation of control over subordinates. An analysis of the transcripts of an industrial negotiation by Francis (1986) demonstrates how the sense of 'team' is conveyed through talk in the negotiations.

Each of these examples illustrates how work is accomplished through language. In each case, it is not only the substance of what is said that is important, but *how* it is said, such as the styles and strategies of users. Herein lies an important difference from much qualitative research, which is usually concerned with the substance of what is conveyed through language, rather than with the nature of its expression. Action is not simply behaviour, since in each of these examples action is undertaken through language. A study by Donnellon, Gray and Bougon (1986) also manifests a concern for the role of language in action, but focuses more on organizational cognition by asking how organized action is possible when there is little shared meaning among participants. The authors observed undergraduates in a simulation of an organization based on a similar framework to that developed by Miles and Randolph (1979), which was also used by Cameron and Whetten (1981). In one of the sessions, around which the article was written, members of one of the departments in the 'organization' (Green – a production unit) moved from disagreement to a consensus which provided a basis for organized action. This shift was prompted by Blue Department (a personnel unit) laying off group leaders in other departments, following a resource cut-back. Eventually, this led to members of Green Department going on strike. Donnellon Gray and Bougon examined the use of language in helping Green members to make sense of their situation and to develop organized action in the form of a strike. One of the linguistic devices employed by participants was metaphor – in the context either of explaining Blue's actions or of generating proposals for action. Regarding the former, Blue's actions were sometimes seen in terms of the metaphor of a power play ('They wanna take over the company') or game playing ('They're playing games'); metaphors used in the context of proposals for action included the notion of striking as principled behaviour ('prove our point'). These linguistic devices enabled participants to make sense of their situation and provided interpretations of prior events which furnished grounds for taking collective action.

The analysis of language provides access to aspects of organizational settings which previously have been either under-developed or not even recognized as appropriate areas of investigation. To many observers, the products of these language studies, particularly those which opt for a more qualitative style of analysis, may appear unrigorous and idiosyncratic. Two points might stand out: how far are the findings a product of the particular inferences drawn by the analyst and what is the generalizability of the findings? It is, of course, true that the results of a language study will be affected by what the analyst makes of the raw materials. It is doubtful whether any method yields findings from which more than one inference cannot be made. Further, an advantage of language studies over much qualitative research is that there is often an emphasis upon 'retrievable data' which permit 'disconfirming evidence' and 'alternative interpretations' to be considered (Mehan, 1978, pp. 36, 37). Considerations of the question of generalizability are essentially no different from those raised in connection with case study research in Chapter 6, in that attention needs to be paid to the adequacy of the theoretical reasoning deriving from language investigations and to the possibility of confirming inferences in different contexts. Possibly more worrying is that, when writing up their materials, language researchers often present just one or two transcripts and appear to forge their analysis in connection with these examples. This approach is evident in a number of studies, as in the cases of Donnellon, Gray and Bougon, Johnson and Kaplan, and Gronn. The representativeness of the portions of text presented is rarely addressed, and the reader is left wondering how far the other interaction exchanges for which data are available would yield the same inferences or whether other, more interesting conclusions could be gleaned. These possibilities are not easily checked unless researchers present large numbers of transcripts, which is rarely feasible. On the other hand,

language studies point to a rich new vein in organizational
research and it is far too early to make pronouncements about
their value. They do not constitute a method of research, in the
sense of a means of generating data; indeed, the methods of data
collection mentioned by Donnellon (1986) in the context of
language studies include ones mentioned in Chapter 5, such as
interviewing and participant observation. The special quality of
language studies lies in their focus on discourse as such and in
their particular emphases on how action is forged through
language and on how language is a vital ingredient of organizational cognition.

Other methods of data collection

Although certain research methods receive greater use than
others (for example, the ubiquitous self-administered questionnaire), it is difficult not to be struck by the immense variety of
techniques in use. Unfortunately, to give detailed attention to all
possible methods would have entailed a radical increase in this
book's size. On the other hand, it is useful for students to be
aware of some of a wide variey of techniques. What follows is a
brief treatment of a number of additional approaches to data
collection which can be found in organizational research. Each
treatment is inevitably slightly cursory but is provided in the
belief that methods of data collection must be tailored to the
problem at hand and that in order to make decisions about the
appropriateness of particular methods some awareness of the
choices to hand is necessary.

Projective techniques
These techniques involve the presentation of ambiguous stimuli
to individuals, whose interpretation of the stimuli is taken by the
researcher to reveal some underlying characteristic of the
individual concerned. An example is the 'sentence-completion
test' in which the individual is asked to complete a number of
unfinished sentences. These tests are often used in the context of
personnel selection exercises such as assessment centres, since
they are used to detect applicants with appropriate characteristics. Miner (1978) developed a sentence-completion test to
measure managerial role motivation. He argues that managerial
effectiveness is a product of a positive attitude to six managerial
role prescriptions. For example, managers must be *competitive*,
in that they must be prepared to do battle for themselves and
their subordinates, and *assertive*, that is, they must be prepared
to assert themselves in relation to discipline, decisions and the

like. The way in which an individual completes a sentence which starts 'Making introductions . . . ' is supposed to reveal something about his or her preparedness to *stand out*, another role prescription. The Miner sentence completion scale comprises forty sentences. Miner (1978) shows that the scale has considerable construct validity in that a host of studies show that high scores on the scale are associated with various indicators of individual performance (for example, the individual's level in the organization and supervisors' ratings of performance). The coding of individuals' answers tends to be a matter of controversy with such tests, since each response has to be translated to discern how far the particular characteristic (such as competitiveness) is in evidence. Brief, Aldag and Chacko (1977) have noted problems with the scale in this area.

Verbal protocols

Following the early work of Newell and Simon (1972) in the area of human problem-solving, the verbal protocol approach has been employed in relation to a number of topics relevant to organizational research (see Schweiger, 1983, for a summary). The approach involves inducing subjects to think aloud while performing a task. The idea is to elicit their thought processes while they are in the throes of making a decision or solving a problem. Subjects' accounts of what they are doing and why they are doing it are usually tape-recorded and transcribed, and then a content analysis is conducted with the aid of a coding scheme to discern fundamental categories of thinking. Verbal protocol analysis has been criticized by Nisbett and Wilson (1977), who doubt whether it is possible for subjects to provide access to higher-order thought processes by simply saying what they are doing. However, the concern that the fact of having to think aloud may have an impact upon individuals' task performance has in large part been discounted by a study by Schweiger (1983), in which two groups of students participated in a business game simulation, one of which provided protocols and the other did not. Isenberg (1986) has used verbal protocol analysis in a study of managerial cognition. Twelve managers were asked to solve a business case in which they had to indicate what the problems were which a focal individual in the case faced and what he or she should do. Three students performed the same task in order to allow the special qualities of managerial problem-solving to be distinguished. Both groups' protocols were analysed in terms of a coding scheme comprising seventeen themes, such as causal reasoning, analogical reasoning, empathizing with others, conditional reasoning and the like. Isenberg found a number of differences between managers and students. Managers were more likely to be reflective, to commence action more rapidly, to ask for specific information and so on.

The diary method

The diary method has been used particularly in the context of studying what managers do (see Stewart, 1967, ch. 1, for a summary). It involves asking individuals to record episodes over a predetermined time period in terms of a prepared set of headings. In Stewart's (1967) research, managers were asked to distinguish between fleeting contacts with other individuals and episodes which lasted more than five minutes. With the latter, they were asked to record for each incident its duration, location, who else participated, how it took place (for example, telephone, inspection tour, or travelling) and the focus of the episode (for example finance or public relations). Stewart argued that the diary method of studying managers' activities enjoys certain advantages over structured observation. It is more economical in terms of time and cost, and so a larger number of managers can usually be studied; activities can be recorded over a longer period; classification is by managers themselves in terms of their own understanding of what they are doing; and information about even confidential discussions (from which an observer might be excluded) is possible. Stewart also recognized some advantages of observation in contrast to diaries. There is time for more detailed and comprehensive recording of information; recording is more likely to be complete, since diary-keepers may omit to fill in information when under pressure; and a consistent standard can more readily be applied. Because diary categories must be easy to apply, so that managers can readily subsume their activities under headings, important but complex categories of information may not be accessible to the diary method. In addition, Mintzberg (1970) has argued that structured observation is superior because it allows access to the content of interaction and not simply the distribution of activities in terms of a number of contextual variables (such as length of meetings). There seems to be a trade-off between the greater amount of information that can be supplied by observation studies (see the section on structured observation, pages 207–13) and the larger numbers of individuals who can be accessed through the diary method (160 in Stewart's case, compared to Mintzberg's 5 CEOs). Researchers' preferences seem to have moved in the direction of observation, whether structured (Martinko and Gardner, 1985) or unstructured (for example, Kotter, 1982).

Critical incident method

One of the commonest applications of the critical incident method is to ask respondents to describe critical incidents which are indicative of both effective and ineffective managerial or leader behaviour. Yukl (1981) cites fourteen such studies. Individuals' responses are coded in terms of categories of managerial behaviour. However, as Yukl notes, there is considerable variety in the kinds of classification scheme which ensue, suggesting that categorizations of leader behaviour tend to be arbitrary. Also, the question of whether respondents understand such terms as 'critical' and 'effective' in similar ways constitutes a problem with many studies. The method has been employed usefully by Yukl and Van Fleet (1982) to compare the findings regarding leader effectiveness deriving from a critical incident study with the more conventional questionnaire method. The authors compared, in a military context, an investigation of attributes of effective and ineffective leader behaviour based on critical incidents with a study of the relationship between leader behaviour and effectiveness using a questionnaire. The same coding scheme for classifying leader behaviour was used in each case. A fair degree of congruence was established; for example, the leader's 'performance emphasis' was a frequently mentioned aspect of effective leadership in the critical incident research and also exhibited fairly high correlations with effectiveness in the questionnaire-based research. This study suggests a useful role for the critical incident approach – as a means of checking findings from more conventional methods – provided that standardization of categories across investigations employing both methods is introduced.

Meta-analysis

Meta-analysis is not a research method or a source of data in the senses used in this book; rather, it provides a means of summarizing the results of large numbers of quantitative studies, although a number of other uses have been identified by the advocates of meta-analysis (see Hunter, Schmidt and Jackson, 1982, for a review of meta-analysis and its uses). Not all commentators agree with this view; Podsakoff and Dalton (1987), for example, treat meta-analysis as a data collection procedure. However, regardless of how meta-analysis is visualized, it provides an interesting approach to reviewing the results of quantitative studies. Ostensibly, all that is needed in order to summarize such findings is to establish whether or not different studies show a particular variable to have an effect. Thus, Locke and Schweiger (1979) summarized the literature on the impact of participative decision-making by indicating whether each investigation had a positive effect (that is, enhanced satisfaction or performance), a negative effect, or no effect, and then examined how many studies fell into each of these three categories. Advocates of meta-analysis argue that such an approach is inadequate. First, it fails to provide information on the size of an effect across all of the studies surveyed. Second, it lacks statistical power; since many studies use small numbers of respondents or subjects, statistically significant results may be difficult to obtain, so that a verdict of 'no effect' may be incorrect. Meta-analysis pools the results of studies in a domain in order to estimate an overall effect size and involves correction for such artefacts as sampling error in arriving at an overall picture. Meta-analyses have been conducted on a number of areas in organizational research which have figured in this book, including the study of the relationship between job characteristics and job satisfaction, based on Hackman and Oldham (1976), from which a number of illustrations were taken in earlier chapters; Loher *et al.* (1985) conducted a meta-analysis on twenty-eight such studies. The average correlation between job characteristics and satisfaction across these studies was .39. In addition, it was found that the correlation was .68 for respondents with a high level of growth need strength (GNS) and .38 for those with low GNS, suggesting that GNS is an important moderator of the relationship. The advantage of meta-analysis can be readily gauged from this example; it provides an overall indication of effect size and allows sub-group differences to be discerned, so that the effects of moderating variables can be assessed in a similar manner. On the other hand, the technique is heavily reliant on all the relevant information being available in publications. Moreover, evidence for overall effect sizes may convey a spurious accuracy, since there is evidence that research which fails to yield positive evidence often does not get published (White, 1982). None the less, meta-analysis is increasing in popularity, and analogues of these techniques are being considered for qualitative investigations (Noblit and Hare, 1988).

9

Issues in organizational research

In this chapter, some recurring problems and predicaments in organizational research will be examined. The issues have been touched upon in earlier chapters but receive a more detailed treatment below. Inevitably, the choice of issues is idiosyncratic, deriving as they do from one writer's views about the state of the field, but it is doubtful whether there would be wholesale disagreement among other writers about what is included; rather, they are more likely to object about what is excluded. None the less, a consideration of the kind of issues examined below would seem necessary in a book such as this.

The problem of level of analysis

This section deals with a cluster of related issues which, while not unique to organizational research, are often revealed in the field. These issues hinge on the degree to which it is possible to draw inferences from data pertaining to one level to another level. The issues both are technical and take a number of forms, so that it is proposed to provide some illustrations of the problem. None the less, it is hoped that the following treatment will permit some familiarity with the relevant issues, as well as allowing some of the worst excesses associated with the problem of level of analysis to be avoided.

One manifestation is the *aggregation problem*. A number of measuring schemes in organizational research entail the derivation of attributes about organizations from individuals' responses to questionnaires. The work of Hall (1968), which was previously encountered on pages 47–8, is an example, in that organization structure scores are built up by aggregating respondents' questionnaire replies to predetermined questions. Similarly, research on technology sometimes uses individuals' replies to questions about their jobs to provide measures of the degree to which technology is routine (Withey, Daft and Cooper, 1983). Such approaches to measurement comprise a shift from individuals' responses about their experiences to another level of analysis: the organization or the job. Taking the example of measures of organization structure, if the degree of variability in individuals' responses in each organization exceeded the variability between organizations, it is not in the least clear how the researcher could be claiming to represent characteristics of organizations. Indeed, the mere presence of a substantial minority view of organization (for example, 25 per cent viewing an organization as rule-bound, 65 per cent viewing it as largely devoid of rules and the remaining 10 per cent adopting an intermediate position) would imply some questioning of the procedure. In a study of social service organizations, Lincoln and Zeitz (1980) sought to establish the degree to which organizational scores deriving from individuals' questionnaire responses could be attributed to real variation between organizations by partitioning out the influence of variations in individuals' responses. In the case of two of the dependent variables examined, the influence of individual variation was small, but with the third variable – a measure of decentralization – the contribution of individual variation exceeded that of organizational variation. They also found that the relationships between the three dependent variables and a number of independent variables differed in terms of whether the results pertained to either the individual or the organizational components of variation. This research casts doubt on research which involves aggregated replies pertaining to different levels of analysis and which fails to separate individual from organizational variation.

Analogous difficulties recur in other areas of organizational research. In the study of leadership, a common approach, exemplified by the LBDQ, is to aggregate subordinates' answers to questions about their superiors' behaviour. Although this approach tends to be congruent with the group-level focus of much leadership research, the process of aggregating individuals' replies may belie important within-group (that is, individual) variation in perceptions of leaders' behaviour, which in turn may be indicative of variation in leaders' ways of dealing with particular subordinates. This recognition prompted an alternative approach which emphasizes leader–subordinate dyads (for example, Graen and Cashman, 1975), although examinations of the evidence deriving from this particular framework suggest that it is not wholly convincing (Bryman, 1986).

A second kind of problem is the *ecological fallacy*, which refers to the problem of inferring relationships relating to high-level entities to low-level ones. Robinson (1950) has shown that findings at an aggregate level need not be the same as those at an individual level; indeed, his research suggested that correlations among variables at the aggregate level tend to be greater than they would be if individuals as such were the focus. Consequently, risks are attached to assuming that inferences from aggregate data referring to individuals or organizations can be made about the individuals or organizations themselves. For example, Rousseau (1985) observes that research on *rates* of turnover in units in organizations suggests that economic factors play a major role, but when individuals' turnover decisions are examined, individual attitudes and intentions constitute the major source of variation.

Third, relationships relating to one level should not be presumed to apply to other levels. The literature on the relationship between technology and organization structure exemplifies this point. This topic has accumulated a great deal of inconsistent findings since the early investigations of writers like Woodward (1965) which suggested that technology has a strong impact on an organization's structure. This early research centred on firms' 'modal' technology, that is, the typical processes employed in work performance. Later researchers emphasized the variety of technological forms which may coexist within a firm, and focused on these as potential sources of variation in organization structure. Both Fry (1982) and Rousseau (1983) have observed that three levels of analysis are currently used by researchers: individual, sub-unit and organizational. The presence of differences in the levels of analysis employed at least in part accounts for the variation in the findings encountered. Studies at the individual level appear to be least likely (and those at the sub-unit level most likely) to produce positive evidence of a relationship with organization structure (Fry, 1982). Moreover, when technology is conceptualized at these different levels, it does not mean the same thing in each case. At the organizational level, for example, technology tends to be conceptualized in terms of the conventional notion of machinery, but at the individual level it is to do with people's perceptions of the nature of the workflow, usually in terms of characteristics like its degree of routineness. This latter approach can be applied to non-manufacturing contexts more readily than the organization-level stance. This example demonstrates that care is needed in such areas of investigation in inferring that identical or similar results will be generated at each level and that the meaning of the findings, even when consistent, is necessarily the same.

Fourth, sampling and choice of unit of analysis point to another source of problems. First, samples of organizations sometimes include a diversity of types of organization, as in the case of the early Aston research (Pugh *et al.*, 1969). While this helps to enhance the generalizability of the findings, when organizations of different statuses are brought together the potential for confusion is considerable. Donaldson (1975) has noted that the West Midlands study, excluding governmental organizations, comprised ten branches, twenty subsidiaries, ten principal units and four head branches. These different types of status represent different levels of analysis and might be expected to reveal different degrees of autonomy. In particular, the measurement of the amount of centralization will be affected, since in branches 'decisions taken by branch managers would be scored as highly centralized (that is, taken at the top of the unit of study) whereas from the point of view of the whole organization the decisions are only being taken at the middle management level, and hence should *really* score medium' (Donaldson, 1975, p. 453). This difficulty raises the question of whether scores from such diverse statuses can genuinely be aggregated. Donaldson found that the correlations between centralization and other dimensions of structure varied markedly as between branches, subsidiaries and principal units. Second, the fit between the level of analysis and theory should be appropriate. The contingency approach to organizations views the organization as the focus of analysis, but some studies confuse this issue slightly. In an investigation of some of the theory's hidden assumptions, Schoonhoven (1981) examined acute care hospital operating suites. Pennings (1987) looked at branches of one bank in his test of the theory. When such diverse and potentially inappropriate levels of analysis constitute the focus, the meaning of the results for the theory can often become a matter of dispute.

Clearly, failure to recognize some of the issues explored in this section may result in erroneous results and inferences, but there is evidence of greater attention being accorded such issues nowadays.[1]

The study of organizational effectiveness

Research on organizational effectiveness (hereafter OE) is paradoxical. The tendency for it to be one of the most central concepts in the field and for a great many studies to be directly or indirectly concerned with it (hence the notion of its being the Holy Grail – see page 4) coexists with an irritation with the fruits of decades of research which has led to calls for the abandonment of OE studies (for example, Goodman, Atkin and Schoorman, 1983). The preoccupation with OE is undoubtedly a product of a commitment among some writers to generating useful, applicable knowledge for practitioners, a tendency which has been intensified by the growing trend towards the location of many organizational researchers in business schools and management departments. Organizational practitioners want to know what factors can enhance OE (Price, 1985), and many researchers have sought to provide relevant knowledge in this light, albeit with apparently limited success. This concern with OE is reflected in a wide variety of studies; for example, much research on individual and work-group performance derives from the fixation with OE. Indeed, the preoccupation is often a focus for theoretical dissent, with writers influenced by Marxist thinking seeing it as indicative of excessive managerialism and as excessively restricting the field's span of interests (for example, Goldman, 1978). While conflicting approaches and an absence of a coherent theory have contributed considerably to some of the dissatisfaction with OE research, methodological issues have played an important part, and it is with such topics that the present section is concerned.

What are some of the chief sources of disillusionment with OE research? First, a variety of different models exists, none of which has produced an agreed approach. The two most commonly cited models are the goal and system resource approaches (Price, 1972). The former construes OE in terms of the degree to which the organization achieves its goals, the latter in terms of the organization's degree of success in extracting scarce and valued resources from the environment. However, most research employs the goal approach, either implicitly or explicitly; but since this approach rarely entails the examination of what people in organizations take to be their goals and what their criteria of effectiveness in achieving them are (for an exception see Cameron, 1978), the nature of organizations' goals is usually assumed. However, there are further difficulties with the goal approach: organizations may have semi-official goals in addition to their formally stated ones, or they may have a number of different goals; it neglects the variety of goals that different sections of an organization may follow; goals frequently change over time (Cameron and Whetten, 1981); different organizational constituencies – owners, shareholders, customers, suppliers, senior managers – may have different conceptions of an organization's goals and criteria of its effectiveness (Friedlander and Pickle, 1968); and goals may be organization- or sector-specific and therefore of limited generalizability.

Second, there is a vast array of different indicators of OE. Campbell (1977) cites thirty indicators: overall effectiveness, productivity, efficiency, profit, quality, accidents, growth, absenteeism, turnover, job satisfaction, motivation, morale, control, conflict/cohesion, flexibility/adaptability, planning and goal setting, goal consensus, internalization of organizational goals, role and norm congruence, managerial interpersonal skills, managerial task skills, information management and communication, readiness, utilization of environment, evaluations by external entities, stability, value of human resources, participation and shared influence, training and development emphasis, and achievement emphasis. Although the meaning of some of these terms is not obvious (brief explanations can be found in Campbell, 1977), this list serves to bring out the considerable variety in types of indicator used.

Third, the nature of the indicators used varies considerably, in that some of the items on Campbell's list might reasonably be thought of as paths to OE, but not as OE as such. Although there may be grounds for thinking that enhancing job satisfaction is a path to better individual performance (though this has long been questioned), treating it as an indicator of OE lacks face validity. Fourth, research on OE has operated in a rather piecemeal fashion with little theoretical rationale for the indicators used or for the variables with which they are supposed to be associated. Consequently, some observers have expressed concern that much OE research has failed to develop a theory of OE, and that many investigations are undertaken in an *ad hoc* manner (Goodman, Atkin and Schoorman, 1983). This tendency, in tandem with the immense variety of indicators employed, many of which seem to be chosen on grounds of availability rather than as operationalizations of OE, has engendered a non-cumulative area of research.

Fifth, researchers often use only one indicator of OE, which is unsatisfactory for such a broad concept. When more than one is employed, it is disconcerting to find that the relationships between them are sometimes not explored, or that, when such analysis is undertaken, the correlations between them are low. However, when measures are carefully developed to reflect different theoretically defined dimensions of OE (rather than *ad hoc* measures which have little rationale other than their availability or that they are easy to measure), the ensuing results can be much more satisfying. For example, Georgopoulos's (1986) study of hospital emergency units emphasizes three major dimensions of OE – economic, clinical and social efficiency – each of which was measured by a variety of indicators. The absence of a relationship between the economic and clinical aspects of OE was attributed to the propensity of physicians to focus on the quality of clinical decisions and to pay less heed to economic issues. However, the relationship between the two criteria was found to be moderated by the presence or absence of emergency personnel training programmes (with those units having such schemes scoring well in terms of both criteria). From such findings, Georgopoulos is able to make a number of recommendations about the simultaneous enhancement of a number of OE criteria. Thus, plausible accounts could be provided for the absence of relationships between some measures of OE rather than simply ignoring it as an inconvenience or as a puzzle.

Finally, regardless of the measurement and other methodological difficulties, the results of OE research are often disappointing; correlations between OE and other variables are often quite small, thereby providing few if any implications for organizational change. For example, although reviews of research on the effects of greater participation at work tend to suggest that it has a positive impact on job satisfaction, when more direct measures of performance are used as dependent variables, such as productivity, the evidence points to minimal effect (for example; Locke and Schweiger, 1979; Miller and Monge, 1986).

From the point of view of methods of data collection, a number of different approaches to the measurement of OE can be distinguished. First, there is widespread use of archival records. Strategic management research makes intensive use of such sources, either in investigations in which data for all variables are collected through documents and archival sources (for example, Rumelt, 1974) or in studies in which data are collected through another source (usually an interview or questionnaire survey; for example, Hitt, Ireland and Stadter, 1982; Lenz, 1980). Intensive use tends to be made of financial/accounting measures of company performance, such as return on capital (ROC), return on equity (ROE), return on assets (ROA), sales volumes and earnings per share. Such financial measures have certain advantages; they are readily available, intuitively indicative of OE, non-reactive and available on a time-series basis (so that retrospective and prospective studies can be envisaged). On the other hand, they provide a very restricted conception of OE and the goals of enterprises, while many would argue about their appropriateness in non-profit, non-commercial organizations. Financial measures of OE are used by various researchers outside the field of strategic management (for example, Pennings, 1987). Other kinds of archival measures of OE are encountered. In his investigation of municipal fire departments in the USA, Coulter (1979) employed measured 'prevention effectiveness' by number of fires per 1,000 population and 'suppression effectiveness' by dollars of property loss from fires per 1,000 population.

Second, self-report measures are sometimes used. Lawrence and Lorsch (1967) asked chief executives to compare their firms' performance to others in their industry. Such evidence might be thought to be too subjective and prone to bias, but an investigation by Reimann (1982) belies such scepticism. Top executives in twenty organizations were asked to indicate their firms' relative performance in connection with eight areas, such as profit growth, product quality, customer service, employee job satisfaction and morale, and competitive strength. More than one informant was used in each case. Informants' answers were aggregated for each firm to form 'competence scores' for each of the criteria as well as an overall measure. Reimann examined the relationship between firms' scores and their subsequent levels of employment and revenue growth nine years later. Three firms had gone out of business; all three were among the bottom five in terms of their competence scores. Among the rest, competence scores were good predictors of subsequent levels of employment and revenue; for example, overall competence correlated .75 with subsequent employment levels, which is indicative of considerable predictive validity.

Third, performance may be assessed by persons in a position to make external assessments. At the individual level, supervisors are often asked to rate the performance of subordinates who are the focus of an inquiry in respect of a number of aspects, such as quality of work, productivity and effort (for example, Brass, 1981). A similar approach can be discerned at the work-group level; Allen, Lee and Tushman (1980) interviewed division managers and laboratory directors in the large R & D facility of a corporation about the performance of those projects with which they were familiar. Like Brass's study, these researchers asked respondents to rate performance on scales. Peers can also be used to provide such judgements; Georgopoulos (1986) asked other hospital physicians about the quality of care in focal hospital emergency units. He also asked patients about their degree of satisfaction with the care they received. Finally, at the organizational level, in their research on social services agencies in the USA, Osborn and Hunt (1974) asked officials in a central co-ordinating unit to rank the relative effectiveness of the agencies. Pennings (1987) interviewed bank branch customers about their degree of satisfaction with ten areas of service (see page 45).

One advantage of using measures of OE deriving from either the first or the third group is that when they are combined with survey interview or questionnaire studies they mitigate the 'common variance' problem, since the sources of data are not the same as those which provide data on other variables. Thus, Allen, Lee and Tushman (1980) established measures of most variables through self-administered questionnaires which were responded to by people in the projects concerned, but in each case assessments of OE were made by others. Similarly, Hitt Ireland and Stadter (1982) devised measures of firms' strategies and other concepts through postal questionnaires, but drew on archival data for indicators of performance. Self-assessed notions of OE, while exhibiting strong predictive validity, can produce a common variance problem if the same respondents are sources of information regarding other variables. However, these reflections raise a further complication; while there is a recognition that variations in findings from OE studies may derive from differences between investigations (such as divergent criteria, phases in the organizational life cycle, models and constituencies being examined), data collection issues are rarely considered important. Cameron (1978) notes that whether organizational records or perceptual measures are used may contribute to divergent findings or to a lack of comparability, but the role of differences in data collection within these two categories cannot be discounted, for example, whether perceptual data are derived from interviews or questionnaires or are based on self-reports or reports by others of OE.

What is distinctively absent in most research is the elucidation of organizations' own notions of OE. Investigations which rely on just one or two indicators may miss firms' notions by a mile, so that it would not be surprising if some of the independent variables are poorly associated with OE; the organizational activities that are deemed to be independent variables may not have been geared to enhancing OE as conceived by the researcher. Further, the use of multiple measures is often a hit-and-miss affair, such as eleven used in a study of public libraries (Damanpour and Evan, 1984). Although multiple-indicator approaches may stand a stronger chance of tapping organizations' own conceptions of OE, we still do not know which are central and which are peripheral; we need to have some idea of organizations' hierarchy of priorities in such a context in order to be able to forge a meaningful interpretation of the ensuing results.

An important start in this direction has been made by Cameron (1978) in the context of institutions of higher education. Semi-structured interviews were conducted with senior officials in a number of organizations, in which general questions such as 'What is it at this institution that makes a difference in terms of its effectiveness?' were asked. From an analysis of the various

OE criteria used, Cameron established nine dimensions of effectiveness: student educational satisfaction, student academic development, student career development, student personal development, faculty (that is, academic staff) and administrator employment satisfaction, professional development and quality of the faculty, systems openness and community interaction, ability to acquire resources and organizational health. Self-administered questionnaires were developed with a variety of questions to tap the extent to which respondents described their institutions as possessing each of these dimensions, and were sent to senior personnel, academic administrators and academic heads in six institutions. The different conceptions of OE at each of the six institutions were explored. Cameron notes that his research strongly suggests that OE is a multi-dimensional concept, and that research in other types of organization should reflect this tendency. A longitudinal study of twenty-nine institutions using the questionnaire has allowed Cameron (1986) to establish some of the variables with which OE is associated.

There can be little doubt that research on OE is in considerable disarray. Much research has become decoupled from the critiques of the literature that have emerged (see the collections edited by Cameron and Whetten, 1983, and Goodman and Pennings, 1977), since many investigations reveal little concern for the issues that have been raised in this section or exhibit mere lip service to them. While the research by Cameron is open to the charge that it does not depart significantly from traditional goal models (Goodman, Atkin and Schoorman, 1983, pp. 169–71), the attempt to ground measures in participants' own conceptions of OE constitutes a significant advance. It is ironic that qualitative researchers exhibit little interest in OE, since systematic, in-depth investigations would provide important insights into people's notions of OE and how these impinge on their everyday activities in organizations in a variety of contexts, though such research would have to recognize the variety of conceptions of OE with which different groupings within organizations operate. Such research could contribute significantly to an ailing area of study which is generally recognized as being of considerable importance.

Problems of time

One recurring theme in this book has been the problem of taking account of temporal processes in organizations. This focus has revealed itself on the following occasions. First, recall the discussion on page 128 of the replication of the first investigation within the Aston Studies programme by Inkson, Pugh and Hickson (1970) which suggested that the pattern of results over time differed from the cross-sectional findings with which the Aston approach is associated. Second, recall the findings from McKinley (1987) which suggested that patterns of findings differed for growing and declining organizations; moreover, this conclusion is similar to earlier research by Freeman and Hannan (1975) which suggested differences in the relationship between organization size and the administrative component in the two contexts. Such evidence suggests that growth and decline comprise different organizational imperatives. Third, recall the discussion in Chapter 4 about the direction of causality in correlational designs, which suggested that inferences about causal processes over time from static designs can be risky. In each of these instances, research demonstrates that temporal processes can lead to profound misinterpretations, although this recognition has not led to a cessation of static research.

On the other hand, there are some countervailing trends. In Chapter 7 it was noted that the increased interest in the analysis of documentary and archival material has led to a growing awareness of the significance of patterns of organizational process over time. In addition, Beyer (1987), in her role as editor of *Academy of Management Journal*, detects a preference among journal referees for 'repeated data collections', that is, data collected at more than one juncture or repeated laboratory experiments. The influence of theoretical positions which emphasize change, and which have gained support since the mid-1970s (such as institutional, population ecology and organizational life cycle approaches), at least in part accounts for the trend towards research which emphasizes temporal change. One of the chief reasons for not conducting survey research in two or more waves has tended to be its cost, but Cameron (1986) suggests a useful approach in following up institutions of higher education that were previously the focus of his research. This tactic offers the opportunity of examining whether results can be replicated, as well as the elucidation of how earlier characteristics are associated with later variables, like organizational effectiveness. One problem is likely to be loss of respondents (only twenty-nine of the initial forty-one in Cameron's case), but the additional information yield is considerable.

While these various tendencies in organizational research are commendable, the relevance of time in another capacity tends to be given scant attention; how far does the passage of time make findings less valid? Is it not possible that findings deriving from a particular time period no longer pertain at a later one (though this possibility does not deter writers from integrating findings relating to different times as though such consideration were irrelevant)? This inattention to time contrasts sharply with the concern that is often expressed about the generalizability of findings to populations and settings and which is denoted by worries about external validity. By contrast, *temporal validity* is given scant attention. Bryman (1989) has shown, drawing on a re-study of religious organizations, that over a period of fourteen years some marked changes could be discerned in the context of distributions of particular variables and of relationships between variables. Lack of temporal validity may be of considerable practical importance in a field like organization studies, because if plans of action are derived from investigations which have not been updated, the context for the application of such results may be inappropriate. Similarly, organizational research is subject to shifts in fashion; currently, work within the rational model (which is exemplified by the Aston Studies, investigations based on contingency theory and similar research) out of fashion (Scott, 1987b, p. xv), though this is not to say that all research within this framework has stopped. It would be very easy for later researchers to assume that the well-known results of investiga-tions within the rational tradition have stood still, even though there may be numerous intervening events (changes in markets, management philosophies, use of consultants and so on) which could substantially alter the nature of the findings.

Moreover, there is much that we do not know about the implications of the passage of time for research practice. There are very few accepted rules of thumb to assist in the tricky issues that confront researchers seeking to address temporal issues. There is virtually no help in deciding the appropriate span of time between waves of measurements. In the context of panel research on leader reward behaviour, Sims and Szilagyi (1979) have shown that the extent of the time lag between administrations of instruments to measure leader behaviour and other variables has a clear effect on the nature of the subsequent results. It would not be surprising if similar considerations applied to before-and-after experimental designs, where the timing of the 'after' measure of the dependent variable is often somewhat arbitrary. Similarly, re-studies like those of Bryman (1989) and Cameron (1986) are invariably based on arbitrarily chosen time-spans which are likely to have implications for patterns of results. Panel studies and re-studies are still so rare that there is little experience to build on to help the researcher in making these decisions. As far as re-studies are concerned, if a short span of time separates the two waves of data collection and a lack of congruence is found with the initial results, it is not obvious what inferences could be drawn; would the findings be indicative of change or of a failure to replicate? Again, such issues are given scant consideration.

The problems that can arise from the selection of a limited time-span can be neatly demonstrated by reference to the hugely successful management text *In Search of Excellence* (Peters and Waterman, 1982). In this book, detailed analyses of forty-three 'excellent' US companies were undertaken, and a number of lessons for management were gleaned. Even though a number of criteria of excellence were employed, some of which were based on financial data covering 1961 to 1980, it is apparent that fourteen of these excellent companies were floundering in the early 1980s (Anon., 1984). In particular, a failure to adapt to market change seems to have been a prominent cause of the sharp turn-arounds in performance revealed by the companies. These trends ostensibly cast doubt on the management principles gleaned from the investigation. Ironically, Price (1985, p. 131) of Hewlett-Packard (even more ironically one of the fourteen excellent companies to have experienced an adverse turn-around) has remarked that books like *In Search of Excellence* are often more appealing to managers than the output of organization studies, because they suggest what is and is not effective management practice, even though they 'may not be accurate'. A number of morals can be drawn from this tale, one of which is that, in conducting rigorous research with a view to providing information about organizational effectiveness, researchers should be prepared to spell out its practical implications, but most importantly for the present discussion, the problem of limited time frames is demonstrated.

Thus far, quantitative research has been the focus for this discussion, but considerations of time are relevant to qualitative research, albeit in different ways. In particular, when research is based on a detailed case study, there are often clear benefits associated with either an extended stay or a return to the organization in question. One of the strengths of qualitative research which is based on detailed case studies is that it is able to capture processes over time. If the sojourn is too short, an uncharacteristic state may be observed. Bresnen (1988) describes his experience in investigating a construction project which enjoyed a fairly buoyant atmosphere and which seemed to be operating well. When he visited it some months later, morale had deteriorated sharply due to a number of unforeseeable circumstances. Focusing solely on the earlier phase of fieldwork would have led to some erroneous conclusions. Further, brief periods of qualitative research may fail to capture some important phases in the organizational life cycle. Most organizations have recurring features which are associated with particular patterns of behaviour and anxieties, such as financial year-ends, budget allocations and annual ceremonial events. Brief forays at the wrong time of the year may mean not only that important information is missed, but also that unrepresentative conditions may be observed and generalized from.

Further, the temporal validity of qualitative research cannot be ignored. Unfortunately, the unstructured nature of much qualitative research tends to mean that it is difficult to generate comparable findings when a re-study is undertaken by another researcher. However, it is not impossible. Burawoy's (1979) 'accidental' re-study of the organization in which Roy (1954, 1960) conducted research in the 1940s allowed him to chart continuities and changes in working practices and the nature of workers' response, which in turn facilitated an elucidation of wider changes to the capitalist mode of production. Similarly, in the second edition of *The Dynamics of Bureaucracy*, Blau (1963) reports some of the chief points deriving from a 'replication' of his initial investigations in a state employment agency by Cohen a decade later. For example, Cohen found that employment officers' preoccupations with their own and others' performance records had intensified and he looked at some of the unofficial practices which were used much more intensively to boost records than when Blau was present. However, the different positions of the two researchers point to some of the problems of interpreting such re-study evidence, since these differences cannot be discounted as at least partial reasons for the contrasting findings (Cohen conducted three years of full participant observation; Blau conducted three months of non-participant and structured observation).

The points raised in this section imply four issues. First, the implications of time for the findings deriving from much static research are not fully understood, and when investigators include a temporal element in their work (such as panel studies) the problems of static studies become very evident. Second, very little is known about organizational change, although there are signs of improvement in this respect. It is striking that detailed case studies covering long time-spans (for example, Johnson, 1987; Mintzberg and McHugh, 1985; Pettigrew, 1985) are particularly adept at bringing out how organizations change and the causes and consequences of change. Moreover, increasing interest in conceptions of time in organizations (for example, Bryman *et al.*, 1987b; Clark, 1985) may promote greater interest in such issues. Third, scant attention is given to the temporal validity of many findings, though this tendency is common to many areas of the social sciences. Fourth, because of the lack of attention to these issues, few guidelines have been developed to assist researchers in decisions about appropriate time-spans.

The problem of applied research

A significant proportion of organizational research is undertaken within an 'applied' context, that is, to provide knowledge that can be used by organizations. This very orientation has been the object of criticism, with writers taking the view that it leads to a discipline that is unconcerned about how the knowledge is used and that the applied emphasis restricts the subject's intellectual development. The notion of applied research implies a contrast with pure or basic research. Scott (1987b) sees a distinction within organizational research between basic research, which is driven by theoretical concerns, and applied research, which is concerned with solving problems. While arguing that practitioners of these two approaches constitute separate groups, Scott also recognizes a group of researchers who reveal both basic and applied elements in their work. This third group tends to be located in departments of business, management, public administration and so on in institutions of higher education. An interesting aspect of the applied emphasis in organizational research has been highlighted by Barley, Meyer and Gash (1988), who note that in the mid-1970s, when interest in organizational culture started to surface, academic and practitioner writers tended to approach the concept differently from each other. After the middle of 1982 (when interest in organizational culture burgeoned) academics' concerns and styles of discourse shifted towards those of practitioners, as revealed by a growing focus on culture as a control mechanism. A number of explanations for this shift can be proffered, but there is a strong possibility that academic writers gradually imbibed practitioners' concerns. While some writers view the applied emphasis with distaste, others are concerned about what they take to be the insufficient practical relevance of much organizational research (for example, Lawler, 1985a; Thomas and Tymon, 1982). In this context, it is interesting to note that Whyte (1987) has bemoaned the supplanting of 'human relations' as a field of research by 'organizational behaviour', because the latter tends to exhibit less concern with applied issues.

This section is not concerned with debates about whether organizational researchers should or should not exhibit an emphasis on generating applied knowledge, but rather, given that some researchers exhibit this orientation, what methodological issues might account for the current unease about the adequacy of this applied knowledge? One problem with examining this issue is that it is not always clear when research is or is not applied. The field of leadership has exhibited a strong concern for generating practical knowledge which would contribute either to the selection or to the training of good leaders (Bryman, 1986), but it is by no means the case that all leadership studies constitute applied research. The point here is that some applied research is undertaken with a direct concern for the solution of organizational problems, such as action research; the bulk of applied research in the field is probably better described as 'potentially applied research'. Further, the distinction between basic and applied (however conceived) is fuzzy (Rossi, 1980) for a number of reasons. The practical relevance of basic research may not be apparent at the outset, as areas of practical importance often come to be recognized at a later stage, the criteria of relevance may shift as circumstances change so that what is basic in one period may be seen as applied in another, and the two – basic and applied – may not always be mutually inconsistent.

One reason for the lack of practical significance of much applied research is that it is ironically too rigorous and sophisticated. The heightened predilection among organizational researchers for investigations in the style of the natural sciences has led to two characteristics which inhibit an easy extraction of practical relevance: the emphasis on variables and their multivariate analysis. The tendency in much organizational research for emphasizing abstract variables often does not lend itself to extracting implications for relevance because there is no 'feel' for the organizational context. Survey investigations are particularly prone to this accusation since they entail research into samples of organizations (often of limited or unknown generalizability), and the variables in question are plucked out of the organizations in which they are embedded. Variables are usually of a high level of abstraction and generality to permit comparisons across organizations. The multivariate analysis of these variables involves looking at independent variables, moderator variables and the like, but goes far beyond the three-variable patterns examined in Chapter 4 in that many variables are simultaneously analysed. The problem here is that it is difficult to envisage what practical significance can be derived from such research, since people who work in organizations are unlikely to have the time or inclination to pick their way through the tangled knots of variables typically engendered by such analysis. Griffin (1980), for example,

246 RESEARCH METHODS AND ORGANIZATION STUDIES

examined the effect of each of five leadership styles on subordinate satisfaction and performance under different levels of task scope and subordinate growth needs. Eight hypotheses, each entailing different combinations of the variables, were generated from a prior examination of the relevant literature. These hypotheses received moderate support – those including performance as a dependent variable were particularly unlikely to be supported. From this study one would derive such conclusions as: when there is high task scope and subordinates have high growth needs, a leadership style combining achievement orientation and participation will lead to overall satisfaction (and also satisfaction with job and supervisor), but not better subordinate performance; when there are low task scope and low growth needs, a maintenance leadership style will lead to better performance, overall satisfaction and satisfaction with the supervisor but not with the job. Further, the results imply that it is rarely the case that more than half of the variation in the dependent variables is being explained and in many instances does not rise above a quarter. In fact, this is a carefully formulated study which has important implications for the factors which moderate the effects of different types of leader behaviour. The point that is being made here is that it is difficult to know what managers could make of these findings for their own behaviour and whether they think that it would be worth analysing every situation in detail to ascertain the correct leadership style in view of some of the incongruent results and also the low levels of variation in the dependent variables being explained. It is worth recalling the previous discussion (page 242) of *In Search of Excellence* (Peters and Waterman, 1982). Multivariate research, when viewed from the perspective of practical relevance, tends to produce results of the 'ifs' and 'buts' kind (for example, if you have situation $a + b$, leadership style X will produce effect 1, but not 2; but if you have situation $a +$ not-b, leadership style X will produce effects $1 + 2$, but not 3). Such findings do not lend themselves to the formulation of concise management 'recipes' (as in the *Excellence* book), and also, when writing up their studies, researchers tend to leave the practical implications of their findings unstated. It is this kind of characteristic that prompts the label 'potentially applied research'.

Second, the prospective consumers of organizational research are rarely involved in the formulation of issues (action research being a notable exception). Were they to be more involved it is possible that the output of organizational researchers would produce findings which would be of greater practical interest. On the other hand, such a trend would substantially reduce the field's intellectual autonomy and therefore, quite properly, would be unacceptable to most researchers, although Lawler (1985a) recommends the involvement of practitioners. Third, the tendency towards using convenience samples tied to particular sectors of the economy (restaurants, electronics firms, libraries and so on), rather than to fairly representative samples covering a number of sectors (for example, Blau *et al.*, 1976), probably limits the prospective relevance of much survey research (and possibly some field experimentation also, albeit in different ways), since it may be difficult for practitioners to perceive the relevance of findings for their sector, because executives often perceive their sector as different and requiring specialized attention. However, in spite of their apparently doubtful generalizability, case studies with a strong qualitative component are often preferred by managers, because, unlike research which emphasizes abstract variables, in-depth research can provide the practitioner with a better feel for organizational reality. Price (1985) of Hewlett-Packard writes:

> Case studies, stories, anecdotes, and field studies are appealing because they have the richness of the situation and have not been filtered through so many abstractions. A reader is able to see much more vividly the richness, ambiguities, and the incongruencies that are part of organizational life.
>
> (Price, 1985, p. 131)

Price argues for the greater use of such research approaches in conjunction with variable-style investigations.

The chief purpose of this section has not been to highlight all of the factors which inhibit the practical relevance of organizational research; much more detailed lists of factors can be found elsewhere (for example, Lawler, 1985a). Rather, its main purpose has been to show how some of the ways in which research is conducted may engender limited practical relevance. In addition, the issue of the ways in which research findings are presented frequently obstructs their applicability, since they often fail to spell out the implications of often complex analyses of variables.

The paradigm problem

One of the themes running through this book is a need to be aware of both the opportunities and the limitations associated with particular methods of data collection. Correspondingly, it has been suggested on a number of occasions that, because the choice of any method involves a trade-off, it has to be recognized that information is lost by dint of not employing another method. The point is to try to reconcile research problem and method as far as possible in order to maximize damage limitation. Of course, the use of more than one method (see Chapter 6) can greatly enhance the process of fusing problem and method, by allowing the researcher to reap the opportunities presented by two or more techniques. However, resource and access considerations, coupled with the predilections of researchers (for example, by virtue of their training, abilities and inclinations), reduce the likelihood that such integration of methods will occur. None the less, the general tenor of this book has been in favour of perusing the whole array of research methods before conducting an investigation and against the 'mono-method monopolies' (Martin, 1989) which seek to peddle one particular approach to the exclusion of others.

However, there is a prominent counter-position to this catholic view. This alternative perspective argues that it is necessary to be aware that research methods are tied to different epistemological positions, that is, different ways of understanding what constitutes acceptable knowledge. Such a view is revealed in the following statement:

> the choice and adequacy of a method embodies a variety of assumptions regarding the nature of knowledge and the methods through which that knowledge can be obtained, as well as a set of root assumptions about the nature of the phenomena to be investigated.
>
> (Morgan and Smircich, 1980, p. 491)

This kind of view owes a great deal to the notion that the study of organizations (and indeed the study of society) exhibits contrasting paradigms which comprise divergent views about the nature of social reality and about what is acceptable knowledge concerning that reality. In this way, the distinction between quantitative and qualitative research is not simply a matter of different approaches to the research process, each with its own cluster of research methods (that is, the view espoused in this book), but it concerns antagonistic views about more fundamental issues to do with the nature of one's subject-matter. The view that quantitative research and qualitative research represent contrasting epistemological positions is usually the result of the suggestion that they bespeak opposing positions regarding the applicability of a natural science model to the study of society. Whereas quantitative research is viewed as suffused with a commitment to the natural sciences, qualitative research is depicted as embracing a different epistemological position that entails a rejection of the scientific method by virtue of an espousal of the notion that people are fundamentally different from the objects which constitute the natural scientist's subject-matter. The distinctiveness of people and social reality, as against the natural order, reveals itself in the capacity of people to attribute meaning to and interpret their social environment and to be active in the construction of that environment, so that the social world is not simply an inert system of regularities waiting to be revealed.

Kuhn's ([1962] 1970) writings within the history of science are in large part the spring from which much of the writing about paradigms has emerged. According to Kuhn, paradigms 'are the source of the methods, problem-field, and standards of solution accepted by any mature scientific field at any given time' (p. 103). Scientific fields are seen as progressing such that long periods of 'normal science', in which scientists work within a common paradigm, give way to periods of 'revolutionary science' whereby a new paradigm emerges and achieves gradual recognition and acceptance. The social sciences, including organization studies, do not reveal a level of consensus which would imply the existence of a paradigm at any stage in their development. However, many authors were taken by Kuhn's suggestion that in the early stages of their development many scientific fields operate at a 'pre-paradigmatic' stage, during which there are competing paradigms (or strictly speaking, pre-paradigms). This contention seems to have struck a cord for many writers who became concerned to map the paradigms in various social scientific fields.

One of the most influential versions of the 'competing paradigms' view is that supplied by Burrell and Morgan (1979). Although their analysis suggests the existence of four paradigms in organization studies, it is proposed to concentrate on two of them – functionalist and interpretive – since they correspond closely to the quantitative and qualitative views of the research process, as elucidated in this book (see Table 9.1 which also mentions other versions of the two paradigms implied by the quantitative/functionalist and qualitative/interpretive pairings). The functionalist paradigm is viewed as influenced by a positivist approach whose leanings towards the natural sciences impel the researcher towards a search for regularities in the social world and for causal relationships among the variables which make up that world. The interpretive approach argues that the social world can only be understood from the perspective of its

Table 9.1   The two 'paradigms' of organizational research

Author	Paradigm I	Paradigm II
Morgan and Smircich (1980); Van Maanen (1982)	Quantitative	Qualitative
Evered and Louis (1981)	Inquiry from the outside	Inquiry from the inside
Burrell and Morgan (1979); Hassard (1986)	Functionalist	Interpretive
Guba (1985)	Positivist	Naturalist

participants. The social world in the functionalist paradigm is seen as an external reality which is beyond the individual. The interpretive paradigm sees the individual as an active participant in the construction of that world and not as something from which he or she is divorced. The latter paradigm emphasizes the need to 'understand the social world by obtaining first-hand knowledge of the subject under investigation' (Burrell and Morgan, 1979, p. 6); the functionalist paradigm emphasizes scientific rigour through following systematic procedures as revealed by the prominence of 'surveys, questionnaires, personality tests and standardized research instruments' (p. 7). An important implication for Burrell and Morgan of the suggestion that each of these two approaches constitutes a paradigm is that they follow Kuhn's suggestion that paradigms are 'incommensurable'; that is, they are not compatible or reconcilable. Burrell and Morgan argue that, contrary to the view that different approaches ought to be integrated, the recognition that they are paradigms denotes that they reflect 'alternative realities' and 'mutually exclusive ways of viewing the world' (p. 398). In fact, as a number of writers have observed (for example, Donaldson, 1985; Hassard, 1988), in his later writings Kuhn softened his views about the incommensurability of scientific paradigms. However, it is not proposed to dwell on this issue in the present exposition.

Two important ramifications of the perception of quantitative and qualitative research (or their synonyms) as competing paradigms, and indeed of any account which regards them as representing competing epistemologies, can be discerned. First, the view would seem to deny the possibility that quantitative and qualitative research can be combined. Second, it suggests that method and epistemology are related, though it is not always obvious how this connection operates. Does it imply that when using a self-administered questionnaire the researcher should realize that he or she is operating within an epistemological framework associated with a quantitative (functionalist) epistemology (that is, method presumes epistemology)? Or does it mean that when seeking to conduct research within a quantitative epistemology the researcher should recognize that only one of the techniques associated with that paradigm (such as a questionnaire) can be employed (that is, epistemology presumes method)? In any event, both of the ramifications of the epistemological version of the differences between quantitative and qualitative research are questionable.

Can quantitative and qualitative research be combined? In Chapter 6 a number of studies were described or cited which in various ways combined methods associated with each of the two approaches. However, Hassard (1986, p. 81) has argued that the kind of exercise referred to in Chapter 6 'only brings together different forms of methodology; it does not extend into research based on the alternative philosophies of major communities [that is, paradigms]'. Hassard has attempted to integrate the quantitative and qualitative approaches *qua* paradigms, an exercise which he deems possible because he denies the incommensurability of paradigms. In a study of a fire service in England, he employed both paradigms (as well as the other two paradigms developed by Burrell and Morgan) as separate phases. However, the practicalities of conducting organizational research impinged on his investigation. The most obvious way forward of employing both paradigms to investigate broadly the same issue was not feasible, because, from the perspective of the organization concerned, little ground would be covered, and hence the research would be of little interest. Moreover, Hassard notes that issues raised by one paradigm may not be appropriate to another. Accordingly, different aspects of work organization were examined through each of the two paradigms. In the quantitative research (that is, within what he calls the functionalist paradigm, following Burrell and Morgan), Hassard administered the JDS to investigate the motivating potential of job characteristics as perceived by fire-fighters. In the qualitative (interpretive) study, he explored the accomplishment of routine tasks through an examination of 'unstructured conversational material'. Hassard views his work as 'multiple paradigm research . . . in which results accrue from quasi-exclusive perspectives' (1986, p. 77).

There are two difficulties with this research. First, it is not obvious what this multiple paradigm research has added up to. It certainly demonstrates that it is feasible to combine Burrell and Morgan's paradigms, but it is not clear what overall view of work organization has been generated. Second, in spite of Hassard's view that his work differs from research which simply combines methods, the differences between his approach and the examples of the integration of quantitative and qualitative research which were cited in Chapter 6 are not great. Indeed, it is not obvious how some of these studies would be classified in terms of Burrell and Morgan's two paradigms. For example, in a study of organizational culture in a large US electronics firm, Siehl and Martin (1988) employed a combination of qualitative research (indirect participant observation, unstructured interviews and analysis of documents) and quantitative research (a questionnaire deriving from the qualitative investigation designed to measure respondents' knowledge of company values, jargon, stories, and so on). Their research was concerned with the impact of training on individuals' cultural knowledge, but they point to other potential uses of their approach which would relate to fundamental issues regarding organizational culture. For example, a questionnaire designed to measure aspects of organizational culture could be developed (following a qualitative investigation of the kind conducted by Siehl and Martin) to provide a more precise delineation of intra-organizational variation (such as between manual workers, routine clerical workers and managers) in the degree of espousal of the measured cultural attributes. In this research, the aim would not be to use the qualitative data as a source of hypotheses which only gain legitimacy when confirmed by quantitative research – a common suggestion which does not constitute a true fusion, since there is an implicit notion that the quantitative information is superior – but to extend the analysis by tracing variation in a more detailed manner than could be provided on the basis of qualitative research alone. How would this research be classified: as quantitative/functionalist or qualitative/interpretive? Also, would it differ greatly from Hassard's study, in that the quantitative and qualitative components would each derive from issues consonant with the two paradigms? Organizational culture has been intensively studied by qualitative researchers (for example, Smircich, 1983), while issues of variation and the correlates of variation are important ingredients of quantitative research. Two points are being made here. First, it is clearly the case, contrary to Burrell and Morgan, that quantitative and qualitative research can be combined. Indeed, one of these writers seems to acknowledge the prospect of inter-paradigm *rapprochement* in his later work (Morgan, 1983, p. 378). Second, the question of whether it is paradigms or simply methods that are being integrated is of little significance. Guba (1985, p. 95) has written that arguments for *rapprochement* 'are based at bottom on a fundamental confusion between paradigm and method'. Since paradigms may be commensurable, and since the fruits of inter-paradigm and inter-method inquiry are not overly different, such a view has to be discounted.

But what of the second ramification: the connection between epistemological position (or paradigm) and method? Morgan and Smircich (1980) were quoted on page 248 for their view about the need to recognize the epistemological implications of a choice of method. They suggest that there is a link between epistemology and method and also that the quantitative/qualitative distinction stands for different epistemological viewpoints. In this latter respect, they differ from other writers who argue that quantitative research and qualitative research represent different approaches to data collection, each of which is appropriate to some issues but not to others (Bryman, 1988a). However, Morgan and Smircich acknowledge that methods may be used in a different epistemological environment:

> any given technique often lends itself to a variety of uses according to the orientation of the researcher. For example, participant observation in the hands of a positivist may be used to document the number and length of interactions within a setting.
>
> (Morgan and Smircich, 1980, p. 498)

This view seems to entail a recognition that methods are more autonomous than the earlier quotation indicated. Participant observation may also be used to test theories (for example, Pinfield, 1986), an activity normally associated with quantitative research. Both quantitative research and qualitative research share a reliance on the researcher's direct experience as a source of data, which is often perceived as an attribute of positivism. The interest among some quantitative researchers in attributions (for example, Staw, 1975) and lay theories (for example, Rush, Thomas and Lord, 1977) suggests that the quantitative tradition has a capacity to address issues of meaning and interpretation, although in a different sense from much qualitative research. Moreover, the examples of integration mentioned in the previous paragraph indicate that methods can be adapted to a variety of different uses.

The gist of this discussion is that methods do not bring a trail of epistemological presuppositions in their wake. Each method should be appreciated for what it is: a means of gathering problem-relevant data. The methods associated with qualitative research have many advantages over quantitative methods which have been mentioned in this book – greater flexibility, better access to hidden aspects of organizations, a greater facility with process and change, good at generating new concepts and ideas and so on – but these are all technical advantages which the researcher may wish to take into account in deciding the best fit between method and research problem. Even two of the central motifs of qualitative research – its emphasis on actors' meanings and interpretations and on the notion that the social world is actively constructed by people – can be treated as important aspects of work and organizations which the techniques associated with qualitative research are superior at revealing. An alternative cluster of technical advantages can be discerned in quantitative research. Similarly, each of the two research traditions exhibits a group of limitations, such as limited generalizability, the problem of interpretation and data analysis difficulties associated with much qualitative research. Good research consists of recognizing such collections of strengths and frailties and not being wedded to a method irrespective of the problem being examined. In the end, a method will be good or bad only in relation to that problem. The advantages of blending methods are considerable, and a major theme of this section has been that the arguments about the epistemological distinctiveness of quantitative and qualitative research is not, and should not be taken to be, a barrier to such integration. It would be ironic if fretting about paradigms – their boundaries and their status – were to act as a barrier to the fusion of methods (where appropriate), since the argument about the connection between epistemology and research method which undergirds the notion of a paradigm constitute a poor statement about how research both is and should be conducted.

Overview

In this chapter, an attempt has been made to explore a number of recurring issues in organizational research. The discussion of whether organizational research needs to examine the connections between epistemology and research method was left until last since it refers to a wide-ranging debate which encapsulates much of this book's subject matter. Each of the five issues refers to a fundamental set of difficulties and dilemmas which researchers confronting many topics are likely to encounter.

In a sense, this chapter does not lend itself to a pithy summary, an attribute that is shared by the book as a whole. The chief message to be extracted is one voiced in the preceding paragraph: that each design and method should be taken on its merits as a means of facilitating (or obscuring) the understanding of particular research problems, and that a fetishistic espousal of favoured designs or methods and an excessive preoccupation with their epistemological underpinnings can only stand in the way of developing such an understanding.

Note

1 There is evidence of an increasing awareness of the problems examined in this section. In particular, the arrival of a complex model for dealing with relationships between variables at different levels of analysis – the *varient* approach developed by Danserau, Alutto and Yammarino, 1984 – is an indication of such concern. So too is research which aims to establish the circumstances in which it is possible to make inferences between levels (for example, Firebaugh, 1978).

Bibliography and author index

The references incorporate an author index; page numbers in bold at the end of each entry indicate where the publication is referred to in this book.

Aldrich, H. E. (1972), 'Technology and organizational structure: a re-examination of the findings of the Aston Group', *Administrative Science Quarterly*, vol. 17, no. 1, pp. 26–43. **126**

Allen, T. J., Lee, D. M. S., and Tushman, M. L. (1980), 'R & D performance as a function of internal communication, project management, and the nature of work', *IEEE Transactions on Engineering Management*, vol. EM-27, no. 1, pp. 2–12. **237–8**

Anderson, C. R., and Paine, F. T. (1978), 'PIMS: a reexamination', *Academy of Management Review*, vol. 3, no. 3, pp. 602–12. **203**

Angle, H. L., and Perry, J. L. (1981), 'An empirical assessment of organizational commitment and organizational effectiveness', *Administrative Science Quarterly*, vol. 26, no. 1, pp. 1–13. **114**

Anon. (1984), 'Who's excellent now?', *Business Week*, 5 November, pp. 47–55. **242**

Arnold, H. J., and Feldman, D. C. (1981), 'Social desirability response bias in self-report choice situations', *Academy of Management Journal*, vol. 24, no. 2, pp. 377–85. **66**

Barley, S. R. (1986), 'Technology as an occasion for structuring: evidence from observations of CT scanners and the social order of radiology departments', *Administrative Science Quarterly*, vol. 31, no. 1, pp. 78–108. **155, 160, 171**

Barley, S. R., Meyer, G. W., and Gash, D. C. (1988) 'Cultures of culture: academics, practitioners and the pragmatics of normative control', *Administrative Science Quarterly*, vol. 33, no. 1, pp. 24–60. **152, 244**

Barnett, W. P., and Carroll, G. R. (1987), 'Competition and mutualism among early telephone companies', *Administrative Science Quarterly*, vol. 32, no. 3, pp. 400–21. **189, 196**

Bateman, T. S., and Strasser, S. (1984), 'A longitudinal analysis of the antecedents of organizational commitment', *Academy of Management Journal*, vol. 27, no. 1, pp. 95–112. **62**

Becker, H. S. (1986), *Writing for Social Scientists: How to Start and Finish your Thesis, Book or Article* (Chicago: University of Chicago Press). **134**

Bennis, W. G., and Nanus, B. (1985), *Leaders: The Strategies for Taking Charge* (New York: Harper & Row). **152, 157**

Bettman, J. R., and Weitz, B. A. (1983), 'Attributions in the board room: causal reasoning in corporate annual reports', *Administrative Science Quarterly*, vol. 28, no. 2, pp. 165–83. **189, 191**

Beyer, J. M. (1987), 'From the editor', *Academy of Management Journal*, vol. 30, no. 4, pp. 621–4. **132, 240**

Beynon, H. (1988), 'Regulating research: politics and decision making in industrial organizations', in A. Bryman (ed.) (1988c), *Doing Research in Organizations* (London: Routledge), pp. 21–33. **162–3**

Blau, P. M. (1955), *The Dynamics of Bureaucracy* (Chicago: University of Chicago Press). **170–1**

Blau, P. M. (1963), *The Dynamics of Bureaucracy*, 2nd edn (Chicago: University of Chicago Press). **243**

Blau, P. M., Falbe, C. M., McKinley, W., and Tracy, P. K. (1976), 'Technology and organization in manufacturing', *Administrative Science Quarterly*, vol. 21, no. 1, pp. 20–40. **46, 115–16, 170, 200–2, 247**

Blauner, R. (1964), *Alienation and Freedom: The Factory Worker and his Industry* (Chicago: University of Chicago Press). **201–2**

Blumberg, M., and Pringle, C. D. (1983), 'How control groups can cause loss of control in action research', *Journal of Applied Behavioral Science*, vol. 19, no. 4, pp. 409–25. **94–5**

Bottomore, T. B., and Rubel, M. (1963), *Karl Marx: Selected Writings in Sociology and Social Philosophy* (Harmondsworth: Penguin). **52**

Bragg, J. E., and Andrews, I. R. (1973), 'Participative decision making: an experimental study in a hospital', *Journal of Applied Behavioral Science*, vol. 9, no. 6, pp. 727–35. **94**

Brass, D. J. (1981), 'Structural relationships, job characteristics, and worker satisfaction and performance', *Administrative Science Quarterly*, vol. 26, no. 2, pp. 331–48. **114, 237**

Brass, D. J., and Oldham, G. R. (1976), 'Validating an in-basket test using an alternative set of leadership scoring dimensions', *Journal of Applied Psychology*, vol. 61, no. 5, pp. 652–7. **215**

Bray, D. W., Campbell, R. J., and Grant, D. L. (1974), *Formative Years in Business: A Long-Term AT & T Study of Managerial Lives* (New York: Wiley). **215**

Brayfield, A., and Rothe, H. (1951), 'An index of job satisfaction', *Journal of Applied Psychology*, vol. 35, no. 5, pp. 307–11. **37, 39–40, 50, 129**

Bresnen, M. (1988), 'Insights on site: research into construction project organizations', in A. Bryman (ed.) (1988c), *Doing Research in Organizations* (London: Routledge), pp. 34–52. **152, 160, 163, 242**

Bridgman, P. W. (1927), *The Logic of Modern Physics* (New York: Macmillan). **36**

Brief, A. P., Aldag, R. J., and Chacko, T. I. (1977), 'The Miner sentence completion scale: an appraisal', *Academy of Management Journal*, vol. 20, no, 4, pp. 635–43. **226**

Brown, C., De Monthoux, P. G., and McCullough, A. (eds) (1976), *The Access-Casebook: Social Scientists Account for How to Get Data for Field Research* (Stockholm: Teknisk Hogeskolelitteratur). **2, 162**

Brown, M. C. (1982), 'Administrative succession and organizational performance: the succession effect', *Administrative Science Quarterly*, vol. 27, no. 1, pp. 1–16. **189–90**

Bryman, A. (1986), *Leadership and Organizations* (London: Routledge

& Kegan Paul). **65, 74, 124, 133, 156, 190, 231, 245**
Bryman, A. (1987), 'The generalizability of implicit leadership theory',
Journal of Social Psychology, vol. 127, no. 2, pp. 129–41. **67, 133**
Bryman, A. (1988a), *Quantity and Quality in Social Research* (London:
Unwin Hyman). **6, 7, 22, 64, 164, 168–9, 213, 253**
Bryman, A. (1988b), 'Introduction: "inside" accounts and social research
in organizations', in A. Bryman (ed.) (1988c), *Doing Research in
Organizations* (London: Routledge), pp. 1–20. **4, 21**
Bryman, A. (ed.), (1988c) *Doing Research in Organizations* (London:
Routledge). **2, 115**
Bryman, A. (1989), 'The value of re-studies in sociology: the case of
clergy and ministers, 1979 to 1985', *Sociology*, vol. 23, no. 1,
pp. 31–53. **164, 241**
Bryman, A., and Pettitt, A. (1985), 'Problems of short scales: the case
of the Aston Studies', *Quality and Quantity*, vol. 19, no. 4, pp.
375–82. **200**
Bryman, A., Bresnen, M., Ford, J., Beardsworth, A., and Keil, T.
(1987a), 'Leader orientation and organizational transience: an investigation using Fiedler's LPC scale', *Journal of Occupational Psychology*,
vol. 60, no. 1, pp. 13–19. **57**
Bryman, A., Bresnen, M., Beardsworth, A., Ford, J., and Keil, T.
(1987b), 'The concept of the temporary system: the case of the
construction project', in N. DiTomaso and S. B. Bacharach (eds),
Research in the Sociology of Organizations, Vol. 5 (Greenwich,
Conn.: JAI Press), pp. 253–83. **243**
Bryman, A., Bresnen, M., Beardworth, A., and Keil, T. (1988),
'Qualitative research and the study of leadership', *Human Relations*,
vol. 41, no. 1, pp. 13–30. **152, 155–6**
Buchanan, D., Boddy, D., and McCalman, J. (1988), 'Getting in,
getting on, getting out, and getting back', in A. Bryman (ed.) (1988c),
Doing Research in Organizations (London: Routledge), pp. 53–67. **2,
162–4**
Bulmer, M. (1982a), 'The merits and demerits of covert participant
observation', in M. Bulmer (ed.) (1982b), *Social Research Ethics*
(London: Macmillan), pp. 217–51. **144**
Bulmer, M. (ed.), (1982b) *Social Research Ethics* (London: Macmillan).
Burawoy, M. (1979), *Manufacturing Consent: Changes in the Labor
Process under Monopoly Capitalism* (Chicago: University of Chicago
Press). **152, 164, 243**
Burgelman, R. A. (1983), 'A process model of internal corporate
venturing in the diversified major firm', *Administrative Science
Quarterly*, vol. 28, no. 2, pp. 223–44. **141, 152, 156, 172–3**
Burgelman, R. A. (1985), 'Managing the new venture division: research
findings and implications for strategic management', *Strategic
Management Journal*, vol. 6, no. 1, pp. 39–54. **25–6, 29–30, 135, 141,
152, 155, 172**
Burns, T., and Stalker, G. M. (1961), *The Management of Innovation*
(London: Tavistock). **201**
Burrell, G., and Morgan, G. (1979), *Sociological Paradigms and
Organisational Analysis* (London: Heinemann). **249–52**

Cameron, K. (1978), 'Measuring organizational effectiveness in institutions of higher education', *Administrative Science Quarterly*, vol. 23, no. 4, pp. 604–32. **234, 238–9**

Cameron, K. (1986), 'A study of organizational effectiveness and its predictors', *Management Science*, vol. 32, no. 1, pp. 87–112. **239–41**

Cameron, K., Kim, M. U., and Whetten, D. A. (1987), 'Organizational effects of decline and turbulence', *Administrative Science Quarterly*, vol. 32, no. 2, pp. 222–40. **109–10**

Cameron, K., and Whetten, D. A. (1981), 'Perceptions of organizational effectiveness over organizational life cycles', *Administrative Science Quarterly*, vol 26, no. 4, pp. 524–44. **217–20, 223, 234**

Cameron, K., and Whetten, D. A. (eds) (1983), *Organizational Effectiveness: A Comparison of Multiple Models* (New York: Academic Press). **239**

Campbell, D. T. (1957), 'Factors relevant to the validity of experiments in social settings', *Psychological Bulletin*, vol. 54, no. 4, pp. 297–312. **73**

Campbell, D. T., and Fiske, D. W. (1959), 'Convergent and discriminant validation by the multitrait–multimethod matrix', *Psychological Bulletin*, vol. 56, no. 2, pp. 81–105. **60–2, 68**

Campbell, J. P. (1977), 'On the nature of organizational effectiveness', in P. S. Goodman and J. M. Pennings (eds), *New Perspectives on Organizational Effectiveness* (San Francisco: Jossey-Bass), pp. 13–55. **234–5**

Campbell, J. P. (1985), 'Editorial: some remarks from the outgoing editor', in L. L. Cummings and P. J. Frost (eds) (1985), *Publishing in the Organizational Sciences* (Homewood, Ill.: Richard D. Irwin), pp. 321–33. **21**

Carroll, G. R. (1984), 'Dynamics of publisher succession in newspaper organizations', *Administrative Science Quarterly*, vol. 29, no. 1, pp. 93–113. **189–90**

Carroll G. R., and Delacroix, J. (1982), 'Organizational mortality in the newspaper industries of Argentina and Ireland: an ecological approach', *Administrative Science Quarterly*, vol. 27, no. 1, pp. 169–98. **189, 195–6, 199**

Carroll, G. R., and Huo, Y. P. (1986), 'Organizational task and institutional environments in ecological perspective: findings from the local newspaper industry', *American Journal of Sociology*, vol. 91, no. 4, pp. 838–73. **189, 197**

Carter, N. M. (1984), 'Computerization as a predominate technology: its influence on the structure of newspaper organizations', *Academy of Management Journal*, vol. 27, no. 2, pp. 247–70. **44**

Cavendish, R. (1982), *Women on the Line* (London: Routledge & Kegan Paul). **144, 152–3**

Champoux, J. E. (1980), 'A three sample test of some extensions of the job characteristics model of work motivation', *Academy of Management Journal*, vol. 23, no. 3, pp. 466–78. **20**

Chandler, A. D. (1962), *Strategy and Structure* (Cambridge, Mass.: MIT Press). **171, 189, 192, 194**

Cherns, A. B. (1969), 'Social research and its diffusion', *Human*

Relations, vol. 22, no. 3, pp. 209–18. **183**

Cherns, A. B. (1975), 'Action research', in L. E. Davis and A. B. Cherns (eds), *The Quality of Working Life*, Vol. 2 (New York: Free Press), pp. 27–32. **186**

Cherrington, D. J., and England, J. L. (1980), 'The desire for an enriched job as a moderator of the enrichment–satisfaction relationship', *Organizational Behavior and Human Performance*, vol. 25, no. 1, pp. 139–59. **116, 130**

Clark, A. W. (1976), 'Introduction', in A. W. Clark (ed.), *Experimenting with Organizational Life: The Action Research Approach* (New York: Plenum), pp. 1–7. **186**

Clark, P. (1985), 'A review of theories of time and structure for sociology', in S. B. Bacharach and S. M. Mitchell (eds), *Research in the Sociology of Organizations*, Vol. 4 (Greenwich, Conn.: JAI Press), pp. 35–81. **243**

Coch, L., and French, J. R. P. (1948), 'Overcoming resistance to change', *Human Relations*, vol. 1, no. 4, pp. 512–32.

Cohen, M. D., March, J. G., and Olsen, J. P. (1972), 'A garbage can model of organizational choice', *Administrative Science Quarterly*, vol. 17, no. 1, pp. 1–25. **174**

Cole, R. E. (1971), *Japanese Blue Collar: The Changing Tradition*, (Berkeley, Calif.: University of California Press). **145–6, 152–3, 171**

Collinson, D. L. (1988), '"Engineering humour": masculinity, joking and conflict in shop-floor relations', *Organization Studies*, vol. 9, no. 2, pp. 181–99. **152, 156**

Converse, J. M., and Presser, S. (1986), *Survey Questions: Handcrafting the Standardized Questionnaire*, Sage University Paper series on Quantitative Applications in the Social Sciences, No. 07–063 (Beverly Hills: Sage). **53**

Cook, T. D., and Campbell, D. T. (1976), 'The design and conduct of quasi-experiments and true experiements in field settings', in M. D. Dunnette (ed.), *Handbook of Industrial and Organizational Psychology* (Chicago: Rand McNally), pp. 223–326. **99**

Coulter, P. B. (1979), 'Organizational effectiveness in the public sector: the example of municipal fire protection', *Administrative Science Quarterly*, vol. 24, no. 1, pp. 65–81. **236**

Crompton, R., and Jones, G. (1988), 'Researching white collar organizations: why sociologists should not stop doing case studies', in A. Bryman (ed.) (1988c), *Doing Research in Organizations* (London: Routledge), pp. 68–81. **162–3**

Cronbach, L. J., and Meehl, P. E. (1955), 'Construct validity in psychological tests', *Psychological Bulletin*, vol. 52, pp. 281–302. **59**

Crowne, D. P., and Marlowe, D. (1964), *The Approval Motive* (New York: Wiley). **66**

Cummings, L. L., and Frost, P. J. (eds) (1985), *Publishing in the Organizational Sciences* (Homewood, Ill.: Richard D. Irwin). **71**

Cummings, T. G., Molloy, E. S., and Glen, R. (1977), 'A methodological critique of fifty-eight selected work experiments', *Human Relations*, vol. 30, no. 8, pp. 675–708. **93**

Cyert, R. M., and March, J. G. (1963), *A Behavioral Theory of the Firm* (Englewood Cliffs, NJ: Prentice–Hall). **218, 220**
Cyert, R. M., Simon, H. A., and Trow, D. B. (1956), 'Observation of a business decision', *Journal of Business*, vol. 29, pp. 237–48. **171**

Daft, R. L. (1980), 'The evolution of organizational analysis in *ASQ*, 1959–1979', *Administrative Science Quarterly*, vol. 25, no. 4, pp. 623–36. **170, 177**
Daft, R. L. (1985), 'Why I recommend that your manuscript be rejected and what you can do about it', in L. L. Cummings and P. J. Frost (eds) *Publishing in the Organizational Sciences* (Homewood, Ill.: Richard D. Irwin), pp. 193–209. **165**
Daft, R. L., and Macintosh, N. B. (1981), 'A tentative exploration into the amount and equivocality of information processing in organizational work units', *Administrative Science Quarterly*, vol. 26, no. 2, pp. 207–24. **116**
Dale, A., Arber, S., and Proctor, M. (1988), *Doing Secondary Analysis* (London: Unwin Hyman). **205**
Dalton, M. (1959), *Men Who Manage* (New York: Wiley). **26, 30, 142, 152, 171**
Damanpour, F., and Evan, W. M. (1984), 'Organizational innovation and performance: the problem of "organizational lag"', *Administrative Science Quarterly*, vol. 29, no. 3, pp. 392–409. **238**
Dandridge, T. C., Mitroff, I. I., and Joyce, W. F. (1980), 'Organizational symbolism: a topic to expand organizational analysis', *Academy of Management Review*, vol. 5, no. 1, pp. 77–82. **176**
Danserau, F., Alutto, J. A., and Yammarino, F. J. (1984), *Theory Testing and Organizational Behavior: The Varient Approach* (Englewood Cliffs, NJ: Prentice-Hall). **255**
Davis, J. A. (1985), *The Logic of Causal Order*, Sage University Paper series on Quantitative Applications in the Social Sciences, No. 55 (Beverly Hills: Sage). **125, 134**
Day, R. C., and Hamblin, R. L. (1964), 'Some effects of close and punitive styles of supervision', *American Journal of Sociology*, vol. 69, no. 5, pp. 499–510. **81, 90–2, 214**
Delacroix, J., and Carroll, G. R. (1983), 'Organizational foundings: an ecological study of the newspaper industries of Argentina and Ireland', *Administrative Science Quarterly*, vol. 28, no. 2, pp. 274–91. **189, 195**
Delamont, S., and Hamilton, D. (1984), 'Revisiting classroom research: a continuing cautionary tale', in S. Delamont (ed.), *Readings on Interaction in the Classroom* (London: Methuen), pp. 2–24. **212**
de Vaus, D. A. (1986), *Surveys in Social Research* (London: Allen & Unwin). **104**
Dillman, D. A. (1978), *Mail and Telephone Surveys: The Total Design Method* (New York: Wiley). **45–6**
Dingwall, R., and Strong, P. M. (1985), 'The interactional study of organizations: a critique and reformulation', *Urban Life*, vol. 14, no. 2, pp. 205–31. **221**

Dipboye, R. L., and Flanagan, M. F. (1979), 'Research settings in industrial and organizational psychology: are findings in the field more generalizable than in the laboratory?', *American Psychologist*, vol. 34, no. 2, pp. 141–50. **87**

Ditton, J. (1977), *Part-Time Crime: An Ethnography of Fiddling and Pilferage* (London: Macmillan). **142, 144–5, 152–3, 166**

Donaldson, L. (1975), 'The Aston findings on centralization: further discussion', *Administrative Science Quarterly*, vol 20, no. 3, pp. 453–6. **233**

Donaldson, L. (1985), *In Defence of Organization Theory: A Reply to the Critics* (Cambridge: Cambridge University Press). **250**

Donaldson, L., and Warner, M. (1976), 'Bureaucratic and democratic structure in occupational interest associations', in D. S. Pugh and C. R. Hinings (eds), *Organizational Structure: Extensions and Replications, The Aston Programme II* (Farnborough, Hants.: Saxon House), pp. 67–86. **105**

Donnellon, A. (1986), 'Language and cognition in organizations: bridging cognition and behavior', in H. P. Sims and D. A. Gioia (eds), *The Thinking Organization* (San Francisco: Jossey-Bass), pp. 136–64. **221, 225**

Donnellon, A., Gray, B., and Bougon, M. A. (1986), 'Communication, meaning and organized action', *Administrative Science Quarterly*, vol. 31, no. 1, pp. 43–55. **223–4**

Dunham, R. B., Aldag, R. J., and Brief, A. P. (1977), 'Dimensionality of task design as measured by the Job Diagnostic Survey', *Academy of Management Journal*, vol. 20, no. 2 pp. 209–23. **20, 39**

Dunkerley, D. (1988), 'Historical methods and organizational analysis: the case of a naval dockyard', in A. Bryman (ed.) (1988c), *Doing Research in Organizations* (London: Routledge), pp. 82–95. **189, 195**

Ebeling, J., King, M., and Rogers, M. A. (1979), 'Hierarchical postion in the work organization and job satisfaction', *Human Relations*, vol. 32, no. 5, pp. 387–93. **37, 38–9**

Edwards, A. L. (1961), 'Social desirability or acquiescence in the MMPI? A case study with the SD scale', *Journal of Abnormal and Social Psychology*, vol. 63, pp. 351–9. **66**

Evered, R. and Louis, M. R. (1981), 'Alternative perspectives in the Organizational Sciences: "inquiry from the inside" and "inquiry from the outside"', *Academy of Management Review*, vol. 6, no. 3, pp. 385–95. **250**

Farris, G. F., and Lim, F. G. (1969), 'Effects of performance on leadership, cohesiveness, influence, satisfaction, and subsequent performance', *Journal of Applied Psychology*, vol. 53, no. 6, pp. 490–7. **96–7**

Faules, D. (1982), 'The use of multi-methods in the organizational setting', *Western Journal of Speech Communication*, vol. 46, pp. 150–61. **175–6**

Fiedler, F. E. (1967), *A Theory of Leadership Effectiveness* (New York:

McGraw-Hill). **55–7**

Finch, J. (1987), 'The vignette technique in survey research', *Sociology*, vol. 21, no. 1, pp. 105–14. **40**

Finlay, W. (1987), 'Industrial relations and firm behavior: informal labor practices in the West Coast longshore industry', *Administrative Science Quarterly*, vol. 32, no. 1, pp. 49–67. **152**

Firebaugh, G. (1978), 'A rule for inferring individual-level relationships from aggregate data', *American Sociological Review*, vol. 43, no. 4, pp. 557–72. **255**

Folger, R., and Belew, J. (1985), 'Nonreactive measurement: a focus for research on absenteeism and occupational stress', in B. M. Staw and L. L. Cummings (eds), *Research in Organizational Behavior*, Vol. 7 (Greenwich, Conn.: JAI Press), pp. 129–70. **198–9**

Ford, J. D. (1979), 'Institutional versus questionnaire measures of organizational structure: a reexamination', *Academy of Management Journal*, vol. 22, no. 3, pp. 601–10. **48**

Francis, D. W. (1986), 'Some structures of interview talk', *Language in Society*, vol. 15, no. 1, pp. 53–80. **223**

Fredrickson, J. W., and Mitchell, T. R. (1984), 'Strategic decision processes: comprehensiveness and performance in an industry with an unstable environment', *Academy of Management Journal*, vol. 27, no. 2, pp. 399–423. **40**

Freeman, J., and Hannan, M. T. (1975), 'Growth and decline processes in organizations', *American Sociological Review*, vol. 40, no. 2, pp. 215–28. **189, 191, 240**

Freeman, J., and Hannan, M. T. (1983), 'Niche width and the dynamics of organizational populations', *American Journal of Sociology*, vol. 88, no. 6, pp. 1116–45. **45, 114**

Friedlander, F., and Pickle, H. (1968), 'Components of effectiveness in small organizations', *Administrative Science Quarterly*, vol. 13, no. 2, pp. 289–304. **234**

Fromkin, H. L., and Streufert, S. (1976), 'Laboratory experimentation', in M. D. Dunnette (ed.), *Handbook of Industrial and Organizational Psychology* (Chicago: Rand McNally), pp. 415–65. **214**

Frost, P. J., Moore, L. F., Louis, M. R., Lundberg, C. C., and Martin, J. (eds) (1985), *Organizational Culture* (Beverly Hills: Sage). **28**

Fry, L. W. (1982), 'Technology-structure research: three critical issues', *Academy of Management Journal*, vol. 25, no. 3, pp. 532–52. **232**

Ganster, D. C. (1980), 'Individual differences and task design: laboratory experiment', *Organizational Behavior and Human Performance*, vol. 26, no. 1, pp. 131–48. **17–20, 22, 28, 71–2, 83, 87**

Geeraerts, G. (1984), 'The effect of ownership on the organization structure of small firms', *Administrative Science Quarterly*, vol. 29, no. 2, pp. 232–7. **48–9**

Georgopoulos, B. S. (1986), *Organizational Structure, Problem Solving, and Effectiveness: A Comparative Study of Hospital Emergency Services* (San Francisco: Jossey-Bass). **235–7**

Gillet, B., and Schwab, D. P. (1975), 'Convergent and discriminant validities of corresponding Job Descriptive Index and Minnesota Satisfaction Questionnaire scales', *Journal of Applied Psychology*, vol. 60, no. 3, pp. 313–17. **60–1**

Gioia, D. A., and Sims, H. P. (1985), 'On avoiding the influence of implicit leadership theories in leader behavior descriptions', *Educational and Psychological Measurement*, vol. 45, no. 2, pp. 217–32. **67–8**

Glaser, B. G., and Strauss, A. L. (1967), *The Discovery of Grounded Theory* (Chicago: Aldine). **167–8**

Glick, W. H., Jenkins, G. D., and Gupta, N. (1986), 'Method versus substance: how strong are underlying relationships between job characteristics and attitudinal outcomes?', *Academy of Management Journal*, vol. 29, no. 3, pp. 441–64. **130–1**

Goldman, P. (1978), 'Sociologists and the study of bureaucracy: a critique of ideology and practice', *The Insurgent Sociologist*, vol. VIII, no. 1, pp. 21–30. **20, 234**

Goodman, P. S., Atkin, R. S., and Schoorman, F. D. (1983), 'On the demise of organizational effectiveness studies', in K. Cameron and D. A. Whetten (eds), *Organizational Effectiveness: A Comparison of Multiple Models* (New York: Academic Press), pp. 163–83. **233, 235, 239**

Goodman, P.S., and Pennings, J. M. (1977) *New Perspectives on Organizational Effectiveness* (San Francisco: Jossey Bass). **239**

Gordon, G. G. (1985), 'The relationship of corporate culture to industry sector and performance', in R. H. Kilmann, M. J. Saxton, and R. Serpa (eds), *Gaining Control of the Corporate Culture* (San Francisco: Jossey-Bass). **139–40**

Gordon, M. E., Slade L. A., and Schmitt, N. (1986), 'The "science of the sophomore" revisited: from conjecture to empiricism', *Academy of Management Review*, vol. 11, no. 1, pp. 191–207. **98**

Goss, D. (1988), 'Diversity, complexity and technological change: an empirical study of general printing', *Sociology*, vol. 22, no. 3, pp. 417–31. **152, 157**

Gottschalk, L., Kluckholm, C., and Angell, R. (1945), *The Use of Personal Documents in History, Anthropology and Sociology* (New York: Social Science Research Council). **198**

Gouldner, A. W. (1954), *Patterns of Industrial Bureaucracy* (New York: Free Press). **147–8, 152, 156, 170–1**

Goyder, J. (1988), *The Silent Minority: Non-Respondents on Social Surveys* (Oxford: Polity Press). **44**

Graen, G., and Cashman, J. F. (1975), 'A role making model of leadership in formal organizations: a developmental approach', in J. G. Hunt and L. L. Larson (eds), *Leadership Frontiers* (Carbondale, Ill.: Southern Illinois University Press), pp. 143–65. **231**

Greene, C. N. (1975), 'The reciprocal nature of influence between leader and subordinate', *Journal of Applied Psychology*, vol. 60, no. 2, pp. 187–93. **123–4**

Griffin, R. W. (1980), 'Relationships among individual, task design, and leader behavior variables', *Academy of Management Journal*, vol. 23, no. 4, pp. 665–83. **245–6**

Griffin, R. W. (1983), 'Objective and social sources of information in task redesign: a field experiment', *Administrative Science Quarterly*, vol. 28, no. 2, pp. 184–200. **19, 97**

Grinyer, P. H., Yasai-Ardekani, M., and Al-Bazzaz, S. (1980), 'Strategy, structure, the environment, and financial performance in 48 United Kingdom companies', *Academy of Management Journal*, vol. 23, no. 2, pp. 193–220. **46, 47**

Gronn, P. C. (1983), 'Talk as the work: the accomplishment of school administration', *Administrative Science Quarterly*, vol. 28, no. 1, pp. 1–21. **171, 223–4**

Gross, N., Giacquinta, J. B., and Bernstein, M. (1971), *Implementing Organizational Innovations: A Sociological Analysis of Planned Organizational Change* (New York: Basic Books). **177**

Groves, R. M., and Kahn, R. L. (1979), *Surveys by Telephone: A National Comparison with Personal Interviews* (New York: Academic Press). **45–6**

Grusky, O. (1963), 'Managerial succession and organizational effectiveness', *American Journal of Sociology*, vol. 69, no. 1, pp. 21–31. **190**

Guba, E. G. (1985), 'The context of emergent paradigm research', in Y. S. Lincoln (ed.), *Organizational Theory and Inquiry: The Paradigm Revolution* (Beverly Hills: Sage), pp. 79–104. **250, 253**

Hackman, J. R., and Oldham, G. R. (1975), 'Development of the Job Diagnostic Survey', *Journal of Applied Psychology*, vol. 60, no. 2, pp. 159–70. **11–15**

Hackman, J. R., and Oldham, G. R. (1976), 'Motivation through the design of work: test of a theory', *Organizational Behavior and Human Performance*, vol. 16, no. 2, pp. 250–79. **10–17, 19, 22, 29, 105, 114, 120, 122, 126, 199, 229**

Hackman, J. R., Pearce, J. L., and Wolfe, J. C. (1978), 'Effects of changes in job characteristics on work attitudes and behavior: a naturally occurring quasi-experiment', *Organizational Behavior and Human Performance*, vol. 21, no. 3, pp. 289–304. **99–101**

Hall, R. H. (1968), 'Professionalization and bureaucratization', *American Sociological Review*, vol. 33, no. 1, pp. 92–104. **47–9, 230**

Halpin, A. W., and Winer, B. J. (1957), 'A factorial study of the leader behavior descriptions', in R. M. Stogdill and A. E. Coons (eds), *Leader Behavior: Its Description and Measurement* (Columbus, Ohio: State University, Bureau of Business Research), pp. 39–51. **38**

Hambrick, D. C. (1983), 'Some tests of the effectiveness and functional attributes of Miles and Snow's strategic types', *Academy of Management Journal*, vol. 26, no. 1, pp. 5–26. **203–4**

Hannan, M. T., and Freeman, J. H. (1987), 'The ecology of organizational founding: American labor unions, 1836–1985', *American Journal of Sociology*, vol. 92, no. 4, pp. 910–43. **189, 196**

Harris, S. G., and Sutton, R. I. (1986), 'Functions of parting ceremonies in dying organizations', *Academy of Management Journal*, vol. 29, no. 1, pp. 5–30. **152, 167–8**

Hassard, J. (1986), 'Paradigm plurality in organisations: empirical opportunities (part two)', *Dragon*, no. 7, pp. 49–91. **250–2**

Hassard, J. (1988), 'Overcoming hermeticism in organization theory: an alternative to paradigm incommensurability', *Human Relations*, vol. 41, no. 3, pp. 247–59. **250**

Hickson, D. J., Pugh, D. J., and Pheysey, D. C. (1969), 'Operations technology and organization structure: an empirical reappraisal', *Administrative Science Quarterly*, vol. 14, no. 3, pp. 378–97. **126, 200–1**

Hickson, D. J., Butler, R. J., Cray, D., Mallory, G. R., and Wilson, D. C. (1986), *Top Decisions: Strategic Decision Making in Organizations* (Oxford: Blackwell). **47, 117**

Hilton, G. (1972), 'Causal inference analysis: a seductive process', *Administrative Science Quarterly*, vol. 17, no. 1, pp. 44–54. **126**

Hinings, C. R., and Bryman, A. (1974), 'Size and the administrative component in churches', *Human Relations*, vol. 27, no. 5, pp. 457–75. **189, 191**

Hirsch, P. M. (1986), 'From ambushes to golden parachutes: corporate takeovers as an instance of cultural framing and institutional integration', *American Journal of Sociology*, vol. 91, no. 4, pp. 800–37. **189, 193–4**

Hitt, M. A., Ireland, R. D., and Stadter, G. (1982), 'Functional importance and company performance: moderating effects of grand strategy and industry type', *Strategic Managment Journal*, vol. 3, no. 4, pp. 315–30. **44, 47, 193, 236, 238**

Hoffman, J. E. (1980), 'Problems of access in the study of social elites and boards of directors', in W. B. Shaffir, R. A. Stebbins, and A. Turowetz (eds), *Fieldwork Experiences: Qualitative Approaches to Social Research* (New York: St Martin's Press), pp. 45–56. **161**

Huff, A. S. (1983), 'A rhetorical examination of strategic change', in L. R. Pondy et al., *Organizational Symbolism* (Greenwich, CT: JAI Press), pp. 167–83. **222–3**

Hull, F. (1988), 'Inventions from R & D: organizational designs for efficient research performance', *Sociology*, vol. 22, no. 3, pp. 393–415. **202**

Hull, F. M., and Collins, P. D. (1987), 'High-technology batch production systems: Woodward's missing type', *Academy of Management Journal*, vol. 30, no. 4, pp. 786–97. **202**

Hull, F. M., Friedman, N. S., and Rogers, T. F. (1982), 'The effect of technology on alienation from work,' *Sociology of Work and Occupations*, vol. 9, no. 1, pp. 31–57. **201–2**

Hull, F., and Hage, J. (1982), 'Organizing for innovation: beyond Burns and Stalker's organic type', *Sociology*, vol. 16, no. 4, pp. 564–77. **201**

Hult, M., and Lennung, S.-A. (1980), 'Towards a definition of action research: a note and bibliography', *Journal of Management Studies*, vol. 17, no. 2, pp. 241–50. **178, 183**

Hunter, J. E., Schmidt, F. L., and Jackson, G. B. (1982), *Meta-Analysis: Cumulating Research Findings across Studies* (Beverly Hills: Sage). **228**

Ilgen, D. R. (1986), 'Laboratory research: a question of when, not if', in E. A. Locke (ed.) (1986b), *Generalizing from Laboratory to Field Settings* (Lexington: Lexington Books), pp. 257–67. **92, 96**

Inbar, M., and Stoll, C. (1972), *Simulation and Gaming in Social Science* (New York: Free Press). **219**

Inkson, J. H. K., Pugh, D. S., and Hickson, D. J. (1970), 'Organization structure and context: an abbreviated replication', *Administrative Science Quarterly*, vol. 15, no. 3, pp. 318–29. **128, 240**

Isenberg, D. J. (1984), 'How senior managers think', *Harvard Business Review*, vol. 62, no. 6, pp. 81–90. **152, 157**

Isenberg, D. J. (1986), 'Thinking and managing: a verbal protocol analysis of managerial problem solving', *Academy of Management Journal*, vol. 29, no. 4, pp. 775–88. **98, 226**

Ivancevich, J. M., and Donnelly, J. H. (1975), 'Relation of organizational structure to job satisfaction, anxiety-stress, and performance', *Administrative Science Quarterly*, vol. 20, no. 2, pp. 272–80. **114–15**

Jackall, R. (1983), 'Moral mazes: bureaucracy and managerial work', *Harvard Business Review*, vol. 61, no. 5, pp. 118–30. **152, 156, 161**

James, L. R., and Jones, A. P. (1980), 'Perceived job characteristics and job satisfaction: an examination of reciprocal causality', *Personnel Psychology*, vol. 33, no. 1, pp. 97–135. **126**

Jenkins, G. D., and Lawler, E. E. (1981), 'Impact of employee participation in pay plan development', *Organizational Behavior and Human Performance*, vol. 28, no. 1, pp. 111–28. **92–3**

Jenkins, G. D., Nadler, D. A., Lawler, E. E., and Cammann, C. (1975), 'Standardized observations: an approach to measuring the nature of jobs', *Journal of Applied Psychology*, vol. 60, no. 2, pp. 171–81. **68, 212**

Jick, T. D. (1979), 'Mixing qualitative and quantitative methods: triangulation in action', *Administrative Science Quarterly*, vol. 24, no. 4, pp. 602–11. **175**

Johnson, F. G., and Kaplan, C. D. (1980), 'Talk-in-the work: aspects of social organization of work in a computer center', *Journal of Pragmatics*, vol. 4, pp. 351–65. **222, 224**

Johnson, G. (1987), *Strategic Change and the Management Process* (Oxford: Blackwell). **152, 157, 243**

Kahn, R., and Mann, F. (1952), 'Developing research partnerships', *Journal of Social Issues*, vol. 8, no. 3, pp. 4–10. **162**

Kamens, D. H., and Lunde, T. K. (1988), 'Institutional theory and the expansion of central state organizations, 1960–80', in L. G. Zucker (ed.), *Institutional Patterns and Organizations: Culture and Environment* (Cambridge, Mass.: Harper & Row), pp. 139–67. **189, 197**

Katz, R. (1982), 'The effects of group longevity on project communication and performance', *Administrative Science Quarterly*, vol. 27, no. 1, pp. 81–104.

Keat, R., and Urry, J (1975), *Social Theory as Science* (London: Routledge & Kegan Paul). **168**

Keller, R. T. (1986), 'Predictors of the performance of project groups in R & D organizations', *Academy of Management Journal*, vol. 29, no. 4, pp. 715–26. **23–4**

Ketterer, R. F., Price, R. H., and Polister, P. (1980), 'The action research paradigm', in R. H. Price and P. Polister (eds), *Evaluation and Action in the Social Environment* (New York: Academic Press), pp. 1–15. **178**

Kidder, L. H., and Judd. C. M. (1986), *Research Methods in Social Relations*, 5th edn (New York: Holt, Rinehart & Winston). **58, 77**

Kilmann, R. H., Thomas, K. W., Slevin, D. P., Nath, R., and Jerrell, S. L. (eds) (1983), *Producing Useful Knowledge for Organizations* (New York: Praeger). **32**

Kotter, J. P. (1982), *The General Managers* (New York: Free Press). **152, 157–8, 227**

Krone, K. J., Jablin, F. M., and Putnam, L. L. (1987), 'Communication theory and organizational communication: multiple perspectives', in F. M. Jablin, L. L. Putnam, K. H. Roberts, and L. W. Porter (eds), *Handbook of Organizational Communication* (Newbury Park, Calif.: Sage), pp. 18–40. **221**

Kruglanski, A. W. (1975), 'The human subject in the psychology experiment', in L. Berkowitz (ed.), *Advances in Experimental Social Psychology* Vol. 8 (New York: Academic Press), pp. 101–47. **89**

Kuhn, T. S. (1970), *The Structure of Scientific Revolutions*, 2nd edn (Chicago: University of Chicago Press); originally published in 1962. **249–50**

LaPiere, R. T. (1934), 'Attitudes vs actions', *Social Forces*, vol. 13, pp. 230–7. **213**

Lawler, E. E. (1985a), 'Challenging traditional research assumptions', in E. E. Lawler (ed.) (1985b), *Doing Research That is Useful for Theory and Practice* (San Francisco: Jossey-Bass), pp. 1–17. **244, 247**

Lawler, E. E. (ed.) (1985b), *Doing Research That is Useful for Theory and Practice* (San Francisco: Jossey-Bass). **32**

Lawler, E. E., and Hackman, J. R. (1969), 'Impact of employee participation in the development of pay incentive plans: a field experiment', *Journal of Applied Psychology*, vol. 53, no. 6, pp. 467–71. **102**

Lawrence, P. R., and Lorsch, J. W. (1967), *Organization and Environment* (Homewood, Ill.: Irwin). **49, 66, 201, 237**

Lazarsfeld, P. F. (1958), 'Evidence and inference in social research', *Daedalus*, vol. 87, no. 4, pp. 99–130. **39**

Leblebici, H., and Salancik, G. R. (1981), 'Effects of environmental uncertainty on information and decision processes in banks', *Administrative Science Quarterly*, vol. 26, no. 4, pp. 578–96. **40, 110, 112–14**

Lenz, R. T. (1980), 'Environment, strategy, organization structure and performance: patterns in one industry', *Stategic Management Journal*, vol. 1, no. 3, pp. 209–26. **141, 204, 236**

Lewis, O. (1951), *Life in a Mexican Village: Tepoztlán Revisited* (Urbana, Ill.: University of Illinois Press). **164**

Lieberson, S., and O'Connor, J. F. (1972), 'Leadership and organizational performance: a study of large corporations', *American Sociological Review*, vol. 37, no. 2, pp. 117–30. **23, 189–90**

Lincoln, J. R. , and Zeitz, G. (1980), 'Organizational properties from aggregate data: separating individual and structural effects', *American Sociological Review*, vol. 45, no. 3, pp. 391–408. **231**

Locke, E. A. (1986a), 'Generalizing from laboratory to field: ecological validity or abstraction of essential elements?', in E. A. Locke (ed.) (1986b), *Generalizing from Laboratory to Field Settings* (Lexington, Mass.: Lexington Books), pp. 3–9.

Locke, E. A. (ed.) (1986b), *Generalizing from Laboratory to Field Settings* (Lexington, Mass.: Lexington Books). **97–8, 128**

Locke, E. A., and Schweiger, D. M. (1979), 'Participation in decision-making: one more look', in B. M. Staw (ed.), *Research in Organizational Behavior*, Vol. 1 (Greenwich, Conn.: JAI Press), pp. 265–339. **228–9, 236**

Lockhart, D. C. (ed.) (1984), *Making Effective Use of Mailed Questionnaires* (San Francisco: Jossey-Bass). **44**

Loher, B. T., Noe, R. A., Moeller, N. L., and Fitzgerald, M. P. (1985), 'A meta-analysis of the relation of job characteristics to job satisfaction', *Journal of Applied Psychology*, vol. 70, no. 2, pp. 280–9. **229**

Lowin, A., and Craig, C. R. (1968), 'The influence of performance on managerial style: an experimental object lesson in the ambiguity of correlational data', *Organizational Behavior and Human Performance*, vol. 3, no. 4, pp. 440–58. **97**

Lubatkin, M., and Pitts, M. (1983), 'PIMS: fact or folklore?', *Journal of Business Strategy*, vol. 3, pp. 38–43. **205**

Lupton, T. (1963), *On the Shop Floor* (Oxford: Pergamon). **26, 30, 152, 171**

Luthans, F., and Lockwood, D. L. (1984), 'Toward an observation system for measuring leader behavior', in J. G. Hunt, D.-M. Hosking, and C. A. Schriesheim (eds), *Leaders and Managers: International Perspective on Managerial Behavior and Leadership* (New York: Pergamon), pp. 117–41. **209–12**

Luthans, F., Rosenkrantz, S. A., and Hennessey, H. W. (1985), 'What do successful managers really do? An observation study of managerial activities', *Journal of Applied Behavioral Science*, vol. 21, no. 3, pp. 255–70. **209–11**

McCall, G. J. (1984), 'Systematic field observation', *Annual Review of Sociology*, vol. 10, pp. 263–82. **207**

McCall, M. W., and Lombardo, M. M. (1982), 'Using simulation for leadership and management research: through the looking glass', *Management Science*, vol. 28, no. 5, pp. 533–49. **216–17, 219–20**

McKinley, W. (1987), 'Complexity and administrative intensity: the case of declining organizations', *Administrative Science Quarterly*, vol. 32, no. 1, pp. 87–105. **202, 240**

Marsh, C. (1982), *The Survey Method: The Contribution of Surveys to*

Sociological Explanation (London: Allen & Unwin). **104**

Marsh, R. M., and Mannari, H. (1981), 'Technology and size as determinants of the organizational structure of Japanese factories', *Administrative Science Quarterly*, vol. 26, no. 1, pp. 33–57. **8**

Martin, J. (1989), 'Breaking up the mono-method monopolies in organizational analysis', in J. Hassard and D. Pym (eds), *The Theory and Philosophy of Organizations* (London: Routledge). **248**

Martin, P. Y., and Turner, B. A. (1986), 'Grounded theory and organizational research', *Journal of Applied Behavioral Science*, vol. 22, no. 2, pp. 141–57. **168**

Martinko, M. J., and Gardner, W. L. (1984), 'The observation of high-performing educational managers: methodological issues and managerial implications', in J. G. Hunt, D.-M. Hosking, C. A. Schriesheim, and R. Stewart (eds), *Leaders and Managers: International Perspectives on Managerial Behavior and Leadership* (New York: Pergamon), pp. 142–61. **209–12**

Martinko, M. J., and Gardner, W. L. (1985), 'Beyond structured observation: methodological issues and new directions', *Academy of Management Review*, vol. 10, no. 4, pp. 676–95. **207–9, 213, 227**

Mehan, H. (1978), 'Structuring school structure', *Harvard Educational Review*, vol. 48, no. 1, pp. 32–64. **224**

Mehan, H. (1983), 'The role of language and the language of role in institutional decision making', *Language in Society*, vol. 12, no. 2, pp. 187–211. **222**

Meindl, J. R., Ehrlich, S. B., and Dukerich, J. M. (1985), 'The romance of leadership', *Administrative Science Quarterly*, vol. 30, no. 1, pp. 78–102. **189, 191**

Meyer, J. W., Scott, W. R., Strang, D., and Creighton, A. L. (1988), 'Bureaucracy without centralization: changes in the organizational system of US public education, 1940–80', in L. G. Zucker (ed.), *Institutional Patterns and Organizations: Culture and Environment* (Cambridge, Mass.: Harper & Row), pp. 139–67. **189, 197**

Miles, M. B. (1979), 'Qualitative data as an attractive nuisance: the problem of analysis', *Administrative Science Quarterly*, vol. 24, no. 4, pp. 590–601. **166, 168**

Miles, R. H., and Randolph, A. (1979), *The Organization Game*, (Santa Monica, Calif.: Goodyear). **217, 220, 223**

Miles, R. E., and Snow, C. C. (1978), *Organizational Strategy, Structure and Process* (New York: McGraw-Hill). **203, 204**

Miller, K. I., and Monge. P. R. (1986), 'Participation, satisfaction, and productivity: a meta-analytic review', *Academy of Management Journal*, vol. 29, no. 4, pp. 727–53. **236**

Miner, J. B. (1978), 'Twenty years of research on role-motivation theory of managerial effectiveness', *Personnel Psychology*, vol. 31, pp. 739–60. **225–6**

Mintzberg, H. (1970), 'Structured observation as a method to study managerial work', *Journal of Management Studies*, vol. 7, no. 1, pp. 87–104. **207, 227**

Mintzberg, H. (1973), *The Nature of Managerial Work* (New York: Harper & Row). **207–12**

Mintzberg, H., and McHugh, A. (1985), 'Strategy formation in an adhocracy', *Administrative Science Quarterly*, vol. 30, no. 2, pp. 160–97. **150–1, 193, 219, 243**

Mitchell, J. C. (1983), 'Case and situation analysis', *Sociological Review*, vol. 31, no. 2, pp. 186–211. **172–3, 178**

Mitchell, T. R. (1985), 'An evaluation of the validity of correlational research conducted in organizations', *Academy of Management Review*, vol. 10, no. 2, pp. 192–205. **64, 112–13, 134**

Mohr, L. B. (1982), *Explaining Organizational Behavior: The Limits and Possibilities of Theory and Research* (San Francisco: Jossey-Bass). **4, 5, 8, 172**

Mook, D. G. (1983), 'In defense of external invalidity', *American Psychologist*, vol. 38, no. 4, pp. 379–87. **96**

Morgan, G. (1983), 'The significance of assumptions', in G. Morgan (ed.), *Beyond Method: Strategies for Social Research* (Beverly Hills: Sage), pp. 377–82. **252**

Morgan, G., and Smircich, L. (1980), 'The case for qualitative research', *Academy of Management Review*, vol. 5, no. 4, pp. 491–500. **27, 159, 161, 169, 248, 250, 253**

Morse, N. C., and Reimer, E. (1956), 'The experimental change of a major organizational variable', *Journal of Abnormal and Social Psychology*, vol. 52, pp. 120–9. **88, 94**

Moser, C., and Kalton, G. (1971), *Survey Methods in Social Investigation*, 2nd edn (London: Heinemann). **104**

Mowday, R. T., Steers, R. M., and Porter, L. W. (1979), 'The measurement of organizational commitment', *Journal of Vocational Behavior*, vol. 14, no. 2, pp. 224–47. **54–64, 68**

Newell, A., and Simon, H. A. (1972), *Human Problem Solving* (Englewood Cliffs, NJ: Prentice-Hall). **226**

Nie, N. H., Hull, C. H., Jenkins, J. G., Steinbrenner, K., and Bent, D. H. (1975), *Statistical Package for the Social Sciences*, 2nd edn (New York: McGraw-Hill). **222**

Nisbett, R., and Wilson, T. (1977), 'Telling more than we can know: verbal reports on mental processes', *Psychological Review*, vol. 84, no. 3, pp. 231–59. **226**

Noblit, G. W., and Hare, R. D. (1988), *Meta-Ethnography: Synthesizing Qualitative Studies*, Sage University Paper series on Qualitative Research Methods, No. 11 (Beverly Hills: Sage). **229**

Oldham, G. R., and Brass, D. J. (1979), 'Employee reactions to an open plan office: a naturally occurring quasi-experiment', *Administrative Science Quarterly*, vol. 24, no. 2, pp. 267–84. **100, 102**

O'Reilly, C. A., and Caldwell, D. F. (1979), 'Informational influence as a determinant of task characteristics and job satisfaction', *Journal of Applied Psychology*, vol. 64, no. 2, pp. 157–65. **19**

O'Reilly, C. A., Partlette, G. N., and Bloom, J. A. (1980), 'Perceptual measures of task characteristics: the biasing effects of different frames of reference and job attitudes', *Academy of Management Journal*, vol. 23, no. 1, pp. 118–31. **69, 126**

272 BIBLIOGRAPHY AND AUTHOR INDEX

Orne, M. T. (1962), 'On the social psychology of the psychological experiment: with particular reference to demand characteristics and their implications', *American Psychologist*, vol. 17, pp. 776–83. **89**

Orpen C. (1979), 'The effects of job enrichment on employee satisfaction, motivation, involvement, and performance: a field experiment', *Human Relations*, vol. 32, no. 3, pp. 189–217. **17–20, 22, 28, 71–2, 77–9, 94**

Osborn, R. N., and Hunt, R. G. (1974), 'Environment and organizational effectiveness', *Administrative Science Quarterly*, vol. 18, no. 2, pp. 231–46. **237**

Pasmore, W., and Friedlander, F. (1982), 'An action-research program for increasing employee involvement in problem solving', *Administrative Science Quarterly*, vol. 27, no. 3, pp. 343–62. **180–3**

Patton, M. Q. (1987), *How to Use Qualitative Methods in Evaluation* (Beverly Hills: Sage). **172**

Payne, R. (1976), 'Truisms in organizational behaviour', *Interpersonal Development*, vol. 6, pp. 203–20. **64**

Payne, S. L. (1951), *The Art of Asking Questions* (Princeton, NJ: Princeton University Press). **52**

Pearce, J. L. (1981), 'Bringing some clarity to role ambiguity research', *Academy of Management Review*, vol. 6, no. 4, pp. 665–74. **129**

Pennings, J. (1973), 'Measures of organizational structure: a methodological note', *American Journal of Sociology*, vol. 79, no. 3, pp. 686–704. **48**

Pennings, J. (1987), 'Sructural contingency theory: a multivariate test', *Organization Studies*, vol. 8, no. 3, pp. 223–40. **45, 233, 236–7**

Peters, M., and Robinson, V. (1984), 'The origins and status of action research', *Journal of Applied Behavioral Science*, vol. 20, no. 2, pp. 113–24. **178**

Peters, T. J., and Waterman, R. H. (1982), *In Search of Excellence: Lessons from America's Best-Run Companies* (New York: Harper & Row). **242, 246**

Pettigrew, A. (1985), *The Awakening Giant: Continuity and Change in ICI* (Oxford: Blackwell). **152, 156–7, 160–1, 197, 243**

Phillips, L. W. (1981), 'Assessing measurement error in key informant reports: a methodological note on organizational analysis in marketing', *Journal of Marketing Research*, vol. XVIII, no. 4, pp. 395–415. **47**

Pinfield, L. T. (1986), 'A field evaluation of perspectives on organizational decision making', *Administrative Science Quarterly*, vol. 31, no. 3, pp. 365–88. **152–3, 159, 166, 174, 253**

Podsakoff, P. M., and Dalton, D. R. (1987), 'Research methodology in organizational studies', *Journal of Management*, vol. 13, no. 2, pp. 419–44. **6, 27, 32, 36, 64, 228**

Pollert, A. (1981), *Girls, Wives, Factory Lives* (London: Macmillan). **152**

Pondy, L. R., Frost, P. J., Morgan, G., and Dandridge, T. C. (eds) (1983), *Organizational Symbolism* (Greenwich, Conn.: JAI Press). **28**

Potter, J., and Wetherell, M. (1987), *Discourse and Social Psychology* (London: Sage). **221**
Powell, W. W. (1985), *Getting into Print: The Decision-Making Process in Scholarly Publishing* (Chicago: University of Chicago Press). **152, 154, 171, 174**
Price, J. L. (1972), 'The study of organizational effectiveness', *Sociological Quarterly*, vol. 13, no. 1, pp. 3–15. **234**
Price, R. L. (1985), 'A customer's view of organizational literature', in L. L. Cummings and P. J. Frost (eds), *Publishing in the Organizational Sciences* (Homewood, Ill.: Richard D. Irwin), pp. 125–32. **24, 234, 242, 247**
Pugh, D. S. (1981), 'The Aston program of research: retrospect and prospect', in A. H. Van de Ven and W. F. Joyce (eds), *Perspectives on Organization Design and Behavior* (New York: Wiley), pp. 135–66. **22**
Pugh, D. S. (1988), 'The Aston research programme', in A. Bryman (ed.) (1988c), *Doing Research in Organizations* (London: Routledge), pp. 123–35. **22, 115, 140**
Pugh, D. S., Hickson, D. J., Hinings, C. R., Macdonald, K. M., Turner, C., and Lupton, T. (1963), 'A conceptual scheme for organizational analysis', *Administrative Science Quarterly*, vol. 8, no. 3, pp. 289–315. **22**
Pugh, D. S., Hickson, D. J., Hinings, C. R., and Turner, C. (1969), 'The context of organization structures', *Administrative Science Quarterly*, vol. 14, no. 1, pp. 91–114. **7, 46, 127–8, 140, 200, 232–3**

Ramanujam, V., and Venkatraman, N. (1984), 'An inventory and critique of strategy research using the PIMS database', *Academy of Management Review*, vol. 9, no. 1, pp. 138–51. **203, 205**
Rapoport, R. N. (1970), 'Three dilemmas in action research', *Human Relations*, vol. 23, no. 6, pp. 499–513. **186**
Redfield, R. (1930), *Tepoztlán: A Mexican Village* (Chicago: University of Chicago Press). **164**
Reimann, B. (1982), 'Organizational competence as a predictor of long run survival and growth', *Academy of Management Journal*, vol. 25, no. 2, pp. 323–34. **237**
Rice, R. W. (1978a), 'Construct validity of the Least Preferred Co-worker scale', *Psychological Bulletin*, vol. 85, no. 6, pp. 1199–237. **65**
Rice, R. W. (1978b), 'Psychometric properties of the esteem for the Least Preferred Co-worker (LPC scale)', *Academy of Management Review*, vol. 3, no. 1, pp. 106–18. **56**
Rice, R. W. (1979), 'Reliability and validity of the LPC scale: a reply', *Academy of Management Review*, vol. 4, no. 2, pp. 291–4. **56–7**
Riecken, H. W. (1962), 'A program for research on experiments in social psychology', in N. F. Washburne (ed.), *Decisions, Values and Groups*, Vol. 2 (New York: Pergamon), pp. 25–41. **89**
Ritti, R. R., and Silver, J. H. (1986), 'Early processes of institutionalization: the dramaturgy of exchange in interorganizational relations', *Administrative Science Quarterly*, vol. 31, no. 1, pp. 25–42. **152–3, 166**

Rizzo, J. R., House, R. J., and Lirtzman, S. I. (1970), 'Role conflict and ambiguity in complex organizations', *Administrative Science Quarterly*, vol. 15, no. 2, pp. 150–63. **129–30**

Roberts, K. H., and Glick, W. (1981), 'The job characteristics approach to task design: a critical review', *Journal of Applied Psychology*, vol. 66, no. 2, pp. 193–217. **18**

Robinson, W. P. (1950), 'Ecological correlations and the behavior of individuals', *American Sociological Review*, vol. 15, pp. 351–7. **231–2**

Roethlisberger, F. J., and Dickson, W. J. (1939), *Management and the Worker* (Cambridge, Mass.: Harvard University Press). **88**

Rohlen, T. (1974), *For Harmony and Strength: Japanese White-Collar Organization in Anthropological Perspective* (Berkeley Calif.: University of California Press). **152**

Rosen, M. (1986a), 'Christmas time and control', *Dragon*, no. 5, pp. 51–73. **152, 154**

Rosen, M. (1986b), 'Some notes from the field: on ethnography and organizational science', *Dragon*, no. 6, pp. 57–77. **146–7, 151–4, 161, 163**

Rosenthal, R., and Rosnow, R. L. (1969), 'The volunteer subject', in R. Rosenthal and R. L. Rosnow (eds), *Artifact in Behavioral Research* (New York: Academic Press), pp. 61–118. **87**

Rosenthal, R., and Rubin, D. B. (1978), 'Interpersonal expectancy effects: the first 345 studies', *Behavioral and Brain Sciences*, vol. 3, no. 3, pp. 377–415. **89–90**

Ross, J., and Staw, B. M. (1986), 'Expo 86: an escalation prototype', *Administrative Science Quarterly*, vol. 31, no. 2, pp. 274–97. **175, 189, 193**

Rossi, P. H. (1980), 'The presidential address: the challenge and opportunities of applied social research', *American Sociological Review*, vol. 45, no. 6, pp. 889–904. **245**

Rousseau, D. M. (1977), 'Technological differences in job characteristics, employee satisfaction, and motivation: a synthesis of job design research and sociotechnical systems theory', *Organizational Behavior and Human Performance*, vol. 19, no. 1, pp. 18–42. **35–6, 40–3, 125–6, 129**

Rousseau, D. M. (1983), 'Technology in organizations: a constructive review and analytic framework', in S. E. Seashore, E. E. Lawler, P. H. Mirvis, and C. Cammann (eds), *Assessing Organizational Change* (New York: Wiley), pp. 229–55. **155, 232**

Rousseau, D. M. (1985), 'Issues of level in organizational research: multi-level and cross-level perspectives', in B. M. Staw and L. L. Cummings (eds), *Research in Organizational Behavior*, Vol. 7 (Greenwich, Conn.: JAI Press), pp. 1–37. **232**

Roy, D. (1954), 'Efficiency and "the fix": informal intergroup relations in a piecework machine shop', *American Journal of Sociology*, vol. 60, no. 3, pp. 255–66. **26, 142, 152, 164, 170–1, 243**

Roy, D. (1960), 'Banana time: job satisfaction and informal interaction', *Human Organization*, vol. 18, no. 4, pp. 158–68. **26, 152, 164, 170–1, 243**

Rumelt, R. P. (1974), *Strategy, Structure, and Economic Performance* (Boston, Mass.: Division of Research, Harvard Business School). **189, 192–3, 236**

Rush, M. D., Thomas, J. C., and Lord, R. G. (1977), 'Implicit leadership theory: a potential threat to the internal validity of leader behavior questionnaires', *Organizational Behavior and Human Performance*, vol. 20, no. 1, pp. 93–110. **67, 133, 253**

Salancik, G. R., and Pfeffer, J. (1977), 'An examination of need-satisfaction models of job attitudes', *Administrative Science Quarterly*, vol. 22, no. 3, pp. 427–56. **18, 129**

Salancik, G. R., and Pfeffer, J. (1978), 'A social information processing approach to job attitudes and task design', *Administrative Science Quarterly*, vol. 23, no. 2, pp. 224–53. **18–19, 21**

Sanday, P. R. (1979), 'The ethnographic paradigm(s)', *Administrative Science Quarterly*, vol. 24, no. 4, pp. 527–38. **139**

Sathe, V. J. (1978), 'Institutional versus questionnaire measures of organizational structure', *Academy of Management Journal*, vol. 21, no. 2, pp. 227–38. **48**

Schall, M. S. (1983), 'A communication-rules approach to organizational culture', *Administrative Science Quarterly*, vol. 28, no. 4, pp. 557–81. **176–7**

Schneider, B. (1985), 'Some propositions about getting research published', in L. L. Cummings and P. J. Frost (eds), *Publishing in the Organizational Sciences* (Homewood, Ill.: Richard D. Irwin), pp. 238–47. **28**

Schoeffler, S. (1977), 'Cross-sectional study of strategy, structure, and performance: aspects of the PIMS program', in H. B. Thorelli (ed.), *Strategy + Structure = Performance*, (Bloomington, Ind.: Indiana University Press), pp. 108–21. **203**

Schoonhoven, C. B. (1981), 'Problems with contingency theory: testing assumptions hidden within the language of contingency "theory"', *Administrative Science Quarterly*, vol. 26, no. 3, pp. 349–77. **233**

Schriesheim, C. A., and Kerr, S. (1977), 'Theories and measures of leadership', in J. G. Hunt and L. L. Larson (eds), *Leadership: The Cutting Edge* (Carbondale, Ill.: Southern Illinois University Press), pp. 9–45. **63, 65**

Schuman, H., and Presser, S. (1981), *Questions and Answers in Attitude Surveys* (New York: Academic Press). **50–1, 54**

Schwab, D. P. (1985), 'Reviewing empirically based manuscripts: perspectives on process', in L. L. Cummings and P. J. Frost (eds), *Publishing in the Organizational Sciences* (Homewood, Ill.: Richard D. Irwin), pp. 171–81. **114**

Schweiger, D. M. (1983), 'Is the simultaneous verbal protocol a viable method for studying managerial problem solving and decision making?', *Academy of Management Journal*, vol. 26, no. 1, pp. 185–92. **226**

Scott, W. R. (1987a), 'The adolescence of institutional theory', *Administrative Science Quarterly*, vol. 32, no. 4, pp. 493–511. **199**

Scott, W. R. (1987b), *Organizations: Rational, Natural and Open Systems*, 2nd edn (Englewood Cliffs, NJ: Prentice-Hall). **241, 244**

Seashore, S. E. (1976), 'The design of action research', in A. W. Clark (ed.), *Experimenting with Organizational Life: The Action Research Approach* (New York: Plenum), pp. 103–17. **179**

Selye, H. (1964), *From Dream to Discovery: On Being a Scientist* (New York: McGraw-Hill). **174**

Selznick, P. (1949), *TVA and the Grass Roots* (Berkeley, Calif.: University of California Press). **170–1**

Serber, D. (1981), 'The masking of social reality: ethnographic fieldwork in a bureaucracy', in D. A. Messerschmidt (ed.), *Anthropologists at Home in North America: Methods and Issues in the Study of One's Own Sociey* (Cambridge: Cambridge University Press), pp. 77–87. **142–3, 152, 163**

Shapira, Z., and Dunbar, R. L. M. (1980), 'Testing Mintzberg's managerial roles classification using an in-basket simulation', *Journal of Applied Psychology*, vol. 65, no. 1, pp. 87–95. **215–16**

Siehl, C., and Martin, J. (1988), 'Measuring organizational culture: mixing qualitative and quantitative methods', in M. O. Jones, M. D. Moore, and R. C. Snyder (eds), *Inside Organizations: Understanding the Human Dimension* (Newbury Park, Calif.: Sage), pp. 79–103. **252**

Sims, H. P., and Gioia, D. A. (eds), (1986), *The Thinking Organization* (San Francisco: Jossey-Bass). **221**

Sims, H. P., and Szilagyi, A. D. (1979), 'Time lags in leader reward research', *Journal of Applied Psychology*, vol. 64, no. 1, pp. 66–71. **125, 241**

Smircich, L. (1983), 'Organizations as shared meanings', in L. R. Pondy *et al.*, (eds), *Organizational Symbolism* (Greenwich, Conn.: JAI Press), pp. 55–65. **134–41, 146, 152, 154–5, 163, 252**

Smircich, L., and Morgan, G. (1982), 'Leadership: the management of meaning', *Journal of Applied Behavioral Science*, vol 18, no. 3, pp. 257–73. **137–8, 152**

Smith, J. E. (1985), 'Computer simulation', in A. Kuper and J. Kuper (eds), *The Social Science Encyclopedia* (London: Routledge & Kegan Paul), pp. 143–4. **218**

Smith, M., and White, M. C. (1987), 'Strategy, CEO specialization, and succession', *Administrative Science Quarterly*, vol. 32, no. 2, pp. 263–80. **198**

Snow, C. C., and Hrebiniak, L. G. (1980), 'Strategy, distinctive competence, and organizational performance', *Administrative Science Quarterly*, vol. 25, no. 2, pp. 317–36. **126**

Snyder, N., and Glueck, W. F. (1980), 'How managers plan – the analysis of managers' activities', *Long Range Planning*, vol. 13, no. 1, pp. 70–6. **212**

Staples, W. G. (1987), 'Technology, control, and the social organization of work at a British hardware firm, 1791–1891', *American Journal of Sociology*, vol. 92, no. 1, pp. 62–88. **189, 194–5**

Staw, B. M. (1975), 'Attributing the "causes" of performance: a general alternative interpretation of cross-sectional research on organizations',

Organizational Behavior and Human Performance, vol. 13, no. 3, pp. 414–32. **132, 253**

Staw, B. M., McKechnie, P. I., and Puffer, S. M. (1983), 'The justification of organizational performance', *Administrative Science Quarterly*, vol. 28, no. 4, pp. 582–600. **189, 191–2, 197–8**

Staw, B. M., and Ross, J. (1978), 'Commitment to a policy decision: a multi-theoretical position', *Administrative Science Quarterly*, vol. 23, no. 1, pp. 40–64. **87–8, 175**

Staw, B. M., and Ross, J. (1980), 'Commitment in an experimenting society: a study of the attribution of leadership from administrative scenarios', *Journal of Applied Psychology*, vol. 65, no. 3, pp. 249–60. **98**

Stewart, R. (1967), *Managers and their Jobs* (London: Macmillan). **227**

Strauss, A. L., Schatzman. L, Ehrlich, D., Bucher, R., and Sabshin, M. (1963), 'The hospital as a negotiated order', in E. Freidson (ed.), *The Hospital in Modern Society* (New York: Macmillan), pp. 147–63. **141**

Sudman, S., and Bradburn, N. M. (1974), *Response Effects in Surveys* (Chicago: Aldine). **42**

Sudman, S., and Bradburn, N. M. (1982), *Asking Questions: A Practical Guide to Questionnaire Design* (San Francisco: Jossey-Bass). **43, 52**

Susman, G. I., and Evered, R. D. (1978), 'An assessment of the scientific merits of action research', *Administrative Science Quarterly*, vol. 23, no. 4, pp. 582–603. **179**

Sutton, R. I. (1987), 'The process of organizational death: disbanding and reconnecting', *Administrative Science Quarterly*, vol. 32, no. 4, pp. 542–69. **2, 149–50, 152, 157–8, 160–1, 167, 171–2**

Sutton, R. I., and Callahan, A. L. (1987), 'The stigma of bankruptcy: spoiled organizational image and its management', *Academy of Management Journal*, vol. 30, no. 3, pp. 405–36. **171, 173, 178**

Thiel, J. (1978), 'A dynamic full system model of business strategy in the brewing industry', PhD dissertation, Indiana University; cited in Lubatkin and Pitts, op. cit. (1983). **205**

Thomas, K. W., and Kilmann, R. H. (1975), 'The social desirability variable in organizational research', *Academy of Management Journal*, vol. 18, no. 4, pp. 741–52. **43, 66**

Thomas, K. W., and Tymon, W. G. (1982), 'Necessary properties of relevant research: lessons from recent criticisms of the organizational sciences', *Academy of Management Review*, vol. 7, no. 3, pp. 345–52. **244**

Thompson, J. D. (1967), *Organizations in Action* (New York: McGraw-Hill). **36**

Thornton, G. C., and Byham, W. C. (1982), *Assessment Centers and Management Performance* (New York: Academic Press). **214–15, 220**

Tolbert, P. S., and Zucker, L. G. (1983), 'Institutional sources of change in the formal structure of organizations: the diffusion of civil service reform, 1880–1935', *Administrative Science Quarterly*, vol. 28, no. 1, pp. 22–39. **189, 196–7, 199**

Turner, A. N., and Lawrence, P. R. (1965), *Industrial Jobs and the*

Worker (Boston, Mass.: Division of Research, Harvard Business School). **10**

Turner, B. A. (1976), 'The organizational and interorganizational development of disasters', *Administrative Science Quarterly*, vol. 21, no. 3, pp. 378–97. **151, 193**

Van Maanen, J. (1982), 'Introduction', in J. Van Maanen (ed.), *Varieties of Qualitative Research* (Beverly Hills: Sage), pp. 11–29. **159, 169, 250**

Van Maanen, J. (1983), 'Epilogue: qualitative methods reclaimed', in J. Van Maanen, (ed.), *Qualitative Methodology* (Beverly Hills: Sage), pp. 247–68. **158, 169**

Van Maanen, J., and Kolb, D. (1985), 'The professional apprentice: observations on fieldwork roles in two organizational settings', in S. B. Bacharach and S. M. Mitchell (eds), *Research in the Sociology of Organizations*, Vol. 4 (Greenwich, Conn.: JAI Press), pp. 1–33. **154, 161–5**

Webb, E. J., Campbell, D. T., Schwartz, R. D., and Sechrest, L. (1966), *Unobtrusive Measures: Nonreactive Research in the Social Sciences* (Chicago: Rand McNally). **66, 143**

Weick, K. E. (1965), 'Laboratory experiments with organizations', in J. G. March (ed.), *Handbook of Organizations* (Chicago: Rand McNally), pp. 194–260. **220**

Weick, K. E. (1968), 'Systematic observational methods', in G. Lindzey and E. Aronson (eds), *Handbook of Social Psychology*, Vol. 2 (Reading, Mass.: Addison-Wesley), pp. 357–451. **207**

White, K. R. (1982), 'The relation between socioeconomic status and academic achievement', *American Psychologist*, vol. 91, no. 3, pp. 461–81. **229**

Whyte, W. F. (1984), *Learning from the Field: A Guide from Experience* (Beverly Hills: Sage). **2, 165, 168, 179**

Whyte, W. F. (1987), 'From human relations to organizational behavior: reflections on the changing scene', *Industrial and Labor Relations Review*, vol. 40, no. 4, pp. 487–500. **244**

Whyte, W. F., and Hamilton, E. L. (1965), *Action Research for Management* (Homewood, Ill.: Irwin). **148–9, 152, 179, 184–6**

Willson, V. L., and Putnam, R. R. (1982), 'A meta-analysis of pretest sensitization effects in experimental design', *American Educational Research Journal*, vol. 19, no. 2, pp. 249–58. **85**

Withey, M., Daft, R. L., and Cooper, W. H. (1983), 'Measures of Perrow's work unit technology: an empirical assessment and a new scale', *Academy of Management Journal*, vol. 26, no. 1, pp. 45–63. **60, 230**

Woodward, J. (1965), *Industrial Organization: Theory and Practice* (London: Oxford University Press). **200, 202, 232**

Yin, R. K. (1979), *Changing Urban Bureaucracies: How New Practices Become Routinized* (Lexington, Mass.: Lexington Books). **44–5, 172, 178**

Yin, R. K. (1984), *Case Study Research: Design and Methods* (Beverly Hills: Sage). **172–3, 178**

Yukl, G. A. (1981), *Leadership in Organizations* (Englewood Cliffs, NJ: Prentice-Hall). **228**

Yukl, G. A., and Van Fleet, D. D. (1982), 'Cross-situational, multimethod research on leader effectiveness', *Organizational Behavior and Human Performance*, vol. 30, no. 1, pp. 87–108. **228**

Yunker, G. W., and Hunt, J. G. (1975), 'An empirical comparison of the Michigan four-factor and Ohio State LBDQ scales', *Organizational Behavior and Human Performance*, vol. 17, no. 1, pp. 45–65. **60**

Zimmerman, D. K. (1978), 'Participative management: a reexamination of the classics', *Academy of Management Review*, vol. 3, no. 4, pp. 896–901. **96**

Subject Index

participant observation 25, 27, 29–31,
135, 138–9, 141–7, 151–3, 155,
160, 164, 166, 177, 221, 225, 243,
252–3
path analysis 200
pilot studies 51, 54, 111
population 107–9, 170, 172
population ecology approach 45,
195–7, 240
positivism 27, 178, 249, 253
postal questionnaires, 41–4, 46–7, 106,
112, 141, 238; *see also*
self-administered questionnaires
probability sampling 87, 107–10, 113,
134
Profit Impact of Market Strategies
(PIMS) programme 203–5
projective techniques 215, 225–6
psychology 1, 21–2

qualitative data, analysis of 165–8
qualitative research:
as preparation for quantitative
research 252
combined with quantitative research
175–7, 248–55
contrast with quantitative research
10, 24–5, 27, 135, 139–41, 158,
168, 178, 242
growth of interest in 26–7, 168
nature of 24–30, 32, 136–8, 159, 170,
221, 223, 239
types of 151–61
Quality of Working Life 95
quantitative research:
combined with qualitative research
175–7, 248–55
contrast with qualitative research
10, 24–5, 27, 135, 139–41, 158,
168, 178, 242
nature of 6–10, 19–24, 32
quasi-experiments 28–9, 73, 94–5,
99–103, 172
questionnaires, *see* self administered
questionnaires
questions in questionnaires and
structured interviews 49–54

random assignment 73, 77, 84, 90, 94,
96, 99–103, 122
random sampling, *see* probability
sampling; simple random sample
reactivity 65–9, 88–9, 143, 145, 197,
206, 211
relationships in the field 3–4, 73, 143,

162–3
reliability 8, 54–7, 62–5, 69–70, 191,
198, 211–12
replication 9–10, 19, 128, 173, 178,
209, 212, 239–40
resources in research 42, 49, 64–5, 70,
85, 110–11, 122, 128, 219, 227,
240, 248
response sets 43, 53, 66–8
respondent validation 164–6
re-studies 163–4, 178, 240–3

sampling issues 9, 46, 107–17, 133–4,
172–3, 193, 213, 232–3; *see also*
probability sampling; simple
random sample; stratified random
sample
scales, *see* multiple-item measures
secondary analysis of survey data 31,
188, 200–6
self-administered questionnaires 2–3,
5, 11, 17–20, 29–32, 36–8, 40–4,
46–52, 61–2, 66, 68–9, 91–3, 104,
106–7, 112, 129–32, 139–41,
175–6, 178, 193, 197, 207–8,
212–13, 225, 228, 230–3, 236–9,
251–2
simple random sample 107–8
simulation 29, 31, 87, 207, 214–20, 226
social desirability effect 43, 66–7, 70
social survey, *see* survey research
sociology 1, 22
spuriousness 119–23, 129
strategic management, studies of 25–6,
40, 46–9, 117, 126, 141, 150, 171,
192–4, 203–5, 236
stratified random sample 108–9, 115
structured interviewing 29–32, 36–7,
40–52, 68–9, 107, 131
structured observation 29, 31, 60, 68,
91, 104, 130–1, 142, 170, 207–13,
220, 227, 243
survey data, analysis of 117–29, 166
survey research 2, 5, 9, 11, 19–20, 22,
25, 29, 36, 40, 69, 71–2, 104–34,
139–40, 142, 158, 170, 175–6, 178,
209, 236–7, 240, 245, 250
systematic observation, *see* structured
observation

technology, studies of effects of 8, 22,
35–6, 40, 100, 126, 155, 160, 162,
200–2, 232
theory:
and qualitative research 25–6,